ISBN 978-1-331-69621-6
PIBN 10222743

1 MONTH OF
FREE
READING

at

www.ForgottenBooks.com

By purchasing this book you are eligible for one month membership to ForgottenBooks.com, giving you unlimited access to our entire collection of over 700,000 titles via our web site and mobile apps.

To claim your free month visit:

www.forgottenbooks.com/free222743

Similar Books Are Available from
www.forgottenbooks.com

Nihil Obstat.

FRANCISCUS M. WYNDHAM,

CENSOR DEPUTATUS.

Imprimatur.

✠ GULIELMUS,

EPISCOPUS ARINDELENSIS,

VICARIUS GENERALIS.

WESTMONASTERII,
Die 28 Oct., 1908.

THE CATECHISM IN EXAMPLES

By *the* REV. D. CHISHOLM

Priest of the Diocese of Aberdeen

THIRD EDITION

IN FIVE VOLUMES

VOL. III.

CHARITY : THE COMMANDMENTS

LONDON

BURNS OATES & WASHBOURNE LTD.

28 ORCHARD STREET   8-10 PATERNOSTER ROW
W. 1————————————————————E.C. 4

AND . AT . MANCHESTER . BIRMINGHAM . AND . GLASGOW

CONTENTS OF VOL. III

CONTENTS OF VOL. III

CONTENTS OF VOL. III

THE CATECHISM IN EXAMPLES

XXV

THE PRECEPT OF CHARITY

I. WHAT IS ENJOINED BY THIS PRECEPT—(1) THE LOVE OF GOD.

CHARITY is a virtue infused by God into our souls, by which we love God above all things and our neighbour as ourselves. Your first great duty, therefore, my child, is to love God. It is not difficult to love God ; all that is required of you is to do everything with the intention of pleasing Him, and in doing this you will love Him with your whole heart.

THE WORDS OF JESUS CHRIST OUR LORD ON CHARITY.

My child, always keep in mind, then, this great commandment of charity, which Jesus Christ Himself has given us.

" Thou shalt love the Lord thy God," He says, " with thy whole heart, and soul, and mind, and strength. This is the first and the greatest commandment ; and the second commandment is like unto it : Thou shalt love thy neighbour as thyself.

On these two commandments depend the whole law and the prophets."

Thou shalt love God—that is His commandment; for this we were made, in time and for eternity. " God made me to love Him." We must love God for His own sake, and we must love all men, whether friends or enemies, for the love of God. This is perfect charity, and greater than this there is nothing on earth nor even in Heaven.

This is what St. Paul says of charity: " Charity will never fail. Faith and hope will pass away, but charity will never pass away. There are three great virtues in this life," he says—" Faith, Hope, and Charity, but the greatest of these is Charity."

In Heaven faith will disappear, because we shall then see things as they are in themselves, in the light of God's countenance; there will be no need of hope there, for what the Saints hoped for they have attained —the possession of God, the beatitude of Heaven; but charity will there be found in all its perfection, for God is there, and " God is Charity," says the Apostle.

THE LITTLE SERVANT MAID.

A holy hermit was once troubled with a temptation of pride; he had spent so many years in the practice of prayer and penance that he began to imagine he was the holiest person in the world.

While he was thinking of this, God made known to him that he was mistaken, and that he was not nearly so holy, nor so far advanced in perfection, and in the love of God, as a certain poor waiting-maid in an hotel in the city.

This astonished the good hermit. " How can it be possible," he said to himself, " that a simple maid in an hotel can be equal to me in virtue, since I have done nothing else for many years but fast and pray continually ? I must go and visit her, and ask her what she does that makes her more agreeable in the eyes of God than I am."

So he went to the city, and easily found the person of whom he was in search. When he had told her what God had revealed to him in the vision, he asked her to let him know what great practices of piety she performed that made God love her so much, and made her more perfect in His eyes than he was.

" My Father," she replied, " I do not know what God can see in me that can please Him so much ; I am only a poor simple waiting-maid, and I have no learning. All that I can say to you is that I endeavour to perform all my actions with the greatest care, in order that I may please God and do His blessed will. When I am carrying wood for the kitchen fire, I think of the love of Jesus in carrying His cross for me, and I tell Him that I love Him because He is so good ; and in the same way, in all my other works, I always try to think of Him in some way or other."

The hermit returned home, thanking God for having put it in the power of even the simplest and lowliest of His children to love Him as much, and sometimes even more than those who have couse-crated themselves entirely to His service.

Lives of the Fathers of the Desert.

BLESSED HENRY SUSO LOVES GOD ABOVE ALL
THINGS.

Blessed Henry Suso was born in the year 1300.
The place of his birth was Suabia, and he was
descended from the noble families of the Bergs and
the Saussens.

God called him to embrace the religious life from
his infancy, for we read that when he was only a
little boy of thirteen he received the religious habit
in the convent of the Dominicans, in the city of
Constance.

At first he was far from being perfect. It is true
that he carefully avoided every grievous sin, as well
as every other outward fault that might in any way
injure his reputation, but he had a great attachment
to the world, and to its opinions and customs.

Still, he did not feel that he was doing right, for
something within him was constantly whispering to
him that God had made him for something far
higher than these empty things, and that he would
never be quite happy until he had given himself
entirely to God.

One day, as God was thus speaking to Him in his
heart, he formed the resolution of becoming a Saint.
" It is not generous in me," he said, " to serve God
as I am doing ; He wants my whole heart, and I will
from this time give it to Him, for I cannot divide it
between Him and the world : He must have it all."

But Satan, who was watching what Henry was
doing, put into his heart thoughts of despondency.
" You must know," whispered the evil spirit to
him—" you must know that it is indeed a very

easy thing to begin to lead a perfect life, but that it is next to impossible to continue in it to the end ; many have begun well, and have ended badly."

Henry answered · " The Holy Ghost, who has put these good thoughts into my heart, is as able to help me in difficult things as in easy ones."

But Satan was not to be so easily overcome. " What you say is quite true : no one can doubt the almighty power of God ; but that which should make you afraid to undertake that perfect life is the thought that perhaps you may not correspond with God's grace. It is not God's grace you are to be afraid of not receiving, but it is your own weakness that should give you cause to tremble at such a step."

Henry replied : " Do you think that God will forsake me, or leave me to myself, since He has called me to serve Him ? He has called me, therefore He will help me. If I throw myself into His arms like a little child, do you think He will cast me away ? Never ; He loves me too much."

But Satan still continued to tempt him. " At least," he said, " you must not think of trying to be a Saint all at once. If you are quite resolved to become a Saint, do so by degrees. Do not forsake the pleasures of the world all at one time, for you will never succeed."

" No," said Henry ; " Jesus Christ said that it was impossible for one to serve Him and the world at the same time."

Satan was vanquished, and retired for a time. He returned afterwards with greater force to tempt him, as we shall soon see.

But God consoled him in his trials, as He does

every one of His children who place their entire confidence in Him. One day, as he was kneeling in the church at his prayers, he felt his soul, as it were, full of holy joy. "O my God, I wish to love Thee alone. My heart must love something, but there is nothing on earth that can satisfy it. Thou alone, O my God, canst fully satisfy it. Therefore from this moment it must belong to Thee alone."

It was now that Satan came to tempt him with the greatest violence. "What are you going to do now?" he said to him in his heart. "What foolishness it is for you to love what you have never seen! Would it not be far better to love the things around you in the world, that you can feel and see, than those which may exist only in your own imagination? Besides, if you really intend to serve that God whom you have never seen, you must consider well what it will cost you. You will have to go against your own inclinations always; you will have to fast, and deprive yourself of your sleep, as well as to give up all your amusements and pleasures, which, indeed, would be the height of folly."

"The love of God," replied the holy man, "makes everything sweet and easy. Besides, look at the troubles and anxieties people of the world experience in attaining these enjoyments, and the remorse they feel when they are over."

This time also Satan was vanquished, and Henry persevered in his holy resolution to love God alone. He is now in Heaven with God, enjoying the eternal reward of those who have served God faithfully in this world to the end. Go, my child, and do thou likewise.

EXCELSIOR ; OR, " HIGHER STILL."

Some people imagine that, living, as they are, in the midst of a sinful world, and in a humble position of life, and occupied with their daily labours, they cannot become perfect. Others think that to be perfect they must live in some desert place, or in a convent, or in a monastery, and must be praying all day. Now, they are all quite wrong in this. For each one may easily become a Saint in the condition of life in which God has placed him. All that is required is to love God.

In the Desert of Thebaides there once lived a holy man named Paphnucius. He was the most holy and the most perfect of all the solitaries who dwelt there, by his austerities and prayers, his purity of soul, and all kinds of virtues and good works. Every day of his life he strove to become more and more perfect, to love God more and more, and to do more and more to increase his reward in Heaven.

Now, one day a thought came into his mind that perhaps he was the holiest man on the face of the earth, and he prayed to God that if there was any-one in the world more perfect than himself, He would be pleased to show him where he was, that he might go and see him, and learn from him to serve God with still greater perfection.

God was pleased to hear his prayer, and let him understand that if he went into a certain city he would find a man much more perfect than he was.

So he left his solitude, and went to the city which God pointed out to him.

When he arrived, he went to the market-place.

There he saw a very poor man playing a street organ, and a crowd of people round about him dancing to his music. God made known to him that this was the man who was more perfect than he.

The holy man was in amazement at this, and wondered in his own mind how it could be possible that one whose whole occupation was going about the streets playing an organ could be more perfect than he, who had spent his whole life in the desert in prayer and in all kinds of austerities. So when he got an opportunity, he took him aside, and said to him :

" My good man, I am very anxious to know how you live. Would you tell me in what way you serve God ? for God has made known to me that you are doing so in a way which is very pleasing to Him."

" Reverend Father," he answered, " I am a very great sinner, and I cannot see how God can be so pleased with me. One time I was a robber by profession, but by the grace of God I repented of my crimes, and now I am trying day by day to make reparation for my past life by this lowly occupation."

St. Paphnucius also learned from his conversation with him that even when he was a robber he had done many good works through charity towards his neighbours, and that perhaps God had rewarded him for them by giving him the grace of repentance.

So he returned to his desert again, and for many years more he studied how to please God better than before, by the practice of every virtue he could imagine ; and his continual prayer to God was this : " O my God, make me become as good in Thy sight as that man who plays the organ on the streets."

After a number of years spent in this way, he began again to wonder if there was in the world anyone who could equal him now in perfection. So God again was pleased to speak to him in his heart, and to let him know that there were, in a little village not far away, a man and his wife who were equal to him in virtue and merit.

So, having a very great desire to become acquainted with them, he went to that village, and easily found out the worthy people of whom he was in search. They had not done anything great in the eyes of the world, but in the eyes of God they had obtained much merit ; for, during the whole course of their married life, which had been for thirty years, they had lived together in the practice of great virtues, good works, kindness to the poor and to strangers, and in perfect peace with each other, both labouring together at their daily employment, and doing all for the glory of God.

Paphnucius returned again to his desert home, ashamed to think that a poor man and his wife, living by the work of their hands and in the midst of a wicked world, should be equal to himself in merit before God ; so he resolved again to do even more than before, that he might become more and more agreeable to Him.

Finally, after some more years spent in this way, he asked God if there was anyone equal to him in merit now ; and God answered him that there was— that there lived in a certain large city a good way off a merchant who stood behind his counter in his shop from morning to night, selling his goods to customers —buying and selling all day long, and that that merchant was as rich in merits before God as he himself was, because he was doing all this for the glory of God, and because it was His holy will.

When Paphnucius saw that people in the world, occupied with the labours of their calling, could become as perfect as a monk in his monastery, and even more so, he gave thanks to God, who has put it in the power of even the lowliest and the humblest person in the world to become so perfect, and to love Him so much.   *Lives of the Fathers.*

" THEE ONLY, O MY GOD, DO I DESIRE."

St. Thomas of Aquin could think only of God, could speak only of God ; nothing gave him any pleasure but to hear about God.

If sometimes he was in the company of those who were conversing about other things, he seemed to take no interest in their conversation ; it was evident his thoughts were on something very different from what they were thinking of.

Once, when residing in Naples, Brother Dominic Caserte beheld him, while in fervent prayer, raised from the ground, and heard a voice proceeding from the crucifix, saying to him : " Thou hast written well of me, Thomas ; what recompense dost thou desire ?"

He answered : " None other than Thyself, O Lord."   BUTLER : *Lives of the Saints*, Mar. 7.

FATHER ALPHONSUS OF SANDOVAL.

Father Alphonsus of Sandoval had a most tender love for the Divine Child Jesus. Christmas was the festival he loved best, because on that day Jesus lay, a little child in the manger at Bethlehem. For the love of the Holy Child Jesus he, although born of a noble family, consecrated his whole life to be the servant of the poor and of the slaves, who were at that time very numerous at Carthagena, in America.

About the year 1615 he fell down exhausted in the midst of his heroic work ; and, afflicted with a painful illness, he lay for a long time suffering the most severe agony.

When anyone went to visit him, he was almost always to be found lying on his back, with his hands joined on his breast, and his eyes fixed on Heaven. In all his sufferings he never uttered a word of complaint, but had always on his lips these beautiful words : " May God be praised ! may God be praised !"

As the festival of Christmas drew near, he became worse, and he earnestly prayed that he might die before that great day, that he might be able to keep it in Heaven. His prayer was heard, for, early on the morning of December 25, he died, full of good works and of merits, at the advanced age of seventy years.

Thus did God reward him for his long life of labour and sufferings, offered up through love for His Eternal Son Jesus.

ST. MARY MAGDALEN OF PAZZI'S EJACULATION.

One day, as St. Mary Magdalen of Pazzi was meditating on the sufferings of her beloved Saviour, and was gazing on the crucifix she held in her hands, she was so much overcome at the thought of how much Jesus loved us poor sinners that she cried out again and again · " O love ! O love ! O love ! No, my dearest Jesus, my heart shall never cease to cry out, ' O love ! O love !' "

Jesus suffered and died for you, my child, as well as for her ; try, then, to love Him as she did : love Him with your whole heart.

THE BEAUTIFUL FLOWER DESTROYED.

St. Rose of Lima loved to be alone, that she might be able to speak continually with God.   Her father had a large garden attached to his house, and this was to her a little Paradise.   In a corner of the garden she built for herself a rustic cell, in which she loved to hide herself, and there, though in the midst of a great city, she lived as if she were in an un-inhabited desert.

Around her little cell she planted the choicest flowers, and cultivated them with great care.   There was one amongst them which she loved more than all the rest.   This was the passion-flower.   It grew up and covered her cell, and its beautiful flowers continually reminded her of what was dearest to her heart—the sufferings of·Jesus.

There was also another flower which she trained up with great care ; she called it her " delight," and she used often to stand beside it for a long time, admiring its beauty and inhaling its sweet perfume.

One morning, when she went as usual to water it, she found it pulled out by the root, and lying on the ground ·quite withered.   This sight filled her with sorrow, and she cried bitterly :

" O my darling flower, who has done this to you ?"

Our Blessed Lord at the same instant appeared to her, and said : " My daughter, what is the matter with you, and why are you so sad ?"

" Don't you see, O Lord, that some cruel person has destroyed my beautiful flower ?"

" Some cruel person !" exclaimed Our Lord. " Well, then, know that it was I Who did it."

" And why, O Lord, did you pull it out ?"

" Why ? Because you are too fond of it. Did you not call it your ' delight,' your ' darling flower '? And did you not say that it was the joy of your heart to look at it ? Now, my child, I want to be the only joy of your heart ; I want you to give your whole heart to Me ; for am I not the Flower of the field, and the Lily of the valley ?"

You see, therefore, my child, how much Jesus desires to live in your soul, and that nothing pleases Him so much as to see you living for Him.

When the hour of death comes, if you have loved God all your lifetime with a tender childlike love, death will have no terrors for you, for you shall then sweetly die in the arms of Jesus, Whom you have always loved.

BLESSED GERARD'S LAST WORDS.

Gerard was a brother of the great St. Bernard, and had served God for many years in the monastery over which his brother ruled.

In the year 1138 he became very ill, and, knowing that his last hour was at hand, received the last Sacraments with great devotion. There was no sadness or fear of death in his soul, and his countenance was radiant with joy.

Just before he expired he raised up his eyes to Heaven and said : " O my God, into Thy hands I commend my spirit." Then, turning towards those who were kneeling around him, he said : " Oh, how good is God to us in making Himself our Father, and what a glory it is for us to be able to call ourselves His children !" Saying these words, he died, and went to dwell with his Father in Heaven.

My child, you can say with truth the same words. What a happiness this should be for you ! Love your Heavenly Father, then, with your whole heart.

ST. PHILIP'S LOVE FOR JESUS.

St. Philip Neri was inflamed with the love of God. " How is it possible," he would often say—" how is it possible that anyone who believes in God, and knows what the love of Jesus has done for him, can ever love anything else but God ?"

If at times he felt this love for Jesus less ardent than it usually was, he would complain to God in this manner : " O my God, Thou art so amiable, and Thou hast commanded me to love Thee. But why hast Thou given me only one heart to do this, and that heart, too, so very little ?"

We also read in his Life that he often received from God in return so many spiritual consolations that, unable any longer to endure so great a fire of love, he was forced to cry out : " No more, O Lord, no more." I know, my child, that you love God, but, ah ! how little is your love for Him when compared to that of St. Philip ! Beg of Jesus, then, to give you the great grace of loving Him daily more and more.

A FAVOURED CHILD OF JESUS.

There lived in Spain a very holy woman whose name was Jane Rodriguez, who from her infancy received from Jesus many miraculous marks of love for our encouragement and instruction.

One day, when Jane was only seven years old, and while she was praying with great devotion before a picture of the Holy Child Jesus, a dazzling brightness filled the room, and the Blessed Virgin appeared to her, holding the Divine Child in her arms. Jane bowed down in profound adoration, and contemplated with admiration the beauty of Mary and the majesty of Jesus.

Our Lady said to her : " My daughter, what do you think of my little Child Jesus ? Do you not think that everyone ought to love Him ? Would you yourself not like to have Him as your own dearest friend ?"

• " Yes, my Lady," answered Jane ; " that is my one only desire."

As soon as she said these words, Jesus stretched out His little hands as if to embrace her, and Mary pressed her to her heart. Jesus then gave her His blessing, and the vision disappeared from her sight, leaving her soul filled with a happiness which it would be vain to attempt to describe.

Jesus is not satisfied with words only. He wishes you to prove by your actions that you really love Him. He says in His Holy Gospel : " If you love Me, keep My commandments."

THE YOUNG CHINESE MAIDEN.

In the year 1841, a Chinese mandarin caused several Christians to be arrested and brought before him, that he might make them apostatize. His promises and his threats were both in vain, and he knew by the firmness of their answers that they would all willingly suffer every torture rather than deny their Faith. But what he could not obtain by words he hoped to obtain by cunning.

Amongst those apprehended was a young girl, who was kneeling at the feet of the mandarin, as is the custom in that country during the time of the trial. Without saying anything to her in answer to her firm refusal to deny her faith, he ordered one of his attendants to trace a circle with his spear on the ground around the girl as she knelt there. When this was done, he said to her : " If you rise up and go beyond that circle, I shall consider it a sign that you have renounced your Faith."

After this he left the place, and in a short time all the others present also departed ; none remained except the girl, who knelt motionless on the ground within the circle.

Towards evening, the secretary of the mandarin, anxious to know how the girl would act when left alone, returned secretly to the place, and watched her for a time unobserved. She was kneeling as before ; and during all the time he watched her from his hiding-place, she seemed not to move.

Filled with admiration, he at last went over to her and kindly said to her : " My child, rise up now and go home."

" No," she replied; " I will die rather than move from this spot."

" But the mandarin was not serious when he drew that circle around you," added the secretary.

" That matters not," she replied; " I heard his words, but I cannot know his intentions. I must understand his words just as I heard them."

The secretary continued to press her to rise up and depart, but she always firmly refused. At length he himself blotted out the circle his master had formed; and then only did the pious child rise from her knees.

Oh, what an example of constancy! Would that all Christians would imitate the example of that young Chinese girl! Then, indeed, would they show that they really loved God.

THE PILGRIM'S DESIRE FULFILLED.

St. Bernardin of Siena tells us of a gentleman, well known for his fervour and piety, who made a pilgrimage to the Holy Land.

He first stopped at Nazareth, where the mystery of the Incarnation was accomplished. He then proceeded to Bethlehem, to kneel at the spot in which Our Lord first deigned to visit this earth as a suffering Infant.

He next walked by the banks of the Jordan, the scene of Our Lord's baptism, and went to the desert which had witnessed that forty days' fast; to the mountain where Jesus was transfigured; to the house at Jerusalem consecrated by the institution of the Holy Eucharist; to the Garden of Olives;

and to Calvary, where Jesus died. He visited the scene of Our Lord's burial and resurrection, and finally ascended Mount Olivet, fondly recalling to mind the blessing which He gave to His Apostles before His ascension. After visiting every place which was in any way connected with Our Lord's life or death, with a heart glowing with love he exclaimed : "O Jesus, Jesus, my much-beloved Saviour, since I can no longer follow Thy footsteps on earth, take me to Thyself in Heaven, that I may see Thee face to face—Thee whom I love with my whole heart."

His prayer was immediately heard, for no sooner was it uttered than he expired. The intensity of his love for Jesus, and his ardent desire of being with Him, had broken his heart ; and after death these words were found engraven on his breast: "Jesus, my Love !"

ST. BENEDICT JOSEPH LABRE'S INSTRUCTION ON HOW TO LOVE GOD.

One day St. Benedict Joseph Labre, having gone to see a poor sick man, spoke to him in words in spired by his own great fervour on the love of God.

When the poor man had listened to him in silence for a short time, he suddenly asked him : "My brother, tell me, I pray thee, how I can love God as much as I ought to do, and as He deserves to be loved."

The Saint said to him · "To love God as He deserves to be loved it is necessary that we should have three hearts joined together in one. The first one, all on fire with the love of God, ought to make us think on Him continually, and, above all other things, to bear with patience during our whole life the sufferings and trials He may be pleased to send us.

" The second heart, made of flesh and blood, ought to make us come to the assistance of our fellow-beings, made as we ourselves are, and to help them in their temporal necessities by affording them all the relief in our power, and in their spiritual wants by instruction, by counsel, by example, and by prayer. This second heart of ours should in a particular manner feel compassion for poor sinners, and should unceasingly ask God to open the eyes of their souls to see the sad condition in which they are placed, and to induce them to do penance for their sins ; it also should be filled with a tender compassion for the poor suffering souls that are in Purgatory.

" The third heart within us ought to be, as it were, of bronze, to be employed in loving ourselves in the manner God desires. It should resist all temptation to self-esteem, or thinking oneself to be of any importance ; it should make us go against our natural desires, and keep our flesh in subjection by fasting and abstinence.

' The more you banish from your soul the thought of self, the more will charity reign in it, and the greater will be your recompense in the world to come."

This was the advice St. Benedict Joseph Labre **gave him.** SCHOUPPE : *Instructions*, ii. 322.

THE HOLY CHILD DOMENICA.

There lived long ago a young maiden called Domenica, who had the great happiness, when only about ten years of age, of having a vision, in which the most holy Mother of God appeared to her, bearing in her arms the holy Child Jesus.

This little girl had ever had an intense love for Our Lady. From the tender age of five years she had been accustomed to impose upon herself little acts of penance in her honour, and every Saturday she secretly gave to the poor part of the food her parents gave her for herself. On that day also she would go to the gardens and the fields in the summertime, and gather the most beautiful flowers she could find. These she arranged in exquisite bouquets, and placed on the altar of Our Lady in her room, on which stood an image of the most holy Mother of God, with the Divine Child in her arms.

One day, when this little servant of Mary stood at one of the windows of her father's house, and was looking down the road, she saw passing beneath a poor but beautiful woman, with a little child at her side. They both looked up towards her, and stretched out their hands to her as if requesting an alms. The little girl hastened at once to the storeroom to procure some bread for them, but when she returned to give it to them, behold, she saw them standing near her in the house, the doors of which had remained shut. The woman now wore an air of graciousness and majesty which quite overawed Domenica, and her wonder was increased when she beheld two wounds on the Child's hands, two on His feet, and one in His side.

" Who has had the cruelty to thus wound your little child ?" she asked of the mother.

· " It is love that caused these wounds," she answered.

" Do these wounds give you much pain ?" she added, addressing the child.

The child did not answer, but only smiled sweetly.

After these and other similar words they turned towards Our Lady's altar, which Domenica had recently adorned with sweet-smelling flowers.

" Tell me, my child," asked the unknown lady, " why do you always place beautiful and fragrant flowers before this image ?"

" It is on account of the love I have for the Divine Child Jesus and His most holy Mother," answered the girl with simplicity.

" And do you love them very much ?"

" I love them," she said, " as much as it is possible for me to do."

" You do well, my child," answered the lady ; " continue to love them, and they will give you Heaven as a recompense."

An odour of the most exquisite perfume came forth from the wounds of the Child.

" Oh, how beautiful is the odour the wounds of your child give forth !" said Domenica. " What is the ointment you use, and where can it be procured ? Could I also buy it ?"

" Yes, my child ; you can buy it by faith and by good works."

Domenica then offered them the bread she had gone to bring them ; but the Mother sweetly said :

" The food my Child prefers is love. Tell Him

that you love Jesus, and you will make Him happy "

At the mention of the word " love " the child began to leap with joy, and, turning towards Domenica, he said to her :

" And do you love Jesus very much ?"

. " Oh yes ; I love Him," she said—" I love Him so much that I cannot think of anything else but Him day and night, and I always try to do all I can to please Him—always, always."

" You are doing well ; continue to love Him with your whole heart, and that love will teach you what to do to make Him love you also."

In the meantime the beautiful odour coming from his wounds seemed to increase. " O my God," she exclaimed, " this odour seems to fill me with love. How beautiful must the odour of Paradise be, since this is so exquisite !"

But in an instant the scene was changed. The unknown woman was suddenly surrounded with brightness and with radiant light. The little Child also shone like the sun in the heavens, and, taking the flowers which adorned the image on the altar, He scattered them over the girl, who had fallen on her knees before Him. Then the heavenly vision disappeared.   *L'Enfant Chrét.*, p. 6.

II. How God often treats those whom He Loves Most.

It is not always those who feel the greatest spiritual consolation that love God most. Sometimes, my child, those who love Him best, and whom

He loves with the greatest affection, are the ones who receive from Him, in this world, the least consolation.

THE THREE YOUNG MAIDENS.

One day a pious lady went to a church to hear Mass. During the Holy Sacrifice God was pleased to grant her the following vision : After the consecration she saw our Divine Lord Himself present on the altar under the appearance of a little child. As she was looking on Him with great love, she saw Him come down from the altar, and go over to three young maidens who were also present at Mass.

When He reached the first one, He appeared to lavish on her many marks of tenderness, and to speak to her in words of endearment. After that, He went towards the second one and smiled on her, but did not treat her in the same affectionate manner in which He had treated the first. Lastly He went to the third one, and, raising up His hand, struck her a heavy blow on the face, which made her fall to the ground. He then returned to the altar and disappeared.

The lady was for a time lost in astonishment at what she had just seen ; and the more she thought about it, the more anxious she became to discover what was meant by the vision.

And as she prayed to God that He would be pleased to manifest to her the meaning of it, she saw standing at her side the holy Child Jesus as she had seen Him on the altar.

" My child," He said to her, " those three young virgins are all most dear to Me ; they are My faithful spouses, and they all love Me with the greatest affection. The first one whom I went to, and to whom you saw Me show so many marks of affection, is only just beginning to advance towards perfection ; I must, therefore, treat her with great kindness, as a mother treats a young child. The second one loves Me with her whole soul, and although I did not treat her as I did the other one she did not complain, because she has more at heart My Divine pleasure than her own satisfaction ; still, from time to time I have to grant her some spiritual consolation, that she may not grow weary in her life of piety.

" As to the third one," continued the holy Child, " she loves Me with the most perfect love, and is willing to receive from My hands afflictions and trials of all kinds, and does not look for any consolation. And although I send her crosses, she is willing to receive them all, not only without complaining, but even with the greatest joy, because it is My will to send them. Therefore I love her more than the other two, although I treat her with greater severity."

The lady was grateful to God for this beautiful lesson, which will be for you also, my child, an encouragement to love your Heavenly Father always, in afflictions as well as in times of joy.

VEN. CESAR DE BUS.

III. THE PRECEPT OF CHARITY COMMANDS US—(2) TO LOVE OUR NEIGHBOUR.

My child, Jesus Christ tells us that the first and greatest commandment of the Law is to love God above all things, and that the second one is like to it : " Thou shalt love thy neighbour as thyself."

BEAUTIFUL WORDS OF ST. JOHN.

" Dearly beloved, let us love one another, for charity is of God. In this is charity : not as though we had loved God, but because He hath first loved us and sent His Son to be a propitiation for our sins. My dearest, if God hath so loved us, we ought also to love one another. If we love one another, God abideth in us.

" Let us therefore love God, because God first hath loved us. If any man say, I love God, and hateth his brother, he is a liar : for he that loveth not his brother, whom he seeth, how can he love God, whom he seeth not ?''

ST. JOHN'S SERMON.

When St. John, the beloved disciple of Our Lord, was a very old man, and not able to walk, the faithful used to carry him to the church, that they might hear him preach to them the heavenly lessons he had heard from the lips of his Divine Master.

He could not preach to them long sermons, because he was so feeble, so they listened to him with the greatest eagerness, that they might hear every word he said. St. John always said to them the same words : " My little children, love one another."

The faithful at length became weary of hearing the same thing so often repeated to them, so they one day said to him · " Master, why do you always preach to us the same words ?"

St. John answered : " My little children, it is the commandment of the Lord; if it is done, it is enough."

History of the Church.

Our Blessed Lord Himself had long before said the same thing : " By this shall all men know that you are My disciples, if ye have love one for the other." From these words, my child, you see what a great virtue the love of our neighbour must be.

THE MONK OF CITEAUX.

In the history of the Abbey of Citeaux, it is recorded that a certain monk of that Order was so good that every time he went to Communion he felt his soul filled with a spiritual sweetness, which lasted sometimes for the whole day on which he had received the Holy Eucharist, and even sometimes for several days afterwards.

It happened that one day this good religious had occasion to reprimand one of the brethren under his care for a small fault he had committed. This he did with a little too much severity. Nevertheless, without considering that he had done anything amiss, but had only acted through zeal for the observance of the rule, he went next morning to the altar to receive Holy Communion as usual. But this time, instead of feeling within him that spiritual sweetness to which he had been accustomed, he was filled with sadness and great dryness, so that he felt no devotion. This distressed him exceedingly, and he began to examine his conscience to discover what he had done to offend God that he should be punished in this way

He soon remembered the words he had used on the previous night to the brother whom he had corrected, and he saw that it was on account of his want of charity to his neighbour that he was so punished. He repented of his fault, and did penance for it, and soon again recovered his accustomed devotion.

IN PRISON FOR CHRIST'S SAKE.

St. Peter Paschal went to preach the Faith to the Mahometans of Grenada. He converted many of them to the true faith. This made the chiefs of that sect hate him. They caused him to be seized and bound with chains, and to be treated as a common prisoner.

His friends at home, hearing of his capture, and of the cruel treatment to which he was being subjected, sent a large sum of money for his ransom. But instead of spending it for his own deliverance, he spent it in freeing a number of women and children who were in danger of losing their Faith.

Our Lord was so pleased with this heroic act of charity that He came once in person to thank him. It was one morning at Mass. A little Boy came to serve him. He was dressed in the garments of a slave. When Holy Mass was over the Saint, as usual, asked Him some of the questions of the Catechism, as was his custom.

The little Boy gave him the answers so correctly, and at the same time with so much ease, that the Saint was astonished. When he asked Him who Jesus Christ was, the child answered · " I am Jesus Christ ; look at My hands, and My feet, and at My side, and you will see the marks of the nails and of the spear. As you in your charity have willingly condemned yourself to be a prisoner for the sake of My people, and have given liberty to them, I have made Myself your prisoner."

Saying these words, Jesus disappeared, leaving the Saint full of joy.

SHE LABOURED FOR GOD'S POOR.

A young lady, who had lived in great purity of heart, took the resolution one day of testifying as often as was in her power her love for God in the persons of His poor.

She was far from being wealthy, and consequently it was beyond her power to give great alms ; but she did that which was of as much benefit to them, and more profitable to herself before God : she spent all the time that she could spare from the duties of her state of life in mending the rags that covered them. This was her only recreation for many years.

One day, as she was passing along the road alone, she met a poor man whom she had never before seen, and who was never seen afterwards. This man, having saluted her respectfully, said to her : " My child, I have some news to give you, for which thank God : in six days you shall die."

This information, instead of filling her with dismay, gave her intense pleasure. She went in great haste to her brother, who was a little older than herself, and to her other relatives and friends, and related to them what the poor man had said to her. They one and all told her to pay no heed to his words, that it was all the effect of her imagination, and that she, who was then enjoying such good health, could naturally look forward to a long life.

But she would not be persuaded to think as they suggested, and from that moment made her immediate preparation for death. She said : " What danger have I to fear in thus preparing to die ? All things must come to pass according to God's holy will, and not one of you will ever succeed in making me disbelieve that this is a warning God from Heaven has sent me. May His holy Name be for ever praised !"

She spent these six days as fervently as she would have done had she been certain that Jesus Christ Himself had spoken to her ; for in her own heart she was persuaded that it was really He who had assumed the appearance of a poor man, to forewarn her that He would soon come and take her to Himself.

She died on the sixth day, in sentiments of great piety, and with her last breath gave thanks to God for having inspired her with so great a love for His beloved poor. *L'Année des Saints*, p. 319.

IV. OF THE REWARD PROMISED TO THOSE WHO LOVE THEIR NEIGHBOUR.

Our Lord has promised a most magnificent reward in Heaven to those who love their neighbours ; the reason of this is because He considers as done to Himself whatever we do to them.

BROTHER BERNARD'S REWARD

Brother Leo, one of the first companions of St. Francis of Assisi, had one day a beautiful vision. He saw coming towards him a great company of Friars Minor, all of whom were surrounded with a bright halo of glory. Their faces, too, were beaming with supreme happiness.

Amongst them there was one brighter and more glorious than all the rest. From his eyes came forth rays of light which dazzled the good brother, so that he could scarcely look at him.

Leo asked the others who this brother was who shone with so much splendour.

One of them answered : " It is Brother Bernard, the first companion of our Father St. Francis. God has rewarded him with this great glory, because when on earth he always thought and spoke well of others, and always judged his neighbour to be better than himself. If he happened to meet a poor man on the street, he would say to himself : ' Bernard, there is a man who bears up with poverty better than you are doing.' If he met one who was clad in rich garments, and who appeared to possess much wealth, he would say : ' There is a man who perhaps is wearing under his fine clothes a rough hair-shirt, and in the midst of his riches is very poor in spirit ; he is certainly doing more for God than you are doing.' As a reward for this charity, God has crowned him with so much glory in Heaven."

Lives of the First Comp. of St. Francis.

ST. MARTIN'S CLOAK.

St. Martin was Bishop of Tours during the latter half of the fourth century. When he was a lad of fifteen, he was obliged to serve in the army. But although he had to live amongst those whose lives were spent in evil, young Martin was never seen to join them in any of their wicked deeds, but was always careful to shun their company as far as he was able.

He was not at that time baptized, but in his heart he believed in Jesus Christ, and tried in all his conduct to imitate His example, and to follow all the maxims of the Gospel so far as he knew them.

The virtue he loved best to practise was that of charity towards his neighbour. He loved the poor because he had learned that they were particularly beloved by Jesus Christ. Every day he distributed among them whatever he was able to save out of his pay ; and that he might make his alms more abundant, he kept for himself only what was strictly necessary for his support.

One day, when he had nothing in his purse, he happened to meet a poor man at the gate of the city of Amiens. The man was almost naked, and was trembling with cold. As soon as Martin saw him, his heart was moved with compassion ; but, having no money to give him, he stood for an instant thinking how he would be able to assist him.

Suddenly a thought came into his mind. He seized his sword, and taking the mantle with which he himself was covered, cut it in two, and gave one half of it to the poor man. With the other half he covered his own shoulders, and proceeded to join the rest of the soldiers, heedless of what they might think of him, or of the jeers they might throw out against him.

On the following night, as he lay asleep, Jesus Christ appeared to him, accompanied by a multitude of His holy angels, and clad in the half of the mantle he had given to the poor man on the previous day. Looking on Martin with a look of gratitude, Jesus said to the angels : " It was Martin who gave Me this garment."

In return for this act of charity Martin received the gift of the faith, became a great and holy Bishop, and is now high among the Saints of God in Paradise.

Life of St. Martin.

V. WE MUST HELP OUR NEIGHBOUR IN HIS NEEDS.

St. John says : " He that loveth not his brother, whom he seeth, how can he love God, whom he seeth not ?" (I John, iv. 21). We are all brethren, and children of one common Father, and we must love each other and help each other in all our needs.

" GOD ALONE FOR ME."

Long ago there lived a woman called Sylvia, who pretended to love God so much that she had no time to think about her neighbour.

" God alone for me," she used to say continually. " I need no one else : what have I to do with other people ?"

Hence she never assisted her neighbours in any of their difficulties, and seemed even to look on them as being quite unworthy of her attention, since she had given her heart entirely to God.

She even went so far as to look with contempt on her parents, her husband, and her most intimate friends, and when they tried to show her that those who really love God love also their neighbour for His sake, she would answer as before : " What have

I to do with you or the things of this world, since I am made for God in Heaven ?   Oh no, I do not need you at all ; God alone is enough for me."

One day as she was walking in the garden near her house she fell into a pond full of water.   Her screams for help soon brought her parents and her neighbours to the spot.   They saw immediately that she was not in any danger, as the water was not deep, and thought that this would be an excellent opportunity for giving her a lesson.

Her mother stood near the edge of the pond, but without stretching out her hand to help her, or showing the least sign of emotion, said to her : " My daughter, don't be afraid ; you do not need my help, since God alone is always enough for you."

The father then came forward and said : " It would be a great act of folly, my child, for me to help you, since you always told me that God alone was sufficient for you at all times."

She next turned to some of her friends who were standing near her parents, and, stretching out her hands towards them, implored them to help her to get out.

But they said · " We **are** altogether unworthy to help you, for we are great sinners and you are so great a Saint, and always thinking of God and speaking to Him.   You must not, therefore, look to us for help."

Her husband, who had just heard of what had happened, came in great haste to the place.   " Come out of the pond," he cried.

" How can I come out when no one will help me ? I cannot get out of myself."

" Ah, my dear wife, I hope you have learned to-day that you do sometimes require the assistance of your neighbour. Come, give me your hand, and I will draw you out."

Saying these words, he dragged her out of the pond. " You see," he continued, when she was standing by his side—" you see that although God alone is to be loved and served, yet it is His holy will that we should love our neighbour also, and help him in his necessities ; and it is by this mark that people will be able to know that we really love God."

From that day Sylvia remembered the lesson she had received, and although she continued to love God as before with all her heart, she joined to it the love also of her neighbour.   *Cesar Celina.*

VI. We must Love our Neighbour even though Ungrateful.

You must love your neighbour not only when he is good and kind to you, but also when he is un grateful, and does you an injury. Has not Jesus Christ said : " If you love them that love you, what reward shall you have ?" (St. Matt. v. 46).

ST. JOHN THE ALMONER AND THE RICH BEGGAR.

In a great city called Adrion, a certain rich stranger who had heard of the compassion of St. John the Almoner for the poor, wished to find out for himself if all that he had heard were indeed true. So one day he put on tattered garments, and stood by the side of the street through which the Saint had to pass in going to the hospital where the sick were, which he did several times every week.

When St. John had come to the place where he was standing, the pretending beggar cried out to him : " Have pity on me, for I am a wretched man just freed from prison."

St. John said to the servant who accompanied him and carried his purse : " Give this poor man six pieces of money."

When the stranger received the money, he thanked him and went away. As soon as St. John was out of sight, he changed his garments and ran by another street, and again met the Saint before he reached the hospital.

Assuming a different tone of voice, he said to him : " Take pity on me, Father, for I am in great destitution."

St. John turned to his servant, and said to him : " Give the poor stranger seven pieces of gold."

The stranger took the gold and went away. When he was gone, the servant said to the Saint : " My Father, you have given alms to that man twice to-day ; it was he who, in the dress of a beggar, met us a few minutes ago."

St. John pretended not to hear what the servant had said ; and when for the third time the same man came under a different guise to ask an alms, the servant said to him : " It is the same man again, Father ; this is the third time he has come to-day."

" Give him twelve pieces this time," was the reply, " for it may be Jesus Christ Himself who has taken **the appearance of this poor man to try me."**

The stranger published everywhere what he had

done to try the Saint's patience and charity, and returned home full of respect and veneration for one endowed with so much virtue.

Life of St John the Almoner.

A POOR MAN SAVES THE LIFE OF A JEW.

A poor charcoal-burner, passing through a wood on a bitterly cold day in the middle of winter, found lying on the ground a man who seemed to be frozen to death. From his appearance, he easily recognized him to be a Jew. Lying at his side was a little basket, in which he carried the small wares by the sale of which he gained his livelihood.

The poor man said to himself: " Perhaps this poor Jew may not yet be dead, and with a little care may revive. Although he is a Jew, he is still a man and my neighbour, and my duty is to do what I can to succour him."

Saying this, and having hidden the basket under the snow, he placed the man on his shoulders, carried him in haste to the nearest inn, and employed the means at his disposal to reammate him. In a short time he was rewarded; to his great joy the Jew opened his eyes, and was soon out of immediate danger.

" Thanks be to God !" the poor man ejaculated. " My labour has not been in vain."

Then he gave the innkeeper what money he had, that he might give the Jew any little nourishment he might need. He next went to the place where he had hidden the things that belonged to him, and brought them to the inn.

On his return the child of Abraham threw himself

upon his neck, and from his inmost heart thanked him for having saved his life. He then requested him to accept, as a sign of his gratitude, the basket with all its contents.

But the charitable charcoal-burner would not take it, saying that what he had done was done for the love of God and for His sake.

The Jew continued to urge him to accept at least a little present from him ; but he did not allow him to finish what he desired to say. Placing the basket in his hands, he affectionately clasped them in his own, saying : " I have only done what was my duty to do ; everyone ought to do the same to his fellow creature, whosoever he may be. May God be your guide, and lead you safely wherever you go."

Saying this, he left him. This good man, in saving the Jew's life, not only performed a good action, but made it more meritorious still by refusing to accept any reward in return. His charity for his neighbour was founded on disinterested love.

Cat. Prat., ii. 28.

XXVI

THE VIRTUE OF RELIGION

I. IN WHAT THE VIRTUE OF RELIGION CONSISTS.

IT is not enough to believe in God, hope in Him, and love Him in our hearts ; we must also manifest these inward sentiments by some outward sign. This is done by the virtue of religion.

The virtue of religion, therefore, is that virtue which arises in our hearts from the consideration of the infinite greatness of God, and produces in them sentiments of the most profound respect for Him, as well as for all that belongs to Him; which also manifests itself outwardly by certain signs, showing forth these interior sentiments of veneration and love.

ST. POLLIO, MARTYR.

Among the almost innumerable multitude of martyrs who sealed with their blood their fidelity to the law of God was one whose name was Pollio, belonging to the city of Rome—a man remarkable for his great faith and piety, of which on many occasions he gave manifest testimony.

Probus, the Governor of the province under Diocletian, had scarcely reached the town in which the generous Christian then resided, when the latter was brought before him, accused of being one of the most zealous disciples of Jesus Christ.

The Governor immediately began to interrogate him, and learned from him that he was one of the lectors of the Church—that is, one of those who at that time were ordained to read the Word of God to the people. The Governor, when he came to know this, began to speak in words of disparagement against the Faith of Christ, and of those who had the courage to embrace it and publicly profess it.

Pollio answered him : " Those only should be considered weak-minded and foolish who forsake the God Who created them, to adopt the superstitions you practise. As for those who listen to the words that we read to them, they become so firmly rooted in their faith that not even the direst torments invented to afflict them will ever cause them to transgress the commandments of their God and King."

" Of what King, and of whose commandments do you speak ?" asked Probus.

Pollio replied : " I speak of the commandments of the Eternal King, Jesus Christ."

" To what do these commandments oblige you ?" said the prefect.

Pollio answered : " They oblige everyone to adore one true and only God, and no other ; they teach us that idols made of wood or stone cannot be gods ; they show us how we ought to live ; they strengthen us to live virtuously ; they teach holy virgins how to tend towards the perfection of their state, and those who have the care of their homes and families to lead a life of constancy and virtue ; they teach masters how to treat their slaves and servants with mildness and humanity, and show these how to serve their masters with fidelity and love. They also instruct subjects how to submit to those who rule over them, and those who are in power to govern with justice. In a word, the commandments of the King of Heaven declare unto us that we must honour our father and mother, assist our friends, pardon our enemies, exercise hospitality towards strangers, help the needy and poor, love all mankind, never do injury to anyone, suffer patiently those who have been unjust towards us, never have any attachment to worldly things, never take from others unjustly what belongs to them, nor even desire them in a covetous manner ; and, finally, that a happy eternity hereafter will be the recompense of him who will have the courage to disregard the death you may inflict upon us."

This beautiful exposition of Christian morality, and the noble profession of faith which accompanied it, did not touch the hardened heart of the judge. The holy martyr, having over and over again refused to offer sacrifice to the idols, was condemned to be burned alive, and by this terrible death went to Heaven to receive the recompense promised to those who in this life prefer to lose all things, even life, rather than transgress the commandments of the Lord."   *Acts of the Martyrs.*

II. WE MUST ADORE GOD, AND HIM ALONE.

You must not forget, my child, that, although God is our Creator and Father, and as such requires that we should love Him with our whole hearts,

He is also our sovereign Master, and, being this, requires that we should adore Him. "The Lord thy God shalt thou adore, and Him only shalt thou serve." The angels in Heaven are all on fire with the love of God, yet St. John saw them prostrate before His throne adoring Him.

ST. JOHN IN PARADISE.

" Behold there was a throne set in Heaven, and upon the throne one sitting. And He that sat was to the sight like the jasper and the sardine-stone, and there was a rainbow about the throne, in sight like to an emerald. And round about the throne were four-and-twenty seats, and upon the seats four-and-twenty ancients sitting, clothed in white garments, and on their heads were crowns of gold.

" And in the midst of the throne, and round about the throne, were four living creatures, and they rested not day and night, saying: ' Holy, holy, holy, Lord God Almighty, Who was, and Who is, and Who is to come !' And when those living creatures gave glory and honour and benediction to Him that sitteth on the throne, that liveth for ever and ever, the four-and-twenty ancients fell down before Him that sitteth on the throne, and adored Him that liveth for ever and ever, and cast their crowns before the throne, saying : ' Thou art worthy, O Lord our God, to receive honour, and glory, and power, because Thou hast created all things.'

" And all the angels stood round about the throne, and the ancients and the four living creatures, and they fell down before the throne on their faces and adored God, saying : ' Amen ; benediction, and glory, and wisdom, and thanksgiving, honour, and power, and strength to our God for ever and ever. Amen.' "

THE ANGELS AT THE ALTAR.

St. John Chrysostom relates the following vision which God granted to himself :

" As soon as the Holy Mass began, I saw a great multitude of the blessed spirits come down from Heaven, clothed in shining garments ; their eyes were reverently cast down towards the ground, their feet were uncovered, and they bowed in profound adoration.

" They stood thus around the altar in silence and awe until the Holy Sacrifice was ended ; they also accompanied the bishops or the priests who administered Holy Communion to the faithful."

In another part of his writings the same Saint relates that a certain old man, to whom God had made known many of the secrets of Heaven, assured him that during the time of Holy Mass he had the happiness of seeing, as far as it is possible for mortal eyes to behold, a multitude of angels, clad in white and shining robes, surrounding the altar and bowing their heads in adoration.

MARDOCHAI AND AMAN THE FAVOURITE OF THE KING.

When Artaxerxes, King of Persia, had given orders that all the members of his Court and the subjects over whom he ruled should bow their knee before Aman, who was his favourite counsellor, and whom he had exalted to the second rank in his kingdom, Mardochai the Jew refused to obey his command, although he foresaw that Aman, who was cruel as well as ambitious, would avenge himself upon him.

Mardochai in his prayer to God declared the motives which had caused him to adopt this resolution. "O Lord, Lord, Almighty King . . . Thou hast made Heaven and earth, and all things that are under the cope of Heaven. Thou art Lord of all, and there is none that can resist Thy majesty. Thou knowest all things, and Thou knowest that it was not out of pride and contempt, or any other desire of glory, that I refused to worship the proud Aman (for I would willingly and readily, for the salvation of Israel, have kissed even the steps of his feet), but I feared lest I should transfer the honour of my God to a man, and lest I should adore anyone except my God." *Esther* xiii. 12-15.

GEYSA, KING OF THE MAGYARES.

The celebrated King Geysa, who reigned over the Magyares towards the end of the sixteenth century, became so favourably disposed towards Christianity, through the influence of his beautiful and heroic spouse Sarobta, that he granted permission to the priests, who were sent by the Bishop of Passau in Hungary, to exercise the duties of their office towards the Germans whom he had taken prisoners.

The zeal and piety of these missionary Fathers, and the devout attention of those to whom they ministered, made so marked an impression on Geysa and some of his courtiers that he and they also desired to be instructed and to embrace the Faith.

After they had received suitable instructions, they were admitted to the Sacrament of Baptism. But Geysa afterwards still continued to offer sacrifices to the idols of his country, as he had done before. On being remonstrated with for doing this, and again told that he must worship only one God—the God of Heaven—he answered in his simplicity " I do not see that in doing this I am doing what is wrong ; for am I not rich enough to offer sacrifices to them all ?"

This way of thinking may be in a way excusable in one who has been brought up in paganism, but should not be entertained by a person educated from his infancy in the truths of Christianity, much less in one who is a member of the faithful. But, alas ! nothing is so common as to see Christians who imagine they are rich in wisdom, virtues, and merits, endeavour to serve God and the world at the same time, and consecrate themselves to the service of both. My child, do not be led by their example, but, since you are God's child, serve Him and love Him alone.

THE OFFICER AND THE MONK.

One day a Capuchin Father was walking in the country, when he was joined by an officer of the army, a man noted for his bravery and skill in war, but who gave himself little or no concern about religion. The Father was about to retire, but the officer immediately spoke to him, and said :

' " Why are you going away, Father ? Does my appearance make you afraid ? Remain with me a few moments ; you have nothing to fear. I am quite aware that persons of my calling are too often accustomed to find their amusement in speaking unbecomingly of men such as you ; but I am not one of these. Indeed, I would consider it a very cowardly act for anyone to insult another who is debarred from replying in a similar tone. It seems to me that such an act would resemble that of a man who would draw his sword to attack one who was unarmed. So, my Father, you need have no misapprehension on that matter. Far from desiring to give you any annoyance, I would, on the contrary, endeavour to offer you some consolation in the severe and laborious life you have chosen, for I know of no state that can be compared to it in hardship and desolation."

Thereupon he began to dilate on the various inconveniences, grievances, and the severity of life to which those of that Order bound themselves—such as walking barefooted, being clad in the coarsest of garments, and subsisting on the plainest of food, as well as the obligation of begging from door to door to obtain it.

The Father permitted him to speak to the end without interruption ; then he replied : " Sir, I am indeed very grateful to you for the kind interest you take in my welfare ; but allow me to say that I am not so much to be pitied as you seem to imagine. I even make bold to say that you are much more in need of commiseration than I am. This may perhaps surprise you ; you may even consider the assertion to be inconsistent. Let me endeavour to prove to you how true it is.

" In the first place, do you yourself not find your

position a trying one, when, at the first intimation of a war having broken out, you are called upon to tear yourself away from the bosom of your family, to whom justly you are so much attached, with the prospect of never again seeing them ? Then, during the time of war, does it appear to you to be sweet and pleasant to encamp, frequently in the middle of the snows of winter, with only a thin canvas tent to protect you from the cold blasts, and to march and countermarch continually over impassable roads and rugged mountains ; to bear the oppressive heats of summer or the biting colds of winter, and to pass the nights so often under the open canopy of Heaven ?

" But these are among the least of what you have to encounter. When, during a siege, you are commanded to occupy the trenches or to scale the walls, or when on the field of battle you are ordered to attack the enemy or to occupy a position exposed to the fire of artillery, without being permitted to retire or advance—in a word, when the cannon-balls and the bullets from the guns of the enemy whistle past your ears, or their shells burst near you, striking and killing many of those who are around you, with the dread that the next minute you may share a similar fate, not to speak of the bayonets and the swords bringing death to so many, and on which you must rush forward—tell me, I ask you, is not your position much more to be deplored than that of the poor Capuchin ? The Capuchin may have plain food and clothing, but his life is not exposed to such dangers as these ; he runs no risk of being wounded or maimed. And I need not add, sir, what is well known to you, that many officers and soldiers, even although they may have escaped with their lives, return home to their families covered with wounds, and not unfrequently deprived of some of the members of their bodies."

Here the officer interrupted him. " And do you account as nothing," he said, with some warmth, " the glory which one acquires for having exposed himself to so many dangers for his Prince and for his fatherland ? It is the desire and the hope of obtaining this glory that sustains us in the midst of all these dangers you have so vividly described."

" I fully expected that this would be your answer," replied the Capuchin, " but I must turn it against yourself. In leading a life which is more severe than the one we live, and in exposing yourself to so many dangers, labours, and wounds, you aspire after a renown which is only temporal ; whereas the Capuchin, in submitting himself to his severe and mortified life, proposes to acquire for himself a greater recompense—one that will never end. It seems to me, therefore, that you are more to be pitied in this instance also than he is."

Those who accompanied the officer assented to the decision of the religious : the officer himself could not deny how truthful it was, and was pleased when the conversation turned on some other matter.

My child, how many people there are who would become great Saints if they only did as much to please God and gain merit for Heaven as they do to please the world and gain the esteem of men ! Endeavour, then, to do as Jesus Christ tells you :

" Lay up for yourselves treasures in Heaven, where neither the rust nor moth doth consume, and where thieves do not break through and steal " (St. Matt. vi. 20).   HAUTERIVE: *Catéchisme de Persévérance*, v. 52.

III. THE NECESSITY OF BELIEVING INWARDLY AND PROFESSING OUTWARDLY OUR FAITH

By the virtue of religion, my child, we believe without doubting all the truths that God has revealed to us, and we also profess outwardly this belief as often as God's honour and our own or our neighbour's good require it. Jesus Christ has said · " He that shall confess Me before men, him shall I confess before My Father Who is in Heaven ; and he that shall deny Me before men, him will I deny before My Father Who is in Heaven." A good Christian will, therefore, be willing to suffer every‐ thing, even to lay down his life, rather than neglect to confess his Faith when duty calls on him to do so.

THE THEBAN LEGION.

Towards the end of the third century the Emperor Maximilian placed himself at the head of an immense army, to wage war against the Begaudes, a people who dwelt among the mountains of Gaul.

In his army was a company of ten thousand soldiers, known by the name of the Theban Legion, because they came from the neighbourhood of Thebes, a country which had received the Christian Faith. All the soldiers in this immense company were Christians, and were renowned for being the bravest troops in the whole Roman army, and many of them had grown old in the service. This legion was commanded by a brave Christian captain whose name was Maurice.

When Maximilian had passed the Alps, he ordered the army to halt, that they might rest a little before engaging in battle with the enemy.

He also issued a command for all the soldiers to join in a solemn sacrifice to the gods to obtain from them a victory in the coming struggle. The Theban Legion alone refused to offer sacrifice.

When the Emperor heard of this refusal, he became very angry, and ordered a thousand of the soldiers to be slain on the spot, in punishment of their disobedience, and as a warning to the rest.

Instead of being dismayed, the other soldiers only envied the fate of their comrades who had been so fortunate as to be chosen to die for Christ's sake, and exhorted them to lay down their lives courageously rather than break the promises they had made to God on the day of their baptism.

When the Emperor was informed of this, he ordered another thousand of them to be put to death. Those who remained alive cried out that they, too, would rather die than disobey God. In the meantime Maurice and the other chief commanders went about among them exhorting them to remain faithful.

The Emperor sent a third time a messenger to tell them that if they did not at once offer sacrifice, they should all be put to death.

When this message was made known to them, these generous soldiers, with Maurice at their head, sent back the following reply: "O Emperor, we are indeed your soldiers, but we are also the servants of the true God of Heaven. Order us to do anything that is not contrary to His law, and our conduct in the past is a sufficient assurance of our obedience in the future. But it is not allowed for any one of us to obey the Emperor when our God, Who is also your God, forbids us. We know how to die for our religion, but we do not know how to deny it ; and following the example of our Divine Master, we will yield up our lives without offering any resistance."

This answer filled the Emperor with rage. He ordered the rest of the army to surround the brave legion that no one might escape, and then to fall upon them and cut them to pieces.

When the hour of combat arrived, all the soldiers of the legion, although they were powerful enough of themselves to put to flight those who came to attack them, calmly laid down their arms at their feet, and allowed themselves to be slain. Not one of them was found to deny his faith. The field was soon covered with the bodies of the martyrs, and the ground was saturated with their blood. On that day ten thousand glorious martyrs were joined to the Church triumphant in Heaven.

History of the Church.

THE NOBLE RELIGIOUS BROTHER.

During the terrible Commune at Paris in the year 1871 a company of armed Communists entered a house of a community of religious Brothers at Picpus, near that city.

As soon as they entered the house the first

person they met was Brother Stanislaus, who was only twenty-six years old, whom they at once seized and brought before their chief.

He began by asking the trembling Brother many questions ; but one of the wicked men, thirsting for blood, suddenly put a loaded pistol to his breast, and cried out : " Swear that there is no God, otherwise I will kill you."

The Brother, raising his eyes to Heaven, calmly but firmly answered : " I swear that I firmly believe that there is one God, and with my whole heart I love Him."

This unexpected answer, so like that made by so many of the early martyrs of the Church, for a moment paralyzed the miscreant, who, instead of firing, turned round to his comrades, and in a tone of rage and anger cried out : " Shall I shoot him ?"

" Yes, kill him," they all exclaimed together— " kill him !"

The man turned to execute their orders, when his eyes met those of his victim, who stood before him calm and heavenly serene in the presence of death. He could not fire ; that gentle look disarmed him, and he lowered his pistol, saying in astonishment : " Look ! he stands there so calmly to allow himself to be killed. What a madman !"

Ask yourself, my child, what you would have done if you had been called upon to die for God as that good Brother was. What answer would you have given ?

Récits Contempor.

GABRIEL, THE PIOUS SCHOLAR.

A pious scholar called Gabriel had the custom every day when going to or returning from school to kneel at the foot of a crucifix erected by the wayside, as is the custom in Catholic countries, and there spending a few moments in pious prayer.

His mother being informed of this, and fearing that he might be performing this action from a motive of attracting the attention of others to himself, asked him one day why he always did what none of his other companions thought of doing.

" I have taken the resolution of doing this, that from my early years I may accustom myself to profess my faith outwardly, so that when greater trials come afterwards, or when I may be called upon to confess my religion before the world, I may not be unprepared. These are the words of the missionary Father to us during our last spiritual retreat."

In after-years he had occasion more than once to profess his faith on important and trying occasions, in the midst of a mocking world, and he found no difficulty in doing so, since from his youth he had accustomed himself to despise the railleries and opinions of men.

MARTIN THO, THE HEROIC MARTYR OF TONQUIN.

In the year 1840 there was arrested in Western Tonquin a virtuous father of a family whose name was Martin Tho. He was seized and imprisoned, not only on account of his faith, but also on account of the influence he possessed among the faithful.

From the day of his apprehension nothing seemed

to find a place in his mind but the thought of how he would best prepare to accomplish the sacrifice of his life for God and his holy religion. His wife was still living, and there were eight children dwelling with her, for all of whom he had an affectionate, fatherly tenderness, and whom he had brought up in the fear of God ; but these he now left under the care and protection of their Father in Heaven.

This pious family, worthy of the admiration of all Christians, grieved indeed that one whom they all loved so well was so soon to be taken from them, and that terrible would be the sufferings he would have to endure at the hands of his impious murderers before death would bring him the palm of victory ; yet their united prayer was not for his deliverance from their hands, for they rejoiced in the thought of him being honoured with the martyr's crown, but that God would give him courage to remain faithful.

Four or five days after his arrest, the children asked permission from their mother to go and visit him in his prison.

She answered them in these heroic words : " My dear children, your beloved father is at present on the battle-field, and no one can tell if he will persevere in confessing his faith and the holy Gospel of Jesus Christ to the end. The thought alone of the terrible tortures they will inflict upon him is of itself a sufficient trial, without us adding to it more trying ones. If you go to visit him, perhaps the very sight of you, whom he loves so much, might unnerve him and make him waver in the faith, or cause him to forget the glory which awaits him. Nevertheless, if any one of you could find means of entering his prison, I will not hinder you, only you must be guided in this by the advice of our catechist : if he permits you to go, I will consent ; if he considers that your visit might prove dangerous, then you will return to me."

But when it was announced to her that the holy confessor had already generously endured most terrible tortures, she, filled with celestial joy, said to her children · " Your father has now gloriously confessed the name of Jesus Christ ; hasten to him, therefore, and give him all the consolation in your power, and by your loving words · encourage him to suffer more still, even death itself, for God's sake."

The two oldest, therefore, a son and a daughter, set forth immediately, and visited him in his dungeon. The Christian hero threw his arms round them, and, embracing them with the greatest tenderness, said to them · " My children, your father will soon be taken from you, and you will see me no more till we meet before the throne of God. This is my last advice to you, my children, and you will repeat it in my name to your brothers and sisters at home. Remember that you have only one soul, and take the greatest care of it. Pray to God to grant you the grace of remaining faithful to your holy religion all the days of your lives, and above all things else, keep yourselves away from the contagion of this wicked world, pure and unspotted before God."

Precious in the sight of the Lord is the death of His Saints.

Annals of the Prop. of the Faith, No. 83.

IV. "Our Help is in the Name of the Lord."

"God has forsaken us."

There was once a young man lying dangerously ill. He was the only hope of his aged parents, who were very poor, and his brothers and sisters were all too young to work.

They tried every means to make him better, but all in vain ; he became weaker every day, and very soon it was apparent to everyone that there was no longer any hope of his recovery. As they were lamenting over this misfortune, a neighbour hap pened to visit them to inquire about the sick man

" Oh, he is dying," they said ; " there is no longer any hope. We have done everything that we could to make him better, but all in vain ;" and they continued to weep bitterly.

" Have you asked God to make him better ?" said the neighbour.

" Oh no," they answered, " God has forsaken us altogether."

" How can you say that God has forsaken you, since you have never asked Him to come to your assistance ? You believe in your hearts that God can help you, yet you have not asked Him to do so. Where is your faith and confidence ? It is not sufficient to believe that God can assist you : you must also, by the daily practice of your lives, act according to your belief. Ask God, therefore, to make your son well again ; most certainly He will do so if He sees that it will be for his good."

After these words of gentle reproof, the unhappy parents knèlt down, and prayed to God to restore their son to health if it were His blessed will.   This they continued to do for several days, and at last they had the happiness to see him rise from his sick-bed. In a short time he became well, and was able to resume his work.

HAUTERIVE : *Catéchisme de Persévérance*, xii. 10.

THE SAINTS AT PRAYER.

St. Paul, the first hermit, although an old man, humbly and reverently knelt on the ground when speaking to God in prayer.   It was in this position that St. Antony found him, even when his holy soul had taken flight to Paradise, his eyes and his hands at the same time being raised heavenwards.

St. Antony, thinking that he was still living, knelt down beside him, and for a long time prayed at his side.   But seeing, after a considerable time, that the Saint did not move, and that he did not hear him utter his usual ejaculations, he gazed upon his holy countenance, and saw that his spirit had gone to take its place among the Saints of God in Paradise.

With reverence he placed all that remained of him on earth in a grave, which two lions from the forest excavated to receive it, and returned home, himself to pray as his beloved master had done, and soon to follow him into the assembly of the Saints.

The Apostle St. James the Less, who was surnamed the Just even by his enemies, was so accustomed to pray to God on his knees that it is recorded of him that after his death they were found hard and rough like the skin of a camel.

When, at the time of his martyrdom, the Jews

had cast him down from a pinnacle of the Temple, and when he was about to breathe his last, he collected his remaining strength, and for the last time placed himself upon his knees. Like his dying Master on the cross, his last prayer was for his enemies who were putting him to death : " Lord, forgive them, for they know not what they do."

Lives of the Saints.

THE YOUNG PRINCE AND THE OFFICER.

The Duke of Bourgoyne, grandson of Louis XIV. of France, was educated by the great Bishop of Cambrai, Fénelon.

He made so much progress under this learned and virtuous tutor that, as he grew up, he was the admiration of the whole kingdom, on account of those qualities which form great princes and prepare them to become eminent kings.

It was impossible, says a historian of the times, to observe him hearing Mass or receiving Holy Communion, without being not only edified, but, moreover, penetrated with profound respect for the holy mysteries. It was commonly said that the example of his piety had converted more people to God than even the eloquence of the great Bourdaloue.

An officer, who had all his lifetime served his king more faithfully than he had served God, and who happened to be at Versailles, where the Duke resided, frequently witnessed him performing these exercises of religion, and was struck by his devotion. But, imagining that it might be more as a matter of form and to attract attention than real piety, he thought he would secretly watch him.

But this only served to convince him that the Duke was really devout and in earnest whenever he performed his spiritual duties, and he became more and more edified. And as he was convinced of this, his conscience began to upbraid him with his own want of fidelity to God, and he resolved upon a change of conduct.

He went to one of the priests of the castle chapel, and kneeling humbly at his feet, said to him : " It is quite impossible to live in a state of indifference in religious matters when one has before his eyes daily the example of a prince so great and so young, in whose heart is rooted so deep and so real a piety."

It was hoped that a prince so accomplished as he was would one day occupy the throne of his ancestor St. Louis, and shed over the whole kingdom the lustre of those virtues which had adorned him, but a premature death put an end to these hopes, and deprived France of a king whose reign might have been recorded in the brightest pages of its history.

JADDUS THE HIGH-PRIEST, AND THE GREAT KING.

When King Alexander the Great was engaged in besieging Tyr, he wrote to the high-priest of the Jews, who was called Jaddus, to ask him to send provisions and auxiliary troops to his assistance. Jaddus refused, saying that his people had bound themselves by a solemn oath made to Darius not to bear arms against him, nor the nations over whom he ruled.

Alexander was very angry at this answer, and threatened that he would march against Jerusalem as soon as he had made himself master of Tyr. This he did, for as soon as he had acquired possession of

Tyr, he marched towards the capital of Judæa, intending to pour out upon the inhabitants the terrible effects of his wrath.

At this information the high-priest offered sacrifices in the Temple, and ordained that public prayers should be offered to God to avert the awful calamity that threatened them.

God heard their earnest supplications, and appeared to Jaddus in a vision, telling him to open wide the gates of the city, and to go out to meet him without fear, clad in his pontifical vestments, and accompanied by all the members of the sacerdotal order.

Jaddus instantly obeyed, and, followed by the priests and the people, he went out to meet Alexander. When they reached a place called Sapha, from which the city and the Temple could be seen they awaited the approach of the Macedonian King.

As he drew near the place a sudden change came over him. The sight of so many people clad in white, of the priests vested in the garments of their office, of the high-priest in his splendid robes, wearing his ephod and his tiara, on which the adorable Name of God was engraved in letters of gold, made so great an impression on the heathen monarch that he commanded his army to halt. Then, going forward alone, he prostrated himself on the ground in adoration of the sacred Name of God, and humbly saluted the high-priest.

" It is not this man whom I adore," said he to Parmenion, his chief officer, who was astonished to behold his invincible prince in this humble posture, **" but it is that great God, whose high-priest he is."**

He then accompanied the people on their return to the city, and ascended to the Temple, where he offered up the sacrifices appointed by the high-priest. On the following day, having assembled together all the people, he asked them what favours they might desire him to bestow on them.

The high-priest answered him in their name that their only desire was to be permitted to be governed according to the laws of their fathers, and to be exempted from paying tribute every seventh year.

Alexander readily granted their petition.

JOSEPHUS, Antiq., lib. xi.

V. THE CATHOLIC CHURCH OUR GUIDE TO THE WORSHIP OF GOD.

God has appointed His one true Church to teach us in what way we are to worship Him. Oh, my child, be careful to learn from it all that God wants you to do, and try with your whole heart to accomplish it.

ST. HERMENEGILD, KING AND MARTYR.

St. Hermenegild, King and martyr, died for Jesus Christ in the year 586, because he would not worship God as the Arians did.

He was the son of Leovigild, King of the Visigoths in Spain, and was brought up in the heresy which his father professed. He reigned along with his father over that nation, and was married to a pious Catholic Princess whose name was Ingonda. By her good example, and more especially by her earnest prayers, he discovered that the religion in which he was born was not the true one. At once, therefore, he abandoned it, and going to St. Leander, asked to be admitted into the one true fold of the Catholic Church.

" O Prince," said the holy Bishop, " have you considered the value of the true faith you wish to embrace ?"

" My Father," replied the King, " I know it well ; it is a treasure that contains everlasting life; it is that pearl, to buy which one ought to sell all that he possesses in this world."

" But if the King, your father, who is an Arian, should try to force you to throw away this precious treasure, what would you do ?"

" With God's help," replied the young King, " I would willingly sacrifice everything that belongs to me rather than do so, because the Catholic faith is of more value to me than all earthly things."

" But he might even deprive you of your crown."

" That matters not," answered Hermenegild, " for the true faith promises me an eternal kingdom."

" He might send away to a distant country your holy spouse Ingonda."

" Both she and I are willing to sacrifice everything for the sake of our holy religion."

" But he might deprive you of your liberty ; he might even take away your life," said the Bishop.

" I accept this also," he answered. " I am willing to go to prison and to death if necessary ; for the true faith contains my sovereign good, and the salvation of my soul, and I am resolved to embrace it at all cost, and to live in it and die in it."

The holy Bishop was satisfied with his answers, and received him into the Church.

When the King his father was informed that his son had become a Catholic, he became very angry. He threatened that if he did not at once return to Arianism he would deprive him of the title of King, take from him all his possessions, and if he still continued obstinate, his very life.

Hermenegild answered respectfully but firmly that he could not deny his religion, because to do that would be to deny God Himself.

Then Leovigild ordered the royal robes his son wore to be taken off, and that heavy chains should be put on him, and that he should be conducted to Seville, and there be confined in a tower. At the same time he gave orders that the darkest dungeon should be chosen as the place of his confinement, and that he should be treated with the greatest harshness, so that he might the sooner be brought to yield.

But the royal confessor of the faith was not to be conquered in this way. From the depths of his dungeon he wrote a letter to his father in these words · " I confess, my King and my father, that your kindness to me has been very great, and to my last breath will I always remember it, and will ever respect and love you. But you cannot imagine that I would ever prefer a greatness that must so soon pass away to my eternal salvation. No, I do not want to wear a crown that would cost me so much, and I am ready to sacrifice my life rather than renounce my faith."

The prison of Hermenegild became for him a

school of virtue, and without ceasing he prayed to God to give him courage to be faithful unto death, and ever obedient to the teaching of His one true Church.

When Easter-time came, Leovigild sent an Arian priest to try to persuade him to yield to his wishes by forcing him to receive Communion at his hands. But the pious Hermenegild would not consent to receive it from one who was a heretic. Then the King, more furious than ever, resolved to shed the blood of his own son, through his hatred for the Catholic faith and the one true Church, and sent soldiers to the prison to put him to death.

When the soldiers entered the prison, they found the young King kneeling at prayer. He seemed to them more like an angel of God than a creature on earth. Instead of being kept back, however, by this angelic appearance, they rushed upon him, and with a hatchet struck him on the head and killed him. His glorious death took place on Holy Saturday, April 13, 586. *Life of S. Hermenegild.*

From the example of this King, my child, you will learn that you must worship God in the manner His holy Church ordains, and not in any other way.

VI. On Atheism.

My child, you have, no doubt, heard of certain people who call themselves Atheists. An Atheist is one who professes to believe that there is no God. But, although such a person may say this with his lips, and try to persuade himself that he believes it, he cannot do so in reality, because all creation proclaims to him that there is a God. " It is only the fool that says in his heart there is no God."

THE GENERAL AT HIS DAUGHTER'S DEATH-BED.

In the United States of America there lived, some time ago, a General in the army, who was known in all that country to be an Atheist, or one who does not believe in God or in the life to come.

His wife was a good Christian, and tried to bring up their daughter, who was their only child, in the fear of God ; and although her father endeavoured to instil into her mind his own wicked principles, the grace of God enabled her to remain firm in her faith, and in the practice of her religious duties.

It happened that she became very ill, and lay in danger of death. Her father, who loved her with intense affection, watched by her bedside continually; but even his love for her could not hide from him what everyone else saw, that she was gradually but surely approaching her end.

" O my dearest father," she said to him one day as he sat beside her, holding her hands in his and tenderly caressing her—" O my dearest father, you see I am now at the point of death, and I must soon leave you. You have often told me that there is no God, and no Heaven hereafter ; and my dear mother has taught me that there is a God, Who will reward us, and make us eternally happy in the next life in His own home above, if we adore and serve Him here on earth. Tell me now, my own dear father, whether I am to believe her or you ?"

This she said, not because she doubted what to believe, but that she might gain her father from his unbelief, and make him a good Christian.

When she had said these words, the General sat motionless, as if struck by a thunderbolt, and for some moments he did not answer. He did not wish to say to his dying child what he knew in his heart to be false, and at the same time he did not want to acknowledge the existence of God in the presence of his associates in unbelief, some of whom were in the room at the time. The contest within him was only for a few moments. He looked on his darling child, and his eyes met hers. In an instant he exclaimed: "O my child, do not heed my words; believe only what your mother has taught you."

Those in the room who heard these words looked at him in amazement. "Surely, General," they said to him, "you do not really mean what you have just now said."

He turned towards them, and, pointing to his dying child, answered, with a thrill in his voice which reached the depths of their hearts: "My friends, it is indeed more convenient to live according to what we had pretended to believe, but at the hour of death it is only the ancient faith in the existence of the one true God that will give us consolation."

Thus did that dying child bring back her father to the truth from which he had wandered, and he lived and died an excellent Christian.

Catéch. Historique.

VII. On Idolatry.

Idolatry, or the worship of idols, is a superstition so monstrous and absurd that we are compelled to ask ourselves, How can it be possible for a man endowed with the gift of reason to venerate as divinities the pieces of wood and stone which have been formed into statues by the hands of men ?

The answer to this enigma is that when man has once rejected the light of faith which he has received from God, he has only the light of reason left to guide him, and this, often extinguished by his passions, causes him to fall into the abyss of every error.

THE PROPHET ELIAS AND THE WORSHIPPERS OF BAAL.

God in His mercy, in order to open the eyes of the blind pagans that they may be able to recognize Him as their only God, has sometimes been pleased to work miracles in their behalf. One of the greatest of these is the one He performed through His prophet Elias on the summit of Mount Carmel, which we read of in the eighteenth chapter of the third Book of Kings.

And Elias answered Achab, King of Israel " Send now, and gather unto me all Israel, unto Mount Carmel, and the prophets of Baal four hundred and fifty, and the prophets of the groves four hundred, who eat at Jezabel's table."

Achab sent to all the children of Israel, and gathered together the prophets unto Mount Carmel. And Elias coming to all the people, said : " How long do you halt between two sides ? If the Lord

be God, follow Him : but if Baal, then follow him."
And the people did not answer him a word.

And Elias said again to the people · " I only remain a prophet of the Lord : but the prophets of
Baal are four hundred and fifty men. Let two
bullocks be given us, and let them choose one bullock
for themselves, and cut it in pieces and lay it upon
wood, but put no fire under : and I will dress the
other bullock, and lay it on wood, and put no fire
under it. Call ye upon the names of your gods, and
I will call upon the name of my Lord : and the God
that shall answer by fire, let him be God."

And all the people answering, said : " A very
good proposal."

Then Elias said to the prophets of Baal : " Choose
you one bullock, and dress it first, because you are
many ; and call on the name of your gods, but put
no fire under."

And they took the bullock which he gave them,
and dressed it : and they called upon the name of
Baal from morning even till noon, saying : " O Baal,
hear us." But there was no voice, nor any that
answered. And they leaped over the altar that they
had made.

And when it was now noon, Elias jested at them,
saying : " Cry with a louder voice : for he is a god,
and perhaps he is talking, or is in an inn, or on a
journey, or perhaps he is asleep, and must be
awaked."

So they cried with a loud voice, and cut themselves
after their manner with knives and lances, till they
were all covered with blood. And after midday was
past, and while they were prophesying, the time

was come of offering sacrifice, and there was no voice heard, nor did anyone answer, nor regard them as they prayed.

Elias said to all the people : " Come ye unto me." And the people coming near unto him, he repaired the altar of the Lord, that was broken down : and he took twelve stones, according to the number of the tribes of the sons of Jacob, to whom the word of the Lord came, saying : ". Israel shall be thy name."

And he built with the stones an altar to the name of the Lord : and he made a trench for water of the breadth of two furrows round about the altar. And he laid the wood in order, and cut the bullock in pieces, and laid it upon the wood. And he said : " Fill four buckets with water, and pour it upon the burnt-offering, and upon the wood." And again he said : " Do the same the second time." And when they had done it the second time, he said : " Do the same also the third time." And they did so the third time. And the water ran round about the altar, and the trench was filled with water.

And when it was now time to offer the holocaust, Elias the prophet came near and said : " O Lord God of Abraham, and Isaac, and Israel, show this day that Thou art the God of Israel, and I Thy servant, and that according to Thy commandment I have done all these things. Hear me, O Lord, hear me that this people may learn that Thou art the Lord God, and that Thou hast turned their heart again."

Then the fire of the Lord fell, and consumed the holocaust, and the wood and the stones and the dust, and licked up the water that was in the trench.

And when all the people saw this, they fell on their faces, and they said : " The Lord He is God, the Lord He is God."

3 *Kings* xviii. 19-40.

VIII. On Sacrilege.

Sacrilege is the profanation of objects or persons or places consecrated to God. Hence, my child, when a person receives any of the Sacraments unworthily, or maltreats a priest or person consecrated to God, or makes a profane use of the sacred vessels, or treats with indignity the sacred emblems of religion, he is guilty of this great sin.

ST. FELIX AND THE ROBBER.

It happened that certain robbers went into the Church of St. Felix at Girone. One of them stole a number of ornaments of gold and silk, as well as others studded with precious stones, and fled away with them.

After he had left the church, he met on the road a man who seemed to be a pilgrim, who asked him whither he was going.

The robber answered : " If you will only keep a great secret, I will show you a rich treasure."

The man promised to do so.

Then the robber showed him the valuable things he had just stolen, saying at the same time · " If only I could sell these things, I would be indeed very rich."

" I have a secret place not far distant," said the stranger ; " and I have many dear and steadfast friends in other places. If you will only bring them to my house, you will be able to dispose of them at your convenience."

The robber agreed, and followed him. But, strange to say, on looking up, he saw before him the town of Girone, from which he thought he had gone a considerable distance. When they entered the town, and were passing the church from which the things had been stolen, the stranger said : " This is my house ; you can go in and leave these things there."

The man raised his eyes in astonishment towards the pilgrim, but at the same instant he disappeared, and he then knew that it was St. Felix himself who had come to make him restore the things he had stolen.

The robber repented on the spot of his sacrilege, confessed his fault, and related to all the people what had occurred to him on the way.

RIBADENEIRA : *Lives of the Saints*, August 1.

IX. ON THE CEREMONIES OF THE CHURCH.

The ceremonies of the Church are the sacred rites and the symbolic actions which have been introduced for the purpose of giving greater solemnity to the Divine offices, and of aiding the soul to raise itself towards God. For when these solemn rites are performed outwardly, they bring before our minds more clearly the invisible things they symbolize, and make it more easy for us to meditate upon them.

ST. ELIZABETH OF PORTUGAL.

St. Elizabeth, Queen of Portugal, had nothing so much at heart as the promotion of those outward signs and ceremonies which are the ornaments of God's worship.

" To enable men to whom God has given a body as well as a soul to fix their minds on heavenly things," she used to say, " it is necessary that outward ceremonies be employed, and that they be performed with all possible decorum and majesty."

She used her influence also in causing them to praise God in hymns and spiritual canticles, as St. Paul advises, that they might be thus enabled to join their voices to the heavenly choirs of the saints and angels, whose happiness for all eternity consists in singing the praises of God. She frequently, also, related what St. Augustine acknowledges in his " Book of Confessions "—that the sweetness of the hymns of the Church contributed much to bring about his conversion.

In these pious canticles she took care that everything should tend to edification, and carefully excluded anything that savoured of the frivolity of the world, or might in any way tend to gratify sensuality.

L'ABBÉ DE CHOISY.

X. ON OUR CONDUCT IN THE HOUSE OF GOD.

The virtue of religion requires of us that we should conduct ourselves with the greatest reverence in the house of God.

ST. JOHN THE ALMONER'S REBUKE.

One day St. John the Almoner saw some people speaking in the church in the presence of the Blessed Sacrament. He went up to them and told them to leave the church at once. They were very much offended at this order of the Saint. But without heeding their angry reply, he said : " My friends, God's house is a house of prayer. If you come hither to pray to Him, do not allow your tongue or your heart to be occupied with any worldly thing, lest you bring upon yourself the terrible punishments inflicted by Him on those who make it a den of thieves."

From his Life.

THE DEVOUT STUDENT.

Claude de Pelletier was the son of a man who occupied a high position in the world. As soon as he had learned to know God he seemed to be altogether penetrated with love and gratitude for Him, and his only thought was how he could make himself more and more agreeable in His eyes.

The sweetest moments of the day were those that he could spend at the foot of the altar ; he loved especially to attend those churches in which the ceremonies of religion were performed most perfectly and with the greatest piety. His very presence in the house of God was a lesson of edification to all who saw him.

If in his walks he passed near a church, he would instantly recall to mind that God dwelt there, and he could not pass without going in to offer Him his homage. His first act on entering was to adore Jesus Christ in His humble tabernacle, and to offer Him all the affections of his heart. The profound respect he had for his Divine Lord's dwelling-place on earth could be read upon his countenance, and recognized by his exterior reverence.

He would generally kneel for a few moments before the altar, and, having there performed his first acts of adoration, faith and love, he would rise and place himself where no one would disturb him, and would remain immovable as long as time would permit in prayer and meditation. Sometimes he would kneel for two or three hours at a time, especially on festivals and the days on which he had received Holy Communion.

Many of his fellow-students, on whom his beautiful example had made a lively impression, used to go to the church expressly to be edified by him, for they knew that they would certainly find him there. Some of them were moved even to tears, and endeavoured to follow his example.

This amiable young man died in the year 1685, at the age of seventeen, having attained in those few years great sanctity. Truly might be said of him what has been said of so many others of God's Saints : " Having been taken away after a few years, he yet lived a long life."   PROYART.

My child, what a beautiful example for your imitation ! Like him, have a great respect for the beauty of God's house and the place where His glory dwelleth.

ST. VINCENT OF PAUL AND THE IRREVERENT MAN.

The love of St. Vincent for Jesus in the adorable Sacrament was very great. Not only did he say holy Mass every day, and frequently visit Jesus present in the holy tabernacle, but he laboured with untiring zeal to make the faithful go often to Holy

Communion ; and many a time did he weep over their coldness and indifference.

One day he saw a person going into the chapel where the Blessed Sacrament was. The man seemed very irreverent, and when passing before the altar he made only a small, unmeaning kind of genuflection.

St. Vincent called him back. " My good sir," he said, " it is Jesus Christ, our Divine Master, Who is present there " (pointing to the tabernacle), " and we must go into His holy presence, not as if we were going into a theatre, but with piety and recollection. This is the way you should kneel." And the good old man knelt down, bending his knee to the very ground.

XXVII

THE ANGELS AND SAINTS: RELICS AND IMAGES

I. On the Honour due to the Angels and in Particular to our Guardian Angels.

THE Catholic Church teaches us, my child, that we should pay to the Angels and Saints an inferior honour or worship, for this is due to them as being the servants and special friends of God.

God made the angels to be partakers of His glory. They are also our guardians. Christ, speaking of the little ones that believe in Him, says: " Their angels in Heaven always see the face of My Father, Who is in Heaven " (St. Matt. xviii. 10).

GOD SENDS HIS ANGELS TO GUARD US.

When you were born, God said to one of His angels : " Go down to the world, and take care of that child ; keep it from harm, protect it against its enemies, assist it in its needs, and bring it safe to Paradise when the day of its trial is over."

That heavenly spirit became your guardian angel, and from that day till now he has never ceased to watch over you. He has offered up to God all your prayers, your alms, your acts of obedience, your labours, and all the good you have ever done for Him. And when the moment of your death draws near, he will watch over you still more tenderly; he will strengthen you against the attacks of Satan; he will inspire you with good thoughts, and will diminish the fears of death. Oh, how happy will he be if he is able to present your soul pure and holy before the throne of God! Then you shall see Him, and be happy for ever with Him.

ST. FRANCES OF ROME SEES HER ANGEL GUARDIAN.

God was pleased to permit St. Frances to see her angel guardian. He seemed to her to be a child of about seven years of age, full of beauty and of dazzling purity, and always had his eyes turned towards Heaven.

When Satan came to tempt her, the angel looked on her with affection, and whispered into her soul words of encouragement, which strengthened her against him.

When she fell into any small fault, the angel disappeared from her sight, and a sadness overspread his countenance; but as soon as she repented of her fault, he returned and appeared full of joy. And when anyone offended God in the presence of St. Frances, she saw the angel cover his face with his hands, as if to show the horror he felt at seeing God offended

Although you cannot see your angel guardian, as St. Frances did, yet he is ever at your side, helping you in your temptations, and inspiring you with good thoughts. How many, in the hour of danger, have been protected from harm by their guardian angels! How many have, by listening to their inspirations, obtained the crown of glory in Heaven!

ST. AGNES NOT AFRAID.

When St. Agnes refused to obey the orders of the heathen judge, who commanded her to sacrifice to the gods, he threatened to send her to a place where every kind of misfortune would fall upon her.

But Agnes only smiled when she heard these threats. " If you knew how great and powerful is the God whom I worship, you would never dare to use such words against me, His servant. I do not fear your threats, for I know the power of my Lord and Master Jesus Christ. Moreover, I have with me an angel of the Lord, whom He has sent to protect me."

And when Symphronius, the son of the judge, went up to her to insult her, the angel who guarded Agnes struck him, and he fell dead at her feet.

Our angel guardian also sometimes assists us in our temporal needs.

ST. GREGORY'S ANGEL.

It is related in the " Life of St. Gregory of Tours " that, when he was a child, his father became very ill. The boy loved his father tenderly, and offered up his fervent prayers to God for his recovery.

One night, as he was asleep, his angel guardian appeared to him and said : " My child, if you want your father to become well do what I now tell you. When you rise in the morning, write the holy

Name of Jesus on a piece of wood, and place it secretly under the pillow on which your father rests his head."

As soon as he awoke the boy ran at once to his mother, and told her what his good angel had said to him. She answered : " Go, my child, and do what he has ordered, and your father will certainly recover."

Gregory wrote the holy Name on a piece of wood, and, without telling his father, slipped it under his pillow. No sooner had he done so than his father recovered. When he learned how he had been cured, he lovingly embraced his son ; but Gregory, falling down on his knees, returned thanks to God, and to his good angel, for this miraculous favour.

Our guardian angel offers up our prayers to God.

ST. GERTRUDE'S GUARDIAN ANGEL. •

One day when St. Gertrude had heard Mass with great fervour, she saw in a vision her angel guardian standing before the throne of God, presenting her prayers to the most Holy Trinity, and at the same time interceding for her. She saw that God was pleased with her prayers, which the angel offered, and that He in return bestowed on her, through the hands of the angel, many graces.

The thought that our good angel is ever at our side should keep us from sin.

WHY HE WAS NEVER ANGRY

One of the Fathers of the desert, being asked one day why he was never angry and always so gay, answered: " I always keep in mind the presence of my guardian angel, who is at my side and assists me in all my wants, who also whispers into my soul what I ought to say and what God wishes me to do, and who writes down the manner in which I have performed each one of my actions. This thought fills me with so much respect for him that I am always careful never to say or do anything that may displease him."

My child, be mindful of your good angel's presence. Pray to him to protect you in all your dangers, and especially at the hour of your death.

THE GUARDIAN ANGEL OF THE DYING MAN.

St. Francis Regis had a tender devotion to the holy angels. He never passed a church without saluting the guardian angels of that church ; and when he saw someone coming to confession, he always besought the angel guardian of that person to obtain for him the grace of true repentance.

One day, passing down a street, he was suddenly stopped by someone. He looked round to see who it might be, but there was no one near him. He tried again to move forward, but he found it impossible. At that moment a window above his head was opened, and he heard a voice of one calling for a priest to attend a dying person. He at once ascended to the room, and, having heard the sick man's confession, he anointed him, and the poor man died in sentiments of great piety. He again attributed this to the intervention of the guardian angel of the dying man.

ST. FRANCIS REGIS PRESERVED FROM A GREAT
DANGER.

The same St. Francis Regis, having spent several
successive nights in hearing confessions in a certain
town, left it to commence a mission in another
place. On the way, being overcome by weariness,
he began to fall asleep, even while walking. There
was a deep pit on the way before him, and as he
proceeded onwards he would have most certainly
fallen into it. But as he was on the brink of
the pit, he felt an invisible hand seize him by the
arm and stop him. This roused him a little, and,
seeing the danger from which he had been preserved,
he threw himself upon his knees and thanked God,
Who had thus been pleased to permit his guardian
angel to show him this manifestation of his loving
care and watchfulness over him.

II. On the Honour due to the Saints, and in
the First Place to Our Lady.

Above all the angels and Saints in Paradise,
placed on the highest throne in Heaven, is Mary
the Mother of God. To her before all others of the
creatures God has made is due the highest honour,
and to her before all the rest should we offer up our
prayers ; because, in the first place, being Mother of
God, she surpasses all the angels and Saints in glory
and dignity, and, in the second place, her prayers
are of immense power and efficacy in obtaining from
God whatever she may ask. The angels and Saints
are only God's servants and friends, but Mary is His
Mother. " Holy Mary, Mother of God, pray for us,"

ST. GREGORY'S PRAYER TO MARY.

Being persuaded of the power of Mary, and desiring to bestow on her all the honour in his power, St. Gregory was accustomed to invoke her in these words :

" The glory which is due to thee, O most holy Virgin, whom the eternal Son of God chose to be His Mother, is ineffable. Every creature that is in Heaven or on the earth is obliged to pay thee homage, for thou art the throne of the Divine Majesty, and thou dost shine with a dazzling brightness, which is diffused throughout the heavenly kingdom, where the eternal Father, Who by His almighty power overshadows thee, is glorified; where the Son Whom thou didst bring forth into this world is adored ; where the Holy Ghost, Who didst by His operation accomplish in thee the Incarnation of the King of glory, is praised and blessed.

" Grant, then, I beseech thee, that I may become participator of Thy graces, and of the perfection of thy virtues, through Jesus Christ, to Whom be given all honour and glory with the Father and the Holy Ghost, throughout the endless ages of eternity. Amen."

ST. CHARLES BORROMEO, THE FAITHFUL SERVANT OF MARY.

We read in the " Life of St. Charles Borromeo " that of all the virtues that distinguished him, there was none so conspicuous as his devotion to the Mother of God.

Not satisfied with reciting daily, on his knees, the Rosary and the Office of Our Lady, he likewise fasted on bread and water on the vigils of her festivals. No one was more exact than he to recite the Angelus whenever the bell announced the hour for that holy prayer. Even when travelling on the road, and during tempestuous weather, he would devoutly kneel down by the wayside and say it on his knees.

In his cathedral church he built an altar, and instituted a confraternity in honour of Mary's holy Rosary. On the first Sunday of every month he organized a procession, in which a magnificent banner of Our Lady was borne in the midst of great pomp. He caused her to be constituted the patroness and special protector of all the works of charity which he established. He also ordained throughout his whole diocese that as often as the name of Mary was pronounced, she should be honoured by some outward sign of veneration.

In order to make all the people confided to his care understand that it was through Mary and by her assistance that they could hope to enter the glory of Heaven—for she is called by the Church " The Gate of Heaven "—he ordained that there should be placed near the entrance of every parish church under his jurisdiction a statue representing the most holy Mother of God. *From his Life.*

CORIOLANUS AND HIS MOTHER.

In the history of the Roman Empire it is recorded that a brave and valiant General, whose name was Coriolanus, having received an offence from the citizens of Rome, resolved, in revenge, to forsake his country and join the army of the enemy.

The hostile army were already drawn up before the gates of the city, and threatened to destroy it. The Romans, on perceiving that their former invincible General led the van, were filled with dismay, and clearly saw that any resistance they could offer would be useless. They sent messengers to him asking for peace, but he refused to grant it. Then ambassadors chosen from the first among the nobility of the city were sent to beseech him to spare the city. But he still refused,.and told them that for the dishonour the people of the city had heaped upon him he would show them no mercy.

Finally, as a last resource, they thought of his mother, who was within the walls ; and, going to her, they besought her to speak to her son, and intercede for them, that for her sake he might spare the city.

When Coriolanus saw his mother approaching, tears came into his eyes ; and when she asked him to have pity upon the ungrateful inhabitants for her sake, he said : " My mother, you have overcome my resentment. For my mother's sake, O country which has so grievously offended me," he added, " I pardon thee."

Thereupon he departed along with his army, and Rome was saved on that day.

Will Jesus Christ do less for us, if His Mother requests Him to show us mercy ? With what sweet confidence can the sinner, as well as the just man, approach to Mary, since she is our loving Mother, and has such power with her Divine Son ! Let us therefore honour Mary.

ST. AMBROSE'S WORDS ABOUT THE SAINTS.

" We should honour all the Saints of God because they are His servants and His friends ; but we should in a particular manner honour those whose relics we possess, for there is a kind of familiarity between them and us, for they seem, as it were, to dwell amongst us. They help us by their prayers, and they protect us whilst we are living, and when the hour of death comes they receive our souls and present them to God."

D. Ambros. in Fest. S. Octav.

It is therefore, my child, by praying to the Saints and venerating their relics that we principally honour them.

III. OF THE POWER OF THE PRAYERS OF THE ANGELS AND SAINTS.

We should ask the angels and Saints to pray for us, because they are our friends and brethren, and because their prayers have great power with God. You can easily understand, my child, the great power of the prayers of the Saints in Heaven when you call to mind how powerful were their prayers even while they were on earth.

PRAYER OF MOSES FOR THE SINFUL ISRAELITES.

" And the people, seeing that Moses delayed to come down from the mount, gathering together against Aaron, said : ' Arise, make us gods that may go before us : for as to this Moses, the man that brought us out of the land of Egypt, we know not what has befallen him.'

" And Aaron said to them : ' Take the golden ear
rings from the ears of your wives, and your sons
and daughters, and bring them to me.' And the
people did what he had commanded, bringing the
ear-rings to Aaron. And when he had received them,
he fashioned them by founders' work, and made of
them a molten calf. And they said : ' These are
thy gods, O Israel, that have brought thee out of
the land of Egypt. . . . And, rising in the morning,
they offered holocausts and peace victims, and the
people sat down to eat and drink, and they rose
up to play.

" And the Lord spake to Moses, saying : ' Go, get
thee down : thy people which thou hast brought out
of the land of Egypt hath sinned : they have quickly
strayed from the way which thou didst show them :
and they have made to themselves a molten calf,
and have adored it, and, sacrificing victims to it,
have said · " These are thy gods, O Israel, that
brought thee out of the land of Egypt." '

" And again the Lord said· to Moses : ' See that
this people is stiff-necked : let Me alone, that My
wrath may be kindled against them, and that I
may destroy them, and I will make of thee a great
nation.'

" And Moses besought the Lord his God, saying :
' Why, O Lord, is Thy indignation enkindled against
Thy people, whom Thou hast brought out of the
land of Egypt with great power and a mighty hand ?
Let not the Egyptians say, I beseech Thee : " He
craftily brought them out, that he might kill them
in the mountains, and destroy them from the earth :"
let Thy anger cease, and be appeased upon the

wickedness of Thy people. Remember Abraham, Isaac, and Israel, Thy servants, to whom Thou swarest by Thy own self, saying : " I will multiply your seed as the stars of Heaven ; and this whole land that I have spoken of, I will give to your seed and you shall possess it for ever." '

" And the Lord was appeased from doing the evil which He had spoken against His people."

Exod. xxxii. 1 *et seq.*

ST. CATHERINE OF SIENA'S INTERCESSION.

In the year 1370 there lived in Siena a rich man who was called Andrew de Naddino, who was noted for his perverse habit of swearing, and for his frequent words of blasphemy against God and His Saints.

He, at that time, became so ill that the physicians declared he could not live ; and his friends, not wishing him to die in the sad state in which he then was, told him that it was time for him to receive the last Sacraments, and prepare for death. But the dying man, who had despised the Sacraments when in health, and who had borne towards the priests of God a special ill-will, refused to receive the last Sacraments, and would not allow a priest to approach him.

St. Catherine heard with the most profound grief that the wretched man was about to die without being reconciled to God. She heard, too, of his great obstinacy, and saw that the only hope of his salvation was in prayer ; so, with much fervour and many tears, she besought her beloved Spouse Jesus to grant him mercy and the grace of conversion.

Our Lord answered her : " My daughter, the sins of this man, and in particular his terrible blasphemies, have ascended to Me in Heaven. Not only has he spoken ill of Me and My Saints, but he has even dared to cast into the fire a picture of Me and My most holy Mother. Is it not, then, just that such a man should be punished eternally for so terrible a crime ? Do not, then, intercede for him, My well-beloved child, for he deserves a thousand deaths."

The servant of God was not discouraged. Like another Moses, she continued to pray and weep. " O my Jesus," she cried out, " remember how Thou didst suffer and die on the cross of ignominy, which Thou didst carry to Mount Calvary on Thy sacred shoulders for the love of poor sinners ; have mercy, I beseech Thee, on this one who needs it so much."

Her prayers were at length heard, yet his conversion was not effected without a miracle of grace.

Our Blessed Lord Himself appeared to him when he had only a few hours to live, and said to him : " My friend, why do you not ask of Me pardon for all the blasphemies you have uttered against Me ? Send for a priest at once, and make your confession, for I am ready to forgive you."

These words of mercy softened the dying man's hardened heart. He made known to those around him the vision he had just had, and sent immediately for a priest, to whom he confessed his sins, and soon afterwards died in sentiments of the most perfect contrition.   *Life of St. Catherine of Siena.*

THE PRAYERS OF ST. DOMINIC.

When the noble Simon, Count of Montfort, was besieging the city of Toulouse at the head of his brave crusaders, a company of forty pilgrims came from England to visit the shrine of St. James the Apostle at Compostella.

Not being able to pass through the besieged city, they had to cross the river in a boat at some little distance from it. But the boat, being too small for the number of men that were in it, was overturned by the force of the current, and the pilgrims were all thrown into the river. Some sank to the bottom, and others were carried away by the stream.

At that moment St. Dominic was praying in a neighbouring church, and, hearing the cries of the drowning men and of the people on the banks, he rose from his knees to see what had happened.

As soon as he was informed of the sinking of the boat, and that forty men were in imminent danger of death, he fell on his face on the ground, and, stretching out his arms in the form of a cross, earnestly prayed to God to preserve those pious pilgrims from death. In a few moments he rose up, and, going to the edge of the waters, he cried out · " I command you all in the name of God to come hither."

" And, wonderful to relate," continues the historian, " no sooner had the Saint said these words than all the pilgrims, rising above the water, came towards the bank. The people who were standing there stretched out their hands to help them, and brought them safely out of the water. Then, raising up their hearts to Heaven, they thanked God, Who had by the merits and prayers of His servant St. Dominic worked so great a miracle in favour of His servants."

Life of St. Dominic.

ST. STANISLAUS KOSTKA AND ST. BARBARA.

As St. Stanislaus Kostka increased in age, he increased also in the love of God. His one great desire was to serve Him in the most perfect manner in his power, and to accomplish this he resolved to consecrate himself to God in the Society of Jesus.

Inspired by a special movement of the Holy Ghost, he made a vow to enter that Order as soon as he had reached a suitable age ; but he did not make it known to anyone, not even to his confessor. At this time he was studying in the college of the Jesuit Fathers in Vienna along with his eldest brother Paul.

During his residence there he became very ill. Satan, who could not bear to see one so fervent, and who feared that if he lived longer, and became a member of that great Society, he would obtain many victories over him, appeared to him in his room, as he lay on his sick-bed, under the appearance of a ferocious dog, and tried to strangle him. But the pious youth, recognizing under this terrible apparition the enemy of mankind, made upon himself the sign of the Cross, and invoked the adorable name of Jesus. Satan immediately disappeared.

The malady, however, became daily more serious, and soon the doctors feared that it might terminate **fatally.**

Stanislaus was resigned to the will of God, and

was ready to die or to live according to His holy will. One thing only gave him trouble : while attending the college for his classes he resided in the house of the senator Kimberker, who was a Lutheran, and who on no account would permit the most Blessed Sacrament to enter within his doors. Moreover, his brother, as well as his tutor, whose religious sentiments were much inferior to those of Stanislaus, had not the courage to insist upon this being done, that they might not give offence to their host.

In his perplexity, he called to mind that he had once read in the Life of St. Barbara, who at the same time was one of the patrons of the college, that those who invoked her help in life would assuredly receive the last Sacraments before they died ; and indeed, on the day of her feast in the year immediately preceding, after having received the Sacraments of Penance and the Holy Eucharist, he had fervently prayed to her to obtain from God that special favour when his last hour approached.

He now again renewed his prayer to her, and it was granted.

On one of the nights following, when his death seemed to be at hand, that great martyr and virgin entered his room, accompanied by two angels robed in resplendent garments, one of whom bore the most Blessed Sacrament.

As soon as he saw this wonderful vision, he informed John Bilinski, his tutor, who was sitting near his bed, and asked him to kneel through reverence for Our Divine Lord, there present in the most Blessed Sacrament, and for the heavenly visitants who were in the room. He then, in the midst of acts of faith, love, and gratitude, received his beloved Master in Holy Communion from the hands of St. Barbara herself.

This favour, great as it was, was followed by another still as remarkable. At the moment which those around him considered would be his last, the most holy Mother of God herself appeared to him with her Divine Son in her arms. She bestowed upon him many affectionate caresses, and assured him that he would not die at that time, for it was the will of her Divine Child that he should enter the Society of Jesus ; and as a testimony of the truth she placed the holy Infant on the bed at his side.

We can easily imagine the fervent love, the respect, the tenderness, the consolation, which the holy young man experienced on this occasion, when he saw his lowly bed the resting-place of the God of Heaven. The sickness under which he had until then laboured could not exist in the presence of Him Who is the joy of all the Saints, and he immediately recovered, contrary to the expectation of his friends, and even of his physicians themselves.

Petits Bolland., xiii. 389.

FLOWERS FROM HEAVEN.

Towards the end of the third century there lived at Cæsarea, in Asia Minor, a Christian lady called Dorothea. When the heathen prefect of that city heard that she was a Christian, he commanded her to be seized and brought before him.

At first he tried by kind words to make her renounce her holy faith ; but seeing all his words were in vain, he ordered her to be tortured and then beheaded.

When she was stretched on the rack, and suffering there most cruel torments, the prefect once more asked her to spare her life by offering sacrifice to the gods.

But the holy virgin said : " I despise your gods ; I pray to the one true God, Who made Heaven and earth. Why do you delay ? Finish quickly what you are to do to me, that I may go to see Him for Whose sake I suffer all these things. For He is my Spouse, and invites me to His Paradise—that land of everlasting happiness."

" Of what land do you speak ?" asked the judge.

" I speak of that land where Jesus Christ dwells with His Saints—a land where there is neither night nor sorrow ; a garden where the fruit is beautiful to the eye and delicious to the taste ; a garden ever fresh and fair, where lilies and roses, and flowers of all kinds, never fade."

There was a man standing near who heard these words of the holy virgin. His name was Theophilus. When he heard them, he laughed and jested like the others, for he also was a pagan, and hated the Christian name.

As she was being led to execution, he met her again. Then, remembering the words she had spoken, he said to her in merriment : " Do you hear me, O you who call yourself spouse of Christ ? When you go into that garden of which you have told us so much, will you have the goodness to send me some of those fruits and flowers which you said are so lovely ?"

Dorothea looked at him as he spoke "I will do it," she said—"I will do it without fail." There was no time for more, for the executioner placed her head upon the block, and with one stroke of his sword it was struck off.

"Those were strange words," said Theophilus to one of his friends, as he was about to leave ; "but Christians are not like other people."

"Their obstinacy is indeed great," said the other. "Even death itself has no terrors for them. But who is this ?" he continued, as there came up to them a boy of such heavenly beauty that the eyes of both were fixed on him in wonder and admiration.

The boy seemed not more than ten years old ; his golden hair fell in ringlets on his shoulders, and in his hand he carried a basket, in which were some most beautiful apples and four roses, two white and two red, of such brilliant colour and of so rich a fragrance that their like had never been seen before.

He held them out to Theophilus. "These flowers are for you," said the child. "Will you not take them ?"

"And whence, my boy, do you bring them ?" asked Theophilus.

"From Dorothea," he said ; "these are the flowers and the fruit she promised to send you."

"Roses in the winter-time !" he cried out—it was then the sixth of February, and a time of great frost —"yes, indeed, and roses such as never blossomed in an earthly garden. Prefect," he said, "your work is not yet done. Your sword has slain one Christian, but it has made another. I also am of the same faith for which Dorothea died."

Within an hour Theophilus was condemned to die ; and on the spot where Dorothea had been beheaded he too poured forth his blood, and went to enjoy God eternally in Heaven along with that holy martyr. *Lives of the Saints*, February 6.

IV. WE MUST HONOUR HOLY RELICS.

We must honour the relics of the Saints—that is, their mortal remains and objects that belonged to them when on earth—because the bodies of the Saints were the temples of the Holy Ghost, and shall one day rise from the dead to everlasting life, and because God has often by the means of relics worked great miracles.

THE BLIND WOMAN OF TIBILIS.

St. Augustine relates the following miracle, which took place in his own days.

" The Bishop Projectus," he writes, " having brought to Tibilis the relics of the glorious martyr St. Stephen, an immense multitude of people went out to meet them. A blind woman who lived in the neighbourhood besought the people to take her to the Bishop who carried the relics. When they had done this, she presented him with a bouquet of flowers, and asked him to touch the sacred relics with them. The Bishop did so, and gave them back to her. As soon as she received them she touched her eyes with them, and recovered her sight, to the joy and amazement of the whole multitude."

ST. AUGUSTINE : *City of God.*

THE BROKEN LEG HEALED.

St. Augustine relates another miracle which was worked by the relics of St. Stephen.

" In the city of Uzales, in Africa, there lived a man whose name was Concordius. One day, by a fall, his leg was broken, and from that time forward he was not able to walk without using a crutch. Hearing of the wonders that were wrought by the relics of St. Stephen, he dragged himself to a church where part of these relics was preserved. There he prayed with great devotion. Suddenly in the midst of his prayers he felt his leg healed, and, rising up, he was able to walk without the help of his crutch. In thanksgiving to the Saint for his cure, he caused a number of candles to be lighted before the shrine, and, going out, published everywhere the wonderful works of God in His Saints."

ST. AUGUSTINE: *City of God.*

WHAT A RELIC OF ST. TERESA DID.

A certain holy man called Dominic had generously gone to the aid of some persons who were struck down by a plague then devastating Spain. He himself was soon seized by the terrible disease. Thinking he was about to die, he prepared himself for death with great piety. Suddenly he remembered that he had in his possession a relic of St. Teresa. Taking it with faith and devotion in his hands, he touched with it the places principally affected by the plague. The pain ceased, and he fell into a gentle slumber, during which St. Teresa

herself appeared to him.   When he awoke he found
that all traces of the malady had disappeared, and
that he was completely restored to health.

Catéch. Historique, ii. 131.

God has at times been pleased to honour His
Saints by preserving their bodies from corruption,
and especially those parts of them by which they
served Him most faithfully.

KING OSWALD OF ENGLAND.

St. Oswald, King of Northumbria, was one day
at table with the holy Bishop Adrian. It was the
great festival of Easter.

During dinner a servant came and said to the
King : " My lord, a multitude of poor people have
just come to the gates, and are asking an alms.
What am I to do with them ?"

The King, taking up a massive silver plate that
was on the table before him, placed upon it as much
food as it could contain, and gave it to the servant,
saying : " Go to these poor people, and distribute
among them this food in my name ; then break the
plate to pieces, and give a part of it to each of
them."

When the servant had gone out to execute the
order, the Bishop took the King by the hand and
said : " O King, may this hand ever remain incorrupt."

Not long afterwards Oswald was slain in battle
and his body was buried with honour. Long afterwards, when the coffin was opened, it was found
that the body had all decayed except the right

hand, which remained incorrupt according to the prayer of the Bishop, because it had been the instrument of so much charity

V. ON PICTURES AND IMAGES.

It is not enough for you, my child, to honour Jesus Christ and the Saints in your heart, but you must also honour the pictures and images which represent them. These pictures and images put us in mind of our Father and our brethren in Heaven ; and if children honour and keep with reverence the portraits of their parents and dear ones, we should certainly with much more reason honour the sacred pictures of God and of His Saints, who are our brethren.

ST. STEPHEN CONFOUNDS THE EMPEROR.

Long ages ago there lived in the East a holy man called Stephen the Young. The Emperor who reigned at that time over that part of the world, and who belonged to the impious sect of Iconoclasts, or image-breakers, endeavoured, first by promises, then by threats, to make the Saint join him in his evil work ; for he knew that if he succeeded in gaining him, many others would be led by his example, and also join him.

But St. Stephen was not to be moved by any promise or threat ; and God worked many miracles by his hands, to show that he was His servant and His champion, as also for the consolation of the faithful and the confusion of His enemies.

One day he gave sight to a man who had been blind

from his birth, by these words · " In the Name of
Jesus Christ, Whom you adore in these holy images,
may sight be given to you."

Another time, when a mother had brought to
him her son, who for nine years had been possessed
by the devil, he delivered him from the wicked
spirit by making him kiss an image of Jesus Christ.

But the miracle that made the greatest noise in
the country was the cure of a soldier who was paralyzed, and who was completely restored to health
by venerating an image of Jesus Christ and His
Blessed Mother.

The news of this miracle reached the ears of the
Emperor. He sent immediately for the soldier,
and said to him in a voice full of anger : " Do you
still continue to venerate images ?"

The soldier, frightened at these words, and fearing
the consequences that he knew would follow if he said
he belonged to the Catholic Faith, fell on his knees
before the Emperor, and said that he did not. At
the same time he began to curse those who did so.

In reward for his base apostasy, the Emperor conferred on him the title of Centurion. But his
honour was short-lived, for as he was returning
home on horseback he was thrown to the ground,
and trampled to death under his horse's hoofs.

This event enraged the Emperor still more against
St. Stephen ; so he commanded him to be brought
to Constantinople and confined in a dungeon, and
his hands and feet to be bound in chains.

A few days afterwards he ordered him to be
brought before him.

As soon as he was led in, the Emperor exclaimed

in a voice of anger : " See, there is the miserable wretch who dared to disobey me and despise my orders ! Tell me," said he to the Saint : " why did you dare to call me a heretic ?"

The Saint replied : " Because you commanded God's holy images to be broken—those images which our forefathers have venerated in all past ages, because they raise up our thoughts to Heaven, and put us in mind of the things and persons they represent. And you have dared, O Emperor, to call the images of Jesus Christ and His most holy Mother idols, and you dared also to trample them under your feet, and to commit them to the flames !"

" You foolish man !" cried out the Emperor ; " do you mean to tell me that in trampling on these images we dishonour the person of Jesus Christ ?"

St. Stephen did not reply, but, taking out his purse, brought forth a piece of money on which was the image of the Emperor ; then, throwing it on the ground, he trampled on it, saying : " Am I dishonouring the Emperor by casting this piece of money on the ground and trampling on it ?"

The attendants of the Emperor immediately rushed upon him, and would have torn him to pieces had not the Emperor ordered them to desist. He commanded him to be led back to prison, and to be brought before another tribunal to be tried for high treason.

Not long afterwards he was brought up again before the court, and, by the Emperor's orders, delivered over to an angry populace, who made him endure the most terrible tortures, and finally put him to death. *Lives of the Saints.*

THE CONVERSION OF KING BOHARIS.

Boharis, King of the Bulgarians, had been instructed in the truths of our holy religion by some fervent missionaries who had gone into his kingdom to preach the Gospel ; but, like many others in his position, he allowed himself to be so much occupied with his temporal affairs that he neglected to embrace the true Faith, and remained a pagan.

Now, it happened, by the providence of God, that a certain famous painter went into that country, and was introduced to the King. The King, who was passionately fond of the chase, asked the painter to paint on the walls of a new palace he had just built a picture representing the chase with all its accompanying pleasures, and recommended him, above all things else, to paint all the animals very fierce and terrifying.

The painter, who was a Christian, thought that this would be a favourable opportunity to try to make the King change his life ; so, instead of painting the picture the King ordered, he painted one of the Last Judgment. Everything in this picture inspired terror. On the one side were the heavens covered with dark clouds, and on the other the earth, which seemed to be all on fire, and the sea, as if changed into blood. The great and terrible throne of the Eternal Judge appeared hanging in the clouds, in the midst of terrible lightning, and surrounded with a multitude of angels, who appeared ready to execute the vengeance of God upon the wicked. All the nations of the earth were represented assembled together on a vast plain, trembling with fear, and waiting the coming of the Judge to pronounce sentence over them. Further down were a great many evil spirits, who waited to receive the souls that were to be condemned, and to take them with them to Hell. Beside them was the mouth of the eternal abyss open to receive them, and vomiting forth flames and clouds of black smoke.

During the time that this picture was being painted no one was allowed to enter. The King more than once asked the painter to show it to him, but he always refused, saying that he wanted to make this painting a great work of art, and that it would not have the same effect upon the King if he saw it before it was finished.

When at length the picture was completed he sent for the King ; and as soon as he arrived, he suddenly pulled aside the curtain that concealed it. The King stood for a few moments gazing at the picture in admiration and terror. Then, turning to the painter, he said · " What does this awful picture represent ?"

" It is but a feeble representation of the terrible Last Judgment Day, when God shall condemn to eternal punishment all those who have not served Him in this world."

He then spoke to the King of the awful judgments of God, of the punishments that God inflicts on the wicked, and the rewards He accords to the good, and with a voice so powerful and so full of earnestness that the King stood as if fixed to the spot. After a short time the King went away in silence, and for many days did not speak to anyone. At last he said : " If the mere painting of the Last

Judgment is so terrible to look at, what must the great reality be ?"   From that moment he gave himself to God by a sincere conversion, embraced the Catholic Faith, and persevered in it to the end.

History of the Church.

THE HOLY PRIEST'S MIRROR.

Frequently artists are accustomed to paint the face of Our Lord like what it must have been during His Passion : the head crowned with thorns, the forehead and cheeks covered with dust and blood, and the eyes swollen with much weeping.   This picture has received the name of " Ecce Homo "— Behold the Man.

A certain priest of Florence in Italy, named Hippolytus, possessed a beautiful painting of the " Ecce Homo," which he caused to be beautifully framed and hung up in his room.   Every day he went thither and gazed upon it as he made his meditation, and it was the means of raising many pious thoughts in his mind.

On the opposite side of the street, and facing this room, dwelt a noble lady, who, unfortunately, was imbued with the spirit of the world, and spent hours every day admiring her personal appearance in her mirror.   Having frequently seen the priest looking for a considerable time on the picture, the frame only of which she could see, she naturally concluded that this also was a mirror, and that he was admiring himself in it ; and, being determined to see if such were the case, she found some excuse for visiting him.   During the visit the conversation fell upon the beautiful mirror.

Hippolytus soon divined her object, but took care not to contradict her, and answered that it was indeed a beautiful mirror, and that it possessed certain properties which no mirror in the world except itself could boast of.

This excited the lady's curiosity more and more. " You see," said the priest, " that other mirrors usually reproduce the countenances of those who gaze at them, just as they are ; but the one I possess has the property of causing to disappear little by little the stains and defects and imperfections which may be there, provided one goes there daily and examines oneself carefully in it."

This information only served to increase her anxiety to know how this could be ; but the priest did not at once take her to see it, but only continued to praise its perfections more loudly. When at length he observed that she was growing impatient to view it, he said · " But come and see it, and you will be able to judge for yourself." And he led her into the room.

One can imagine the disappointment of this worldly lady when she discovered that it was only a picture. The priest now took the opportunity to show her that it was not the defects of the countenance that could be revealed in this mirror, but those of the soul that is created to serve God alone, yet is occupied in pleasing itself and serving the world.

The lady, we are told, was so much moved at these words that from that time she lived a Christian life, and died a holy death.   SCHMID *et* BÉLET.

ST. VINCENT AND THE DYING MAN.

St. Vincent, having for a long time in vain exhorted a hardened sinner to repent before he should meet his Judge, gave him one day a little picture representing our Saviour falling under the weight of His cross. " Take this little picture, my friend," he said to him, " and keep it in remembrance of the words I have just spoken to you, and, as a favour, I beg of you to promise me that you will look at it for a few moments every night before retiring to rest, and think at the same time of the sufferings which Jesus endured for you when He carried His cross and fell so frequently under it. You will then say to yourself : ' How long shall I, by my sins, leave Him to lie under the heavy cross ? How long shall I see Him suffering for me, without freeing Him from them, since it is in my power ?' "

We know not if the poor sinner kept his promise, but it seems that he did, for when the Saint returned to visit him he found him entirely changed. " O my Father," he said, " I could get no peace when I thought of my Saviour suffering when it was in my power to relieve Him. So I am resolved to sin no more, and to make up by my good life for the time to come for all that I have caused Jesus to suffer by my sins."

Lives of the Saints.

THE PICTURE OF THE CHILD JESUS.

There was once a girl who, though not bad, was very giddy, disobedient to her parents, and loved her amusements more than her lessons.

One day the priest gave her a little picture of the

Child Jesus, and asked her to place it before her eyes when she sat down to her lessons. She did this, not so much that she might keep in her mind the presence of God, as to please the priest who gave her the picture.

As it was always before her, she saw it every time she raised her eyes from her books. At first she did not think much of the Holy Child Jesus Whom it represented, but by degrees she began to think oftener of Him, and even sometimes to say a short prayer to Him.

One day, as she was looking at it longer than usual, she said to herself, " Oh, how good Jesus has been to me, and I am so sinful and ungrateful !" Then the tears came into her eyes. " He came into this world," she continued, " that I might get to Heaven, and I think so little about Him and Heaven. But, my dear little Jesus, it shall be so no longer, for I must become a Saint, and love Thee more than I have yet done."

The girl kept her resolution : she became obedient and pious, to the astonishment of her parents, who could not tell what had produced the change in their child. But the priest who had given her the picture knew the cause of it, and in his heart thanked God, and prayed to Him that she might persevere. This prayer was heard ; for she grew up piously, and, after living for a time in the world, and edifying everyone by her virtuous life, she consecrated herself to God in the religious state.

VI. THE CRUCIFIX.

The sight of the crucifix, on which we behold the image of Jesus nailed to the cross, should put us in mind of the great love He has for us, and should make us grieve for our sins which caused Him to suffer so much.

THE CROWN OF GOLD AND THE CROWN OF THORNS.

It was the great feast of Our Lady's Assumption. The people of Hungary were celebrating it with the greatest pomp, for they venerated the most holy Mother of God as the special patroness of their kingdom, and loved her with the deepest devotion.

St. Elizabeth of Hungary was at that time a child nine years old. She lived in the royal palace under the care of the Duchess Sophia, whose daughter Agnes was her constant companion.

On the morning of that great festival the Duchess said to Agnes and Elizabeth : " Let us go down to Eisenach to the church of our dear Lady, to hear the High Mass of the Teutonic knights who honour her specially ; perhaps we may also hear a sermon in her praise. Put on your richest robes and your golden crowns."

The young Princesses, being adorned as she had ordered, descended with her to the city, and, entering the church, knelt before the great crucifix.

At the sight of the image of the dying Saviour, Elizabeth took off her crown, and, laying it on a bench, prostrated herself without other ornament on her head than her hair.

The Duchess, seeing her thus, said rudely to her : " What ails you, Lady Elizabeth ? What new whim is this ? Do you wish that everyone should laugh at you ? Young ladies should hold themselves erect, and not throw themselves upon the ground like fools or old women. Can you not do as we do, instead of behaving like an ill-reared child ? Is your crown too heavy ? Why do you remain thus stooped like a peasant girl ?"

Elizabeth, rising, humbly answered : " Dear lady, do not blame me. Behold before my eyes my God and my King, the sweet and merciful Jesus, crowned with sharp thorns ; and can I, who am but a vile creature, remain before Him wearing pearls, gold, and jewels ? My coronet would be a mockery of His thorny wreath."

Then she began to weep bitterly, for already the love of her Divine Saviour had wounded her tender heart. She then knelt humbly as before, leaving Sophia and Agnes to speak as much as they pleased, and continued to pray with such fervour that, having placed a fold of her mantle before her eyes, it became saturated with her tears.

The two other Princesses, in order to avoid a contrast so disadvantageous to them in the eyes of the people, were obliged to imitate her, and to draw their veils over their faces, " which," adds the chronicler, " it would have been much more pleasing to them not to do."   *Life of St. Elizabeth.*

THE BOOK OF THE CRUCIFIX.

When St. Bonaventure was teaching theology with great repute in Paris, and was drawing upon himself the admiration of everyone by his learned writings, it happened that St. Thomas of Aquin went to see him one day. He asked him to show him the books out of which he drew so much profound learning.

St. Bonaventure led him into the little room where he studied, and showed him a few ordinary books that lay upon the table.

But St. Thomas told him that he desired to know the names of the other books from which he drew his deep learning.

The Saint then showed him a little oratory, in which was suspended a crucifix. " This, my Father, is my only other book ; it is the principal one I use, and from which I learn all that I teach and all that I write. Yes, it is in casting myself upon my knees at the foot of the crucifix, and in praying here for light in all my difficulties and doubts, and by assisting at Holy Mass, that I have made more progress in the sciences, and have obtained more true knowledge, than I should have done by reading all the books in the world."

RODRIGUEZ : *Perfect. Chrét.*, iii. 189.

" MY SOUL IS FULL OF CONSOLATION."

In the Life of Charles Clarentine, who was born in Picardy, in France, about the middle of the seventeenth century, we read that from his infancy he had the happiness of experiencing the power of the Cross of Jesus.

At the college of Amiens, where his parents had placed him for his studies, he applied himself with so much diligence to his lessons that nothing else seemed ever to occupy his attention.

When the intense cold of that Northern climate, or any other inconveniences, were for his comrades a pretext for interrupting their studies, and when they invited him to do as they did, his invariable answer was : " Oh no ! Should we not suffer something for the love of Jesus Christ, Who has suffered so much for us ?"

God submitted this love of Him to great trials. Charles became dangerously ill, and suffered so much pain that he thought his last hour could not be far off. Then he asked that they should place a crucifix at the foot of his bed, on which he could fix his eyes.

It happened that his confessor came to visit him on one occasion when he was suffering acute pain. He asked him how he felt. " My Father," replied Charles, placing his two hands upon his breast, " with regard to my body, I acknowledge that I am suffering very much pain ; but my soul is full of every consolation, so much so that I can scarcely contain my joy."

Then, taking into his hands the crucifix which the Father offered him, he devoutly kissed it, and said several times : " See, my Love is crucified, and I still live."

The confidence which the sight of that crucifix infused into his soul was as strong as his love was

tender.   He pressed it against his heart and upon
his lips, and said : " What enemy can now overcome
me, since I have this to defend me ?   It is my sword,
my protection ; it is my shield and my breast-
plate."

The terrors of death can never make the disciple
of Jesus Christ afraid, and he looked forward to his
death as the gate through which he had to pass
to reach Heaven ; and when the end did come, with
the crucifix in his hand, he repeated the words of
his dying Saviour : " Father, into Thy hands I
commend my spirit."   *Catéch. Historique*, i. 282.

XXVIII

THE SECOND COMMANDMENT

I. We must Speak with Reverence of God.

THE Second Commandment is, " Thou shalt not take the Name of the Lord thy God in vain " This commandment commands us to speak with reverence of God and of all things that belong to Him, for He says that He will punish with the greatest severity those who speak of Him in an unbecoming manner, or who take His Name in vain.

" THAT IS NOT THE WAY TO SPEAK OF GOD."

A mother was once on a journey along with her child, a girl of four years. Although so young, the child had learned from her mother to know and love God, and many people who were much older learned from her example to be ashamed of their carelessness, and to live more piously.

One day they were at dinner in an inn, where there were a number of travellers ; these were also at table with them. Among them were two young men, who by their dress and appearance seemed to belong to the better class of society. They had scarcely sat down to table when they began to

III

speak with the greatest irreverence of God, to take His holy Name in vain, and to say profane words.

The child was very much displeased when she heard them speaking in this way. She looked round to see if any one of those who were at table would have the courage to tell them to cease ; but every one of them remained silent, although there must have been some present to whom the words that were uttered were as displeasing as to her.

When the child saw that no one checked them, she rose up from her place, and, going over to the men who were speaking, said to them : " It is not right of you to speak in that way ; no one ought to speak of the good God in such a manner. It is, indeed, very wrong of you."

The two men were astonished to hear these words from a little girl. They said no more, but their faces became flushed with shame, for they saw that every eye was upon them, and that everyone present was glad to see the courage of the child ; so they at once rose up and left the place.

An old man who was present broke the silence that followed, by saying aloud : " My child, you are right : that is not the way to speak of the great and Almighty God."

HAUTERIVE : *Catéchisme de Persévérance*, xii. 243.

ST. LOUIS AND THE HOLY NAME OF GOD.

St. Louis, King of France, was one of the gentlest and most pious of monarchs. One thing only did he punish with great severity, and this was disrespect to, and profanation of, the Holy Name of God.

At that time, as in our own days, nothing was

more dishonoured than God's holy Name. To put an end to this great evil, as far as lay in his power, he formulated a law for the punishment of all who were found guilty of this great sin. Then, having assembled all the members of the great Court in one of the largest apartments of the palace, the doors of which he caused to remain open, he read in a loud voice the terms of the decree ; after which he pronounced an eloquent discourse, setting forth the enormity of the crime, and his determination to punish without mercy all who would wilfully be guilty of it.

Most of those who came to the knowledge of the new law carefully refrained from every form of blasphemy or word of disrespect to the Name of God ; but there were some who, trusting to the well-known clemency of the King, placed no restraint upon their tongues. Among these was one who occupied a high position in the city of Paris. The King, hearing of this, summoned the offender to his presence, and having in words inspired by his zeal for the honour of God showed him the malignity of the sin, ordered his tongue, the member through which it had been committed, to be pierced with a red-hot iron.

Many of the inhabitants showed great indignation at this action of the King, and did not hesitate to shower upon him the heaviest maledictions.

He was in a short time informed of their conduct towards him ; but he would not consent to their receiving any punishment, saying that from his heart he pardoned them, because the words they uttered were not against God, but only against himself.

Afterwards, referring to this matter, he said " Would to God that my tongue should be pierced with a hot iron, if only by suffering this I might be able to root out of my kingdom every word of blasphemy or dishonour against God's most holy Name !" And when someone praised him for his zeal, he answered : " I prefer to hear the maledictions that are poured forth against me when I cause to be executed the law I have passed, than to hear the words of praise you are lavishing upon me."

HOW ST. FRANCIS ESTEEMED THE NAME OF GOD.

St. Francis of Assisi always pronounced the Name of God with profound veneration. If by chance he saw lying on the ground a piece of paper on which the Name of God was written, he reverently took it up, and placed it carefully in his cell. He also counselled all his disciples to do so likewise.

From his Life.

II. God's Chastisements on those who take His Name in Vain.

God often punishes, even in this life, those who take His Name in vain, or who speak of Him with irreverence.

A SUDDEN PUNISHMENT.

A zealous priest relates the following terrible story ⋅ " I was preparing the children of my congregation for their first Communion. Amongst them there were two boys who were very wicked. They had never learned their Catechism, and had very seldom gone to Sunday-school; and I told them that if they did not listen very attentively to the instructions I was about to give them, and did not change their conduct, I would be obliged to make them wait a year longer, for I could not permit them to receive Jesus Christ into their souls without sufficient instruction, and without seeing a great change in their conduct.

" This threat seemed to make no impression on them—they only laughed at it—and I was obliged to send them out of the church that they might not distract the others. When they reached the street they began to quarrel, and were heard to blaspheme and to take God's holy Name in vain.

" A workman who was passing at the time, hearing the terrible words they were uttering, chid them and tried to make them cease; but instead of obeying they turned towards him and called him many wicked names, at the same time cursing and swearing even more than before.

" The man continued on his way, but he had not gone far when he heard the noise of something heavy falling, and screams for help. He looked round, and saw that a wall on the side of the street, on the spot where he had passed the boys, had fallen down, that the screams must have come from them, and that they must at that moment be buried under the ruins.

" He ran back along with the crowd that were rushing to the place, and on removing the fallen stones and lime, they found the two boys crushed and dreadfully mangled. They were at once taken to a neighbouring house, but they were both quite dead.   The wall had fallen on them whilst the words of blasphemy were yet upon their lips, and they had to appear in this state before the dread tribunal of Jesus Christ to be judged."

A MAN WHO OPENLY DEFIED GOD.

Not many years ago there was a certain inn-keeper, who was, like many men of the world, without religion, and who thought of nothing but making money.   He was accustomed to swear by God's holy Name every hour of the day, and to speak with the utmost disrespect of holy things.   It was his great boast that he had not said even the Lord's Prayer for many years.

One day he said to those to whom he related this " Although I have lived in this way for so long a time, I am as prosperous, and even more so, than those who pretend to live piously.   Even if this house were to be burned to the ground, I would not be much annoyed, for I have sufficient money laid past to build another and a still better one."

Some years afterwards it happened that a terrible tempest broke over the town in which this impious man lived.   The noise of the thunder and the vivid flashes of lightning caused the hearts of even the bravest to be full of fear.   In the midst of the tempest the lightning struck the house of the inn-keeper and set it on fire.   The man himself, who had sought refuge from the storm inside the house, escaped with great difficulty ; and when he saw all his property being consumed before his eyes, a sudden frenzy took possession of him, and he became mad.   After living for some time, a terror to all who had formerly known him, he died in despair.

The people of the town, who had so often heard his blasphemous words, looked on his death as a punishment sent by God on account of his wicked life, and especially of the impious manner in which he had so often spoken of God.

PUNISHED BY GOD'S COMMAND.

The chastisements which God in the Old Law inflicted on those who took His holy Name in vain, and the laws, both civil and religious, that were enacted against them, show us how great was this crime, not only in the eyes of God, but also in the eyes of men.

" And behold," says the Scripture, " there went out the son of a woman of Israel, and fell at words in the camp with a man of Israel. And when he had blasphemed the Name [of God], and had cursed it, he was brought to Moses. And they put him into prison, till they might know what the Lord would command.

" And the Lord spoke to Moses, saying : ' Bring forth the blasphemer without the camp, and let them that heard him put their hands upon his head, and let all the people stone him. And thou shalt speak to the children of Israel : " The man that curseth his God shall bear his sin ; and he that blasphemeth the Name of the Lord, dying, let him die." All the multitude shall stone him, whether he be a native or a stranger. He that blasphemeth the Name of the Lord, dying, let him die.'

" And Moses spoke to the children of Israel ; and

they brought him that had blasphemed without the camp, and they stoned him. And the children of Israel did as the Lord had commanded Moses."

Lev. xxiv. 10-23.

III. ON BLASPHEMY.

Blasphemy means speaking evil of God or of His Saints, or speaking of them with contempt, or of the truths revealed by God, or of anything sacred, such as the Sacraments and the Holy Sacrifice of the Mass. This is a very great sin, my child, and one that is punished by God with His most terrible punishments.

"YES, I DO FEAR GOD."

One day a number of young men were together in a public conveyance. They belonged to the class of those who think it manly to ridicule everything that is sacred; so they spent their time in mocking God, and in laughing at what He has been pleased to reveal to us in His Church.

During the conversation, one of them, bolder than the rest, said : " As for me, I do not fear either God or the Devil. As for the Devil," said he, smiling, " I do not fear him, because there is no Devil ; and as to God—well, as He does not trouble me, I do not trouble Him."

This made the others who were present laugh, and they all declared that he was acting very wisely.

But it happened that a poor countryman was sitting in a corner of the carriage who was of a very different disposition. He listened for a time to the words of the young man in silence ; but as soon as the man had said these last words he could not contain himself any longer, and showed by his manner how displeased he was. The young men soon noticed his looks of displeasure, and one of them, by way of jest, asked him if he believed in anything, or feared anything.

" Yes," he answered, " I fear God ; and I tremble when I think of the terrible evils that shall one day fall upon those who do not fear Him."

These words, pronounced with a tone of great firmness, seemed to fill the young impious men with fear, for they all hung down their heads, and did not say another word.

THE BLASPHEMER CONDEMNED TO DEATH.

During the terrible Revolution in France at the end of the eighteenth century, there was among the revolutionists a man notorious among all the evil men of his time for the terrible blasphemies he uttered. His name was Chaumette.

One day, in a company of men of similar dispositions to his own, he cried out aloud, so as to be heard by them all : " If there is a God, let Him crush me by His thunders !"

Not long after this the party to which he belonged was overcome by one still more powerful, and Chaumette was made prisoner and condemned to death.

.As they were conducting him to the scaffold, a voice was heard in the crowd, exclaiming : " Here comes that wretch who dared to say there was no

God. The curse he then called down upon his
head has now fallen on him. Surely you must now
acknowledge that the thunder of God's Divine
ustice has fallen on you !"

Chaumette recalled to mind the words he had
uttered. He grew pale, and died an ignominious
death—a death he truly deserved as a fit punishment for his impiety and blasphemy.

HAUSFREUND.

THE DREAM OF KING ROBERT OF FRANCE.

The saintly King Robert of France praying one
day to God that He would be pleased to maintain
peace in his kingdom, Our Blessed Lord was pleased
to appear to him in a dream, and thus spoke to him
" It is in vain, Robert, that you pray to me for
peace. Peace will never reign in your kingdom
until you have banished from it all blasphemers."

And experience attests that in those countries
where this vice prevails, and where people have no
respect for the Name of God, all authority is
despised, and the people fall into a state of indifference to the whole law of God. Peace and true
happiness are unknown among them.

NACH HUNOLT.

A TERRIBLE PUNISHMENT OF GOD.

Two young soldiers, who lived without any fear
of God, had obtained leave to return home for a
time to visit their friends. It was in the year 1533.
Their way led them through an immense forest,
situated in the Lower Lausitz.

When they had accomplished half of their journey through the forest, they were overtaken by a furious tempest. The thunders rolled, and the brilliant flashes of lightning lit up the heavens above them, while the silence of the grave seemed to forebode some great evil. Suddenly the rain began to fall, and the two soldiers ran forward with great speed, that they might reach some place of security where they could rest until the tempest had abated.

They had not gone far when they came upon a young shepherd, who was kneeling beside his sheep, his head uncovered, and his hands devoutly joined together. He was saying his prayers to God aloud, and beseeching Him to protect himself and his flock from the dangers which threatened them.

The soldiers, on seeing him thus occupied, began to mock him and to laugh at him. One of them said to him : " O foolish boy, put on your hat, and go home as quickly as you can with your flock. Why do you kneel there, losing your time in muttering prayers which can never do you any good ?"

The young shepherd, on hearing these words of blasphemy, was pierced to the heart with sorrow, and cast upon the one who said them a sad look of displeasure. But they had not advanced more than a dozen steps when a flash of lightning struck them, and the one who had uttered the words was cast lifeless upon the ground, and his hat thrown to a great distance. The other was stunned, and for a time lay unconscious. In a short time, however, his senses returned, and he stood up, now no longer the impious wretch he was before, but a sincere penitent ; for he had experienced in his own person what a terrible thing it is to expose oneself to the vengeance of God by words and sins of blasphemy.

CHIMANI.

IV. On Swearing and Cursing.

My child, do not go with those who curse and swear, or who say bad words, because they will teach you also to be wicked like themselves. God cannot love a child who says bad words, or who goes with those who say them. It is better to have poverty with Christ than riches with those who curse and swear and profane God's holy Name.

THE LITTLE NEWSBOY.

One evening, after the tidings of a victory gained during a time of war, the city was filled with excitement, and a brisk business was created among the news-dealers. One little boy came into the sitting-room of an hotel to sell his papers.

" Papers, sir ? Papers ?" said he.

A man was sitting by. He seemed to be attracted by the intelligent looks of the boy, and said to him, with an oath : " Come here, my lad ; you are a fine boy. Let me have a paper ;" and he drew the boy to his side.

The boy gave him the paper, and received for it an extra penny, the man swearing again that he was a fine boy.

" What is your father's name ?" he asked.

" My father is dead," said the boy.

" Well," said the man, " I must take you, and you

will be as my own boy;" and again he swore. " I'll
make a man of you," said he.

The boy made no answer, but still seemed rather
shy of his new-found friend.

" I say, my little fellow," said the man, who kept
swearing at almost every word he spoke, " how
would you like to come and live with me, and be a
great man some day ?"

" I think," said the boy quietly, " that I should
not like to live with a man who swears as you do."

The man was silent. What could he say ? And
the little boy went on to sell his papers.

Ave Maria, vii. 744.

" FATHER, STRIKE ME AGAIN, BUT OH, 'DO NOT SWEAR."

There lived at Namur, a town in Belgium, a boy
of ten years of age, who attended a school taught
by the Christian Brothers. In this school he
learned not only his lessons with care, but also
how to please God and keep away from evil.

This boy's father was not a good Christian, and
was in the habit of flying into a great passion when
he met with any contradiction, and swearing by
the holy Name of God.

One day it happened that the boy did not reach
home at the accustomed time after school, either
because he had been detained for his lessons longer
than usual, or because he had lingered too long by
the way.

When he entered the house, he met his father,
who was very angry. He raised up his hand and
struck the boy a heavy blow that nearly stunned

him ; at the same time he swore and took God's holy Name in vain.

The good child fell on his knees at his father's feet, and, with tears streaming from his eyes, begged of him not to say these words again.

" O my father," he said, " give me another blow like the one you have just given me, but oh, do not swear like that again."

The father did not expect this answer ; he was moved when he saw his son kneeling at his feet and heard these words. He felt ashamed of his cruelty to the boy, and still more at the reproof he had received, which he knew he so well deserved. He turned away to hide his tears, and from that moment he was never again heard to swear, nor even to say an angry word.

V. How to Overcome the Habit of Swearing.

My child, when one has acquired the bad habit of swearing, it is indeed very difficult to overcome it. Yet, with care and perseverance, this may be effected, as the following examples will show.

" O LORD, HAVE MERCY ON ME."

There was once a young soldier who had been brought up piously, but had forgotten the lessons of his childhood by mingling with bad companions.

· Among the other wicked things they taught him was the bad custom of swearing and taking God's holy Name in vain.

But his conscience told him he was doing wrong, and God was always speaking to him by His grace, asking him to break off the bad habit, and to begin again to love Him as he had done in his child-hood.

One day he happened to hear a sermon which inspired him with the good resolution of going at once to Confession. He humbly accused himself of his great sin, and promised for the time to come never to be guilty of it again.

"Father," he said to his confessor, "tell me what I must do to overcome that bad habit."

"My child," he answered, "whenever a word of that kind falls from your lips, bow your head towards the ground, as if to kiss the footprints of our dear Lord, and say at the same time this prayer : 'O Lord, have mercy on me.'"

The soldier promised to do as his confessor advised him, and in a very short time he almost entirely overcame his wicked custom.

One day he had to go to fight against the enemy It was a fierce contest, and many of his comrades were struck down at his side. In the midst of the fight his sword fell from his hand. At the same instant, in the excitement of the moment, by forget-fulness, he uttered an oath which took the holy Name of God in vain.

He had scarcely uttered the word, when, remem-bering that he had done wrong, he at once, according to his custom, bowed his head towards the ground, and said his usual prayer : "O Lord, have mercy on me."

While bowing down and saying this prayer, it happened that a bullet from a gun of the enemy passed over his head, and had he been standing erect at the time, it would have most assuredly struck him, and very likely killed him on the spot.

Through gratitude to God for his marvellous escape, he became more and more careful of his words, and strove for the rest of his life to hinder others from falling into this bad custom.

The Catechism Illustrated.

THE SOLDIER CURED OF AN EVIL HABIT.

A certain soldier was in the habit of cursing and swearing, and almost every time he opened his mouth to speak, he was sure to say an unbecoming word. One of his comrades, seeing the bad habit he had acquired, and wanting him to overcome it, said to him one morning : " My good friend, I will give you a shilling to-night if you do not curse or swear during the whole of this day."

The soldier said he would willingly keep from swearing, that he might gain the promised shilling. With an effort, he succeeded in keeping his good resolution, and in the evening received the reward which had been promised him.

His companion then said to him : " Since you have overcome your evil habit to-day for the sake of a little worldly gain, surely to-morrow, for God's sake and for an eternal reward, you will take the same good resolution."

The soldier was ashamed of his past conduct, and from that moment kept so strict a guard upon his lips that he never afterwards was heard to say an unbecoming word.

Catéch. en Histoires.

VI. On Oaths.

An oath, my child, consists on calling God to witness the truth of what we say, and to punish us if we say what is false.　It is lawful to take an oath sometimes, but only when God's honour, or our own or neighbour's honour, defence, or good require it.　How often, alas! is an oath taken without just cause!　How careful we should be never to take any false, rash, unjust, or unnecessary oath!　The Saints of God are our models in this as in all other virtues.

HE WOULD NOT TAKE AN OATH.

Clotaire II., King of the Francs, being filled with admiration for St. Eligius on account of his honesty and piety, as well as his diligence in performing the duties he had entrusted to him, desired him to become one of his immediate attendants.

" Would you not desire to be always in my palace and to become one of my chief ministers ?" he said one day to him.

" My liege," he answered, " such an honour is greater than I could ever presume to hope for."

" But the King replied : I am so pleased with your fidelity in the service of God that I am sure you will be equally faithful in mine.　Therefore you may consider yourself from this time forward attached to my household."

St. Eligius thanked the King for this great act of his favour, and was about to retire, when Clotaire called him back.

" It is my invariable custom," said the King,

" when I confer a similar favour on anyone, to exact from him a solemn oath on the relics of the Saints that he will always be faithful to me."

" My King and my master," replied Eligius, " I beseech you not to require this of me. The respect I have for the Name of God and for His Saints is great, and above all other things, and I would consider it a mark of irreverence if I were to do what you ask me."

But the King said : " What I ask of you to do I have asked of many others who are good and holy, and they have never refused. It cannot, therefore, be wrong for you to do as they did."

" It is true, O King," replied Eligius, " that in this act there may be no sin ; but I humbly beg of you not to require it of me. I will, indeed, be faithful to you." And the Saint wept, for he was afraid, on the one hand, to offend the King, who had been so kind to him, and, on the other, he was afraid that if he took such an oath God might be angry with him.

The King, seeing his great delicacy of conscience, did not press him further. Eligius remained for a long time in the service of the King, and was the most faithful of all those who dwelt in his palace.

Life of St. Giles.

VII. On Perjury.

My child, when a person swears that something is true which he knows to be false, that is called perjury. It is a great sin, and terrible punishments have been inflicted even in this life on those who have been guilty of it.

THE ENEMIES OF ST. NARCISSUS.

There was once a holy Bishop called Narcissus. He dwelt at Jerusalem, and was a model of piety not only to his flock, but to the many pilgrims who came to visit the holy places once sanctified by the presence of Jesus Christ.

The Devil was full of wrath because of the multitude of souls the Saint was daily snatching out of his hands, and resolved to ruin his reputation. For this purpose he put it into the hearts of three wicked men to accuse him of a grievous crime of which he was innocent.

One of them, after speaking of this supposed crime, said : " May I be burned alive if what I say is not true !"

The second one added : " And may I be seized with a most dreadful malady if I have spoken falsely l"

The third one said : " May I become blind if what I have stated be not true l"

The people, deceived by these men, began to think that the accusation must be true, since they had sworn to it with such terrible oaths, and they no longer looked upon their Bishop as a Saint, but, on the contrary, from that moment began to call him a hypocrite.

Narcissus very soon perceived the effects of the calumny of these men ; he protested that he was innocent, and then left the matter in the hands of God. In the meantime he left the city and went into solitude, that he might be alone with God, Who knew his innocence. And God, Who watches with a jealous eye over the fame of His children on earth, in His own good time brought to light the innocence of His servant.

The first of his calumniators was burned to death, for his house took fire, and he could not escape. The people remembered the words he had said when he accused Narcissus—" May I be burned alive if what I say be not true !"—and they repented of having so readily given heed to his words against the man of God.

Almost at the same time the second one who had called on God to send him some dreadful malady if his words were false was seized with a terrible disease ; he was covered from head to foot with ulcers, and his whole body became a mass of corruption.

The third one was so moved at what had happened to his two companions that he repented and confessed his crime.   Then the holy Bishop was looked on with far more admiration than before.   Nevertheless, the abundant tears shed by this man, now so repentant, made him lose his sight.

Lives of the Saints, October 29.

GOODWIN, EARL OF KENT.

Edward, King of England, gave a great feast to his nobles and the princes of his Court.   Among the guests present was one called Goodwin.   He was Earl of Kent, and commonly believed to be the murderer of Alfred, brother to the King, although it had been impossible to prove it.

It happened during the banquet that as a page in the service of the King was giving the Prince a goblet of wine, his foot slipped on the floor, and he would have fallen had he not supported himself on his other foot.

"Oh, how fortunate it was for me to have another foot to support the one that slipped!" he said. "It is indeed true that when one has a brother to come to one's aid in his necessities, he is immovable as a rock."

These words of the page, said in a tone of amusement, caused all the guests to laugh. But the King suddenly became sad ; the remembrance of his beloved brother was brought back to his mind by these thoughtless words, and he said in the hearing of them all : "Ah! if my brother Alfred were yet living, he would indeed be of great assistance to me."

In saying this, the eyes of the King turned towards Goodwin. The other guests also looked at him in silence. Goodwin saw that, although no one dared to accuse him of being the cause of Alfred's death, yet they all believed him to be the guilty one.

"O King," he said, "perhaps you think that I was accessory to your brother's death, but I am innocent of it. Let this morsel of food be the last that ever I eat if I had any hand in that most detestable crime."

Saying these words, he put the food into his mouth and tried to swallow it, but it became fixed in his throat and choked him. He fell back on his seat **dead.**

The people who were present were filled with awe at this terrible death, and looked on it as a punishment **sent from Heaven.**

VIII. On Vows.

A vow is a deliberate promise made to God to do something that is pleasing to Him. Before making a vow it is necessary to consider well what you are about to do, my child, because when once made it is sinful to break it. It is always prudent to obtain advice before making a vow. This is the counsel of the Saints.

THE BROTHER OF THE CHRISTIAN SCHOOLS.

Not many years ago there was a mother who had two sons. The elder one was a soldier, who had distinguished himself by his bravery in the Crimean War. After the Siege of Sebastopol he obtained permission to spend some time at home with his mother.

When he reached home he was grieved to find his little brother Henry, who was only ten years old, lying at the point of death. His mother sat weeping by his bedside, every moment expecting to see him breathe his last.

"O my darling Henry," she exclaimed, "if you die, I must die also, for I cannot live without you; you were my life, my only joy."

These words seemed hard to the young soldier, but he said to himself: "She is his mother as well as mine, and if I were lying dying as he is, she would have said the same to me, and love me just as much."

All that the doctors could do to restore the boy to health had been in vain. His eyes were already glazed in death. He saw not his mother and brother,

who held his cold hands in theirs. " He is dying ;
he is dying !" exclaimed the disconsolate mother.

The priest, who was there already, spoke of resignation to God's most blessed will, and how happy
those are whom God takes to Heaven in their innocence ! These words were full of consolation, but
they were spoken to a mother whose son was in the
agonies of death.

The dying boy gave one more convulsive movement. Everyone thought it was his last. " Let us
pray," said the priest ; and everyone knelt round
the bed and prayed.

The soldier also prayed. No one near him heard
what he said, but God in Heaven heard him. " O
my God," he prayed, " if you make my little brother
better, I solemnly vow to consecrate my whole life
to the education of children of his age. I will teach
them to love You and bless You. . . . O my God,
I will love You and bless You all the days of my life,
if you cure my little brother and console my mother."

The child suddenly began to breathe more regularly. Soon afterwards he opened his eyes ; they
met those of his mother, and he smiled. A cry of
joy burst from her lips. " He is not going to die,"
she exclaimed ; " see, he is already better !"

Joy now filled that happy home. Day by day
the child grew stronger, and was soon able to leave
his bed.

Then did the elder son make known to his mother
the vow he had made " Here, dearest mother, is
my sword ; give it to Henry when he grows older ;
he will be able to use it. As for me, I must leave
you again to go and fulfil my vow to God—that vow

which brought from Heaven my brother's life.   I
go now to teach the children who are like him to
love God and serve Him."

The mother threw her arms round the neck of her
son, and pressed him to her heart.   He saw now that
she loved him even more than his brother.   " You
must not go," she cried out in her maternal love for
him.   But he remembered the vow he had made,
and not even his mother's tears could hinder him
from fulfilling it.   He is now a Brother of the
Christian Schools.

HAUTERIVE : *Catéchisme de Persévérance,* vi. 37.

JACOB'S VOW.

The first vow of which the sacred Scriptures make
mention is the one that Jacob made when he was
on his journey to Mesopotamia to escape the wrath
of his brother Esau.

" And when he was come to a certain place," says
the sacred text, " and would rest in it after sunset,
he took of the stones that lay there, and putting
under his head, slept in the same place.

" And he saw in his sleep a ladder standing upon
the earth, and the top thereof touching Heaven ·
the angels also of God ascending and descending by
it, and the Lord leaning upon the ladder, saying to
him : ' I am the Lord God of Abraham thy father,
and the God of Isaac : the land wherein thou sleepest,
I will give to thee and to thy seed.   And thy seed
shall be as the dust of the earth ; thou shalt spread
abroad to the west, and to the east, and to the north,
and to the south ; and in thee and thy seed all the
tribes of the earth shall be blessed.   And I will be

thy keeper whithersoever thou goest, and will bring thee back into this land ; neither will I leave thee, till I shall have accomplished all that I have said.'

" And when Jacob awaked out of sleep, he said : ' Indeed the Lord is in this place, and I knew it not.' And trembling, he said : ' How terrible is this place ! This is no other but the House of God, and the gate of Heaven.'

" And Jacob, arising in the morning, took the stone which he had laid under his head, and set it up for a title, pouring oil upon the top of it. And he called the name of the city Bethel, which before was called Luza.

" And he made a vow, saying : ' If God shall be with me, and shall keep me in the way by which I walk, and shall give me bread to eat, and raiment to put on, and I shall return prosperously to my father's house : the Lord shall be my God : and this stone which I have set up for a title, shall be called the house of God : and of all things that Thou shalt give to me, I will offer tithes to Thee.' "

Gen. xxviii. 11 *et seq.*

ST. FRANCIS OF SALES AND THE ROSARY.

St. Francis of Sales had always a great devotion to Our Blessed Lady. To testify to her how much he loved her, he made a vow to say every day of his life a certain portion of the holy Rosary in her honour, which vow he carefully fulfilled all his lifetime.

Now it happened that a certain young man, who was very pious, and who also had a great love for the most holy Mother of God, having heard of this vow that St. Francis had made, thought he would prove the sincerity of his love for Mary in the same manner.

But, being prudent as well as virtuous, he went to the Saint to tell him of his intention. He was surprised at the first words that fell from St. Francis' lips as soon as he had begun to speak to him on the subject. " Don't do it," said he. " Be careful never to make that vow."

The young man said to him · " You, my Father, did so when you were young like me, and why do you refuse to allow me to follow your example in this good work ?"

" It is just because I was young when I made that vow that I say to you now so earnestly not to make it. I am older now, and it is because I have learned much by experience that I give you this advice. I do not tell you not to say the Rosary ; on the contrary, I advise you and exhort you to say it every day, because it is a prayer which is exceedingly dear o the Blessed Mother of God. Let this be a firm resolution on your part, but not a vow, because then if you did sometimes omit it, you would not commit a sin."

THE VOW OF BLESSED MARGARET OF HUNGARY.

Bela IV., King of Hungary, seeing that he was in danger of being driven from his kingdom by the Tartars who had invaded it, made a vow to God in concert with Mary, his wife, that if He would be pleased to deliver him from his enemies, he would dedicate for ever to His holy service the child that was soon to be born to him. His prayer was heard, and his vow accepted, for the Tartars left the kingdom as suddenly as they had entered it.

Not long after this event the Queen gave birth to a daughter, who was called Margaret. Faithful to their vow, her parents, when she was three years old, took her to the Dominican convent of Veszprim, and placed her under the care of the Countess Olympiada, who herself took the religious habit, that she might the more easily watch over her little charge. The child, thus given to God in her infancy, daily grew up in wisdom and grace, and her life was a series of wonders from beginning to end.

THE ROBBERS OF AUBRAC.

During the twelfth century, Adalard, Viscount of Flanders, having set out on a pilgrimage to the shrine of St. James in Galicia, as was the custom of the pious knights in the Middle Ages, fell into an ambuscade of robbers on the way thither.

This place was situated on the summit of a high mountain, far away from any inhabited town, and often inaccessible on account of the snow and mist which covered it during the greater part of the year. It was known by the name of the mountain of Aubrac.

Seeing himself in danger of losing his life, Adalard made a solemn vow that if he escaped his present danger, he would found on that same place a hostel, where pilgrims might find shelter and rest, and at the same time banish from the mountain the robbers who had made it their stronghold.

This pious vow was registered in heaven, and the Viscount gained a complete victory over his enemies. Many of the robbers lay dead on the declivities of the mountains, and all the others took refuge in flight.

Full of gratitude to God for coming to his assistance, Adalard called together the young knights who had accompanied him, by whose prowess also the enemies were repulsed, and made known to them the vow he had made.

" My friends," he said, " if even brave knights like yourselves could not effect your passage through the defiles of these mountains unless by force of arms, how can it be possible for those who are entirely unarmed, and the old men, and the women, and the children, to reach in safety the end of their pilgrimage ? Is it not a work worthy of a Christian to purge these mountains of the hordes of evil men which infest them, and to establish on the very spot where we have gained our victory a house of refuge for these pilgrims ?"

The knights, having with one accord applauded this generous resolution, continued their route, and soon reached the place of intended pilgrimage without further molestation.

Adalard, having reached the tomb of the Apostle of Spain, and having laid the offering he had brought on the altar of the shrine, received, in return, the staff of the pilgrim. When he had finished his devotions he left the town, and began to retrace his steps homeward. Mindful of his vow, and the glorious events which had occurred on the mountains, he went thither a second time with all the speed at his command. God was waiting for him there. When he reached the place where the robbers had attacked him, a violent tempest, such as frequently break out in these places, arose, and a gust of wind, more fierce than the others, raised him from the ground and cast him, along with his horse on which he rode, into a deep crevice hidden by the snow.

This new danger brought again even more vividly before him the remembrance of his vow, and he renewed it with the utmost fervour, at the same time adding that, if he should escape this new danger, he would for the rest of his life consecrate himself to God in that same place.

God again heard his prayer and accepted his vow. In a short time his followers were able to reach him, and bring him out of his perilous position. It is related that Our Lord Himself, to confirm him in his good resolution, appeared visibly to him, and showed him near the highway a cave in which lay the bodies of nearly thirty pilgrims whom the robbers had slain in order to obtain what money they possessed, and ordered him to found there a noble church to His honour and to that of His blessed Mother, wherein many would find rest and security in the day of peril.

Faithful to the orders vouchsafed him by God, he, on that very day, caused a humble cabin to be erected, covered with branches of the dwarf trees that grew upon the mountain, and took up his abode within it. Adalard soon saw that God blessed his work abundantly. In it His holy Name was glorified by all the people, the poor found comfort, the grieving **ones consolation, and the pilgrims rest and safety.**

Aubrac, once the stronghold of robbers, and the scene of many murders, soon offered to the world an image of the heavenly Jerusalem.

Histoire de l'Hôpital d'Aubrac.

THE VOW OF DUKE LOUIS, HUSBAND OF ST. ELIZABETH.

The pious Duke Louis, husband of the dear St. Elizabeth, took the cross at the head of many other noble crusaders, to endeavour to rescue the Holy Land from the power of the infidels. This he did, unknown to his wife, who, he feared, might be deeply grieved at the step he had in duty taken, although he knew that in the end her piety would secure for him her consent. So he resolved, by degrees, tenderly to inform her.

But one evening, as they sat alone side by side, Elizabeth, in a moment of tender familiarity that existed between them, unloosed her husband's belt, and began to search the alms-purse attached to it. Immediately she drew from it the cross, the usual badge of the crusader.

At this sight she at once felt the misfortune that threatened her, and, seized with grief and affright, she fell senseless to the ground.

The Duke raised her up, and strove to calm her sorrow by the sweetest and most affectionate words. He spoke to her for a long time, using the voice of religion, and even the language of the Holy Scriptures, to which she was never insensible.

" It is for the love of our Lord Jesus Christ," he said, " that I go. Thou wilt not prevent me from doing for God what I should do for a temporal prince, for the Emperor or the empire, if they required my services."

After a long silence **and** much weeping, she said to him : " Dear brother, if it be not against God's will, remain with me."

But he replied : " Dear sister, permit me to set out, for I have made a vow to God."

Then, entering into herself, she immolated her will to God, and said to her husband · " Against God's will I wish not to detain thee. I have offered thee and myself as a sacrifice to Him. May He in His goodness watch over thee ! May all happiness attend thee for ever ! This shall be my prayer each moment. Go, then, in the name of God."

MONTALEMBERT : *Vie de S. Eliz.*

THE RASH VOW OF JEPHTE.

The most striking example that can be found of a vow made without reflection, and the terrible consequences of it, is given us in the sacred Scriptures, in Judges, chapter xi.

Jephte, one of the judges of Israel, was at war with the Ammonites, and went forth to meet them in battle. His first thought was to pray to God that he might obtain from Him the strength and courage necessary to overcome them. In his anxiety to secure this help from Heaven, he imprudently made a vow that if he should gain the victory, he would sacrifice to God whatsoever he should first meet on his return home.

Jephte gained the victory. When the news had reached the camp of the children of Israel, there was great joy among the people. The only daughter of

Jephte, immediately assembling together her companions, went forth joyously to meet him with timbrels and dances, and was the first to approach him.

As soon as he saw her coming towards him consternation fell upon him at the remembrance of his vow. " Whom, when he saw," says the Scripture, " he rent his garments, and said : ' Alas ! my daughter, thou hast deceived me, and thou thyself art deceived, for I have opened my mouth [vowed] to the Lord, and I can do no other thing.'

" And she answered him : ' My father, if thou hast opened thy mouth [vowed] to the Lord, do unto me whatsoever thou hast promised, since the victory hath been granted to thee, and revenge of thy enemies. . . .' And he did to her as he had vowed."

The sacred Scriptures tell us no more. Some of the Fathers of the Church are of opinion that he offered her up as a holocaust to the Lord ; but most of them think that he consecrated her to God in the service of the Tabernacle. But they all consider that the vow he made was rash, and that it will be for all time to come an example to Christians to make their vows to God with prudence and discretion.

IX. On Speaking Irreverently of Holy Things.

A LEARNED DOCTOR HUMBLED.

The following example will show you, my child that sometimes God punishes with great rigour Christians who dare to speak irreverently of the truths of religion.

Simon Turiajus was born in England, at the beginning of the thirteenth century. In after-years his great reputation for learning caused him to be chosen one of the professors in the great schools of Paris, where his eloquence procured for him so great renown that his name was known throughout the West of Europe.

But the applause he daily received caused the demon of pride to find an entrance into his heart, and led him to speak contemptuously of the Church of God, its doctrine, and its practices.

One day he dared publicly to assert that he could easily prove the doctrines of the Church to be true, and just as easily prove that they were all false.

But God was pleased to punish even in this world his audacious presumption. His memory suddenly failed him, and his intellect became so obscured that he could not distinguish even the letters of the alphabet one from the other, or repeat even the Lord's Prayer. The learned Nicholas of Durham informs us that he himself was an eyewitness of his own little son endeavouring to teach him the letters of the alphabet.   Dr. Brunner.

THE JUDGMENT OF GOD.

In the village of Edinghausen, not far from the town of Bielefeld, in Prussia, one of the men who dwelt there arranged with his companions to give, in a hotel, a parody of the Last Supper.

When everything was ready, he sat down at a table, around which his associates in iniquity were **seated.** Then, taking the bread and the chalice into **his hands, he** pronounced over them the words of consecration, and distributed the bread and the wine among them.　When it came to his turn to partake, he became suddenly ill, placed his head upon the table, and became motionless.　His companions came to his assistance, but it was too late ; he was dead.　　　　　　　　*Catéchisme Pratique*, ii. 168.

THE TERRIBLE PUNISHMENT OF NESTORIUS.

Nestorius, the author of that terrible heresy which endeavoured to deprive Our Blessed Lady of her glorious title of Mother of God, was punished by God by an awful death.

When he became near his end, his sufferings were frightful to behold.　His body began to fall into pieces by corruption, and his tongue, which had uttered so many blasphemies against Jesus Christ and His Holy Mother, was eaten with worms.　One day he mounted his horse to escape from the anger of the people which had been aroused against him, but he fell from it and died on the spot.

BARON : *Annals anno*, 436.

X. What the Second Commandment Ordains.

By this commandment we are commanded to speak with reverence of God and of all holy things. How often, in times of danger, does God protect those who act in this manner !

THE CHRISTIAN PASSWORD.

On the day of the famous battle of Bull-Run, General Smith, who commanded the army of the

South, arrived along with his division too late to know what was the password.

He foresaw that if he advanced without it he would be fired upon by his own army, and if he remained where he was he would most likely be attacked by the enemy.

Seeing the danger he was in, both from friend and foe, he came in front of the division, and asked if there was any man amongst them who would volunteer to sacrifice his life for the salvation of the rest.

A young man immediately came forward and said he would do it.

" Do you know what will happen to you ?" said the general.

" Yes, general," he replied.

" You will be shot."

" I know it," he answered.

Then the general wrote these words on a piece of paper : " Send me the countersign : General Smith," and gave the paper to the heroic soldier. He knew that as soon as they had shot him they would search him, and finding the paper, would carry it to General Beauregard.

When the young soldier received his message, he departed amidst the cheers of his comrades, who admired his bravery. He was a good Catholic, and on the way he prepared himself to die as became a Christian by acts of contrition and by recommending his soul to God.

When he reached the outposts of the army he heard the cry, " Who goes there ?"

" A friend," he replied.

" Give the countersign," they cried.

He went forward towards them without saying a word.   In an instant all the guns were raised to fire upon him.

Thinking that his last hour had come, he stood, and, raising up his hand, made the sign of the cross.

Immediately every gun was lowered, and the soldier was told to pass.

It happened that the sign of the Cross was the countersign that Beauregard had that morning appointed, as he himself was a good Catholic, and so, by using it, the pious soldier escaped death.

XI. OUR IMPRECATIONS.

Imprecations are words of hatred or of anger, by which one calls upon God to send to oneself or others death or damnation or some other terrible evil. This is a terrible sin, because it is directly opposed to our own spiritual welfare, and to the charity due to our neighbour, as also on account of the injury it does to God, to the honour due to His holy Name.

A MOTHER'S MALEDICTION.

St. Augustine narrates the following account of a terrible event which occurred in Cæsarea, and in which he himself bore a conspicuous part.

There dwelt in that city a mother who had ten children, of whom seven were boys and three were girls.   One day the oldest son became very insolent towards his mother, and even struck her with his hand.   The other children were present, but none of them interfered to prevent him.   The mother was filled with anger at this undutiful conduct of her offspring, and in her fury ran to the church, and, with her hair in disorder, and the breasts from which they had been nourished in their infancy exposed, she cursed them, and prayed that God might make an example of them to the whole world.

This awful prayer, said in an hour of passion, was heard. First the oldest son, who had struck her, then the other children, one after another, were seized with a strange trembling in every limb. They could not rest anywhere, but wandered from place to place, and from town to town, over all the Roman Empire.

The mother, seeing, but too late, the terrible consequences of her curse, was filled with shame and remorse. Everyone who heard of what she had done hooted her, and would not even speak to her, so that, being unable any longer to bear their reproaches, she hanged herself in despair.

Two of the children, Paul and Palladia, his sister, in their wanderings came to the city of Hippo, of which St. Augustine was Bishop. Every day for two weeks they went to a chapel there where the relics of St. Stephen were preserved, and prayed for their cure.

At the end of the second week, on Easter Sunday morning, as Paul was praying in the presence of the congregation, he fell into a swoon. After a little time he came to himself, and rose up perfectly cured. The joy of the people was very great when they saw this miracle, and they sang hymns of praise and thanksgiving to God for His mercy to him.

But Palladia still remained in the same sad condition as before. On Easter Monday Paul and his sister went together to the church, the one in perfect health, the other trembling in every limb. St. Augustine ascended the pulpit and told the terrible story of the mother's curse to the entire congregation. He exhorted parents to take a warning from what they had heard and seen, and not to be rash and angry with their children, and never ask God to hurt them, but rather to bless them. He also told the children present to reverence and honour their parents and be obedient to them, lest they should be punished as these had been.

When the sermon was ended Palladia went to the chapel of St. Stephen, and most earnestly prayed to him and to God that the terrible curse of her mother might be removed. Her prayer was at length heard, for she, like her brother, fell into a swoon, and afterwards rose up perfectly cured.

XXIX

THE THIRD COMMANDMENT

I. What is Commanded by this Precept.

" Remember that thou keep holy the Sabbath Day." These are the words by which God ordered His people to sanctify the day which He had appointed to be dedicated to Him. By this commandment we are commanded to keep holy the Sundays and the holidays of Obligation, on which we are to give our time to the service and worship of God.

TERRIBLE END OF THE IMPIOUS NICANOR.

The impious Nicanor having resolved to fight against the Jews on the Sabbath Day, some of the Jews who were in his camp went to him and reminded him that it was not lawful to do so on the day consecrated to the service of God. Nicanor, puffed up with pride, and thinking in his present greatness that he could do whatever he wished, answered them : " Is there some Mighty One in Heaven Who hath commanded the Sabbath day to be kept holy ?"

" Yes," they reverently answered, " there is the **living Lord Himself in Heaven**, the Mighty One that **commandeth the seventh day** to be kept."

149

Then Nicanor replied : " And I, who am mighty upon the earth, command you to take up arms to obey the order of the King."

He began the battle, and although his army was superior in numbers to that of the Jews, it was entirely overthrown, and he himself was found among the slain.   Thus was punished one who neglected to keep holy the day of the Lord.

2 *Mach.* xv. 3-5.

II. How Sundays and Holidays are to be Sanctified.

The way in which we have to sanctify the Sunday and holidays of Obligation in the New Law is by hearing Mass, by prayer, and by other good works.

" stop ! whither are you going ?"

" Lukewarm Christians," writes a pious author, " may take example from the conduct of a certain young woman who lived in the first centuries of the Church.   One day when she was on her way to hear holy Mass, one of the guards of the Emperor met her, and, being struck by her great modesty, went over to her, and, seizing her in a very rough manner, said · " Stop !   Whither are you going ?"

" The young woman was frightened, because she thought that he was about to insult her.   So she made on her forehead the sign of the Cross, in order to obtain the Divine protection, and did not answer him.

" The soldier, deeming himself insulted by her silence, shook her violently, and said : ' Speak ! Who are you ? and whither are you going ?'

"She courageously answered : ' I am a servant of Jesus Christ, and I am going to the assembly of the Lord.'

" ' You shall not go,' said the soldier ; ' you must come and sacrifice to the gods, for to-day we worship the sun ; you must worship with us.'

"He then attempted to pull off the veil that covered her face. But, fortified by grace from on high, she would not permit him, and cried out to him : ' O wretched man, Jesus Christ will punish you.'

"At these words the soldier became furious, and, drawing his sword, plunged it into the breast of the pious maiden.

"She fell dead at his feet, but her holy soul flew up to heaven, there to receive an unfading crown of glory."   *History of the Church, Fourth Century.*

DROWNED IN THE FLOOD.

Certain traders of Gubbio had gone to a public fair held in the town of Cisterno, and, having succeeded in selling all their wares, two of them began to speak of returning home, and arranged to set out on their return next day at dawn, so as to arrive by evening in their own neighbourhood.

But a third one, who was from the same place, would not agree to start so early, saying that next day being a holiday, he could not think of commencing his journey without first having heard Mass according to the command of the Church. " We can hear Mass early in the morning," he said, " and then, after a little food, we can take our departure more to our satisfaction ; and even if we do not succeed in getting to Gubbio before nightfall, there are good inns by the way where we can rest for the night."

His companions did not yield to this wise and salutary counsel, but, being determined to reach their homes the next day, they answered : " Almighty God will have compassion on us if we omit Mass for this once."

So next morning, before dawn, without even entering the church, the two travellers took their way on horseback towards their home, and left the other one behind.

They in course of time reached the banks of the River Corfuone, over which they had to pass. But the heavy rain which had fallen during the night caused the waters to rise and rush along in a torrent, so that, flowing with great force against the wooden bridge, they undermined and weakened it.

The two travellers, however, in their anxiety to reach their homes, advanced upon it with their horses ; but no sooner had they reached the middle than a still more furious rush of the waters broke down and swept away the whole structure. The unhappy traders were instantly plunged with their horses into the flood and drowned, losing at one time their money, their lives, and most likely their souls.

At the sound of the crash, and the sight of the terrible havoc, the peasants ran to the spot, and contrived with hooks to draw out the bodies of the drowned men, leaving them lying on the bank, in order, if possible, that they might be recognized and receive burial.

Soon afterwards the third trader, who had been detained by his wish to hear Mass, and who then set forth on his journey with great alacrity, came up to the river, and, beholding the two bodies on the bank and the crowd of people around them, went to see what had occurred. He at once recognized them as his two companions, and heard from the bystanders the sad story of their terrible end.

Then, lifting up his hands to Heaven, he returned thanks to the Most High, Who had so mercifully preserved him, and he blessed a thousand times the hour in which he assisted at the holy Sacrifice, since it was the source of his preservation.

When he reached his destination he announced the sad intelligence to the relatives of the unfortunate men, who went and gave them suitable burial. From that hour all the people of that country were most careful never to absent themselves from Mass on the days appointed by the Church. You also, my child, take warning from this example, because, if God does not always punish in this world those who disobey this command, He will most certainly do it in the next life. *The Hidden Treasure*, p. 120.

III. How We should Hear Mass.

It is not enough to be present in body at Mass on Sundays, but we should hear Mass with very great devotion and attention if we desire to please God, and procure for our souls the fruits of that great **sacrifice.**

THE COUNTRYWOMAN'S DISMAY.

There was once a woman who lived in a country village at some little distance from a church.

In order to obtain from God some favour which she greatly desired, she took the resolution of hearing a certain number of Masses during the course of the year. So, whenever she heard in the distance the bell announcing that a Mass was about to begin, she would immediately interrupt her occupations, and run to the church through rain and snow, without taking at all into account the inclemency of the weather or any other inconvenience.

On her return home, in order to keep count of the Masses she had heard, she was accustomed to slip a bean into a box through a small slit in the lid like that commonly seen in money-boxes.

When the year was ended, confident of having fulfilled her vow, and of having acquired no little merit by having heard so many Masses, she went to open the little box, when, to her dismay, of all the beans she had deposited, she found only one.

Confounded and amazed beyond measure, she took it to heart and became very sad. Turning to God, she said with tears : " O Lord, how is it that out of so many Masses at which I have assisted, I find the record of only one ? Nor have I ever failed to be present, as Thou dost well know, even at great inconvenience to myself, never being kept back by any obstacle, but hurrying through rain or hail, or whatever seemed to oppose me."

Then Almighty God inspired her to go to consult a wise and pious priest, who at once asked her in what spirit she had accomplished this devotion, her demeanour on the way, and the attention with which she had assisted at the Holy Sacrifice.

To all which she had to acknowledge that on the

way to church she had always been thinking about her affairs, or chatting in a light manner with those whom she met, and that while assisting at the Divine Mysteries she had passed much of the time in whispering with some friend or neighbour, or had occupied her mind with her domestic affairs.

"Behold the cause," said the priest, "of so many Masses being lost. Chatting, idle curiosity, and wilful distractions have taken away all your merit. Either the Devil has taken away the beans you deposited in the box as a record against you, or your angel guardian has carried them off that you might see how works are lost if not done in the right way and with the right spirit. But be sure you return thanks to God that one at least of the Masses you assisted at seems to have been well heard, and has remained profitable to you."

The Hidden Treasure.

THE KING OF JAPAN'S SEVERE SENTENCE.

Long ago there lived in Japan a King who had been brought up in the errors of his people, but who, on the preaching of the zealous missionaries who went thither to extend the kingdom of Jesus Christ, was one of the first to embrace the faith.

It happened one day that he was informed that one of his servants had been guilty of some acts of disrespect during the offering of the Holy Sacrifice of the Mass. This filled the King with great anger, and he at once sent for the offender. When he had acknowledged that he was guilty, the King condemned him to death, to the astonishment of all who were present.

The princes of the Court, thinking this an act of too great severity, went to the King to ask him to revoke his sentence, telling him at the same time that the sentence was far too severe for so small an offence.

" What do you say ?" he exclaimed. " Do you call it a small offence to be guilty of disrespect in the presence of the great God of Heaven ? If that servant had shown the same disrespect in my presence, would you not say that he deserved the severest chastisement ? And yet, what am I when compared with the Eternal King of Heaven ?"

The servant was spared at their petition, but this was a lesson for all who heard of it ; and for many years afterwards in that country it was never known that anyone ever showed disrespect in the church during the Holy Sacrifice.

O my child, would to God that the same might be said everywhere ! At least, do you what lies in your power, both by word and by example, to see that God is honoured in your presence during the offering up of the Sacred Mysteries.

Letters of Fr. Charlevoix.

THE CHILDREN OF ST. MARGARET AT MASS.

The historian of St. Margaret of Scotland, who had the happiness of residing in her Court for many years, has written down some of the simple instructions she daily gave her children as they stood around her or sat by her side. They are her own words, and he says he himself was often present, and heard them.

" My beloved children, fear the Lord, for they that fear Him shall never want all kind of good things. Love God, for if you love Him He will give you prosperity in this life, and eternal happiness with His Saints in that which is to come."

Then, when the hour for the Holy Mass came, she would lead them into the church, and kneel in the midst of them before the altar, as if she saw God visibly present ; and they, too, like her, bent themselves down with reverent humility till Mass was ended. One of those who sometimes had the privilege of being present on these occasions, and who had seen the devotion and reverent piety of the Queen and her children, used to say : " If you desire to know how the angels of God in Heaven pray, go to the church and look at the queen and her children, praying during the offering up of the Holy Mass."

From St. Margaret's Life.

IV. Hearing Mass the Cause of Many Blessings.

The Most Holy Sacrifice of the Mass is the source of innumerable graces to those who assist at it devoutly. To the sinner it offers the grace of repentance, and to the just that of perseverance. It also frequently is the source of many temporal blessings.

" strike ! strike !"

St. Anthony, Archbishop of Florence, relates that two young men went out to hunt on Sunday ; the one had heard Mass, but the other had neglected to do so, and both of them were very careless Christians. The sky was cloudless ; not a leaf was stirring. Presently they heard the low rumbling of distant thunder. A dark, smoke-like vapour spread

over the face of the Heavens.   Flashes of lightning
succeeded one another with alarming rapidity, and
the voice of the thunder was now heard in one con-
tinuous roar.   In a few moments the sky grew black,
and was shrouded in darkness.   Soon the vivid
flashes of lightning lit up the Heavens with a
lurid glare.   At times the whole universe seemed
to be on fire, and the peals of thunder were terrible
to listen to.   Many trees were struck with lightning
within view of the hunters, and as they were looking
on in terror, one of the largest trees immediately in
front of them was shivered to fragments.

Suddenly they heard above them in the air a wild,
unearthly cry.   "Strike ! strike !" cried the voice,
and instantly a flash of lightning killed one of the
men, the one who had not heard Mass.

The other young man was panic-stricken at this,
especially as he heard the same terrible voice crying
out   "Strike him too !"   A little after, he was
encouraged by another voice, which said : " I cannot
strike him, because he heard Mass this morning."

Life of St. Anthony, Archbishop of Florence.

THE CONSCIENTIOUS JEWELLER.

When the allied armies entered France in the
year 1814, they remained in that country for a considerable time, especially those who resided in the
capital.   Some of the latter took advantage of the
opportunity thus afforded them of purchasing in
Paris various objects which they intended to bring
home with them to their friends in their own
countries.

Among these was a Prussian officer, who possessed ample means, and was anxious to procure valuable gems and other rich objects of art. One Sunday he visited the house of one of the wealthiest and most distinguished jewellers in the capital.

" Sir," he said, on entering the house, " I have come to you for the purpose of purchasing some of your choicest gems and other works of art, for which, I am told, your house is so famous. Would you kindly show me some of them ?"

The jeweller answered · " I would be very much pleased to do so, but to-day being Sunday, my ware-rooms and business premises are closed. Be so good as to return to-morrow, and I will be at your service."

" I fully appreciate your conscientious scruples, but, unfortunately, to-morrow I shall be busily engaged elsewhere," said the officer.

" I am very sorry indeed," replied the merchant ; " but on no account will I transgress the commandment of God and His Church by transacting business on Sundays."

" I would only add this observation," said the officer, " which I hope will make you reconsider your decision in the circumstances. The purchases I intend to make will reach the sum of between six hundred and eight hundred pounds."

" Certainly that would be a profitable transaction," returned the jeweller, " yet I prefer to forego all the profits that would arise from it rather than stain my conscience by doing what is sinful."

" Ah, then, if such is your determination," added the other, " I shall be obliged to make my purchases elsewhere."

Thereupon the officer, bowing politely to the jeweller, took his departure.

He had not gone far from the house when this consideration entered his mind · " Here is a man who is indeed very scrupulous in his observance of the precept to keep the Sunday holy ; this gives me every reason to conclude that he will be equally scrupulous in his commercial transactions, and that I may entirely trust to his honesty in the purchases I intend to make, for it is well known that in matters of this kind one can be so easily imposed upon."

Under the influence of this reflection, the officer deferred the day of his departure. On the Monday morning he returned to the conscientious jeweller, not himself only, but accompanied by many of his countrymen, to whom he had related the incident, and all of whom made important purchases.

Catéch. en Exemples, No. 948.

TWO TRADESMEN.

In the " Life of St. John the Almoner " we read the following example : In a certain town there were two tradesmen who followed the same occupation. The one was burdened with a family—wife, children, and grandchildren. The other lived alone with his wife, for he had no family. The first brought up his family in great comfort, and all his transactions were crowned with success. Thus he went on till he found that he had laid past in the bank a large sum of money, which would serve in time as marriage portions ·for his daughters.

The other, who was without children, got very

little employment, was half famished, and, in short, was a ruined man.

One day he said confidentially to his neighbour : " How is it that you have succeeded so well in your business ? On your home there seems to be showered down every blessing of God, while I, a poor wretch, cannot hold up my head ; and every kind of misfortune seems to fall upon my house."

" I will very willingly tell you the secret of my success," said the other. "Come with me to-morrow morning, and I will point out to you the place whence I draw all my wealth."

Next morning as soon as it was light he went to his house, and they both set out together to hear Mass ; and when it was over, the pious man led the other one to his workshop. This he did for several days, till at last the poor man said · " When are you going to tell me where you get your wealth ? for you promised me that you would tell me whence it came."

" It is by going to Mass every morning," replied the other.

" Oh, if that is all that is needed, I know the way to the church well enough without putting you to the inconvenience of taking me."

" Well, my friend," he said, " if you go to Mass every day, you will very soon see a great change come over your condition."

The prophecy of the good man was soon verified ; for, beginning to hear Mass every morning, he was soon well provided with work, shortly paid all his debts, and was soon in a prosperous condition.

Life of St. John the Almoner.

V. On the Consequences of Assisting at Mass Carelessly.

It is a pity to see so many Christians assisting at Holy Mass with so little devotion, and behaving so irreverently during the celebration of these " most tremendous mysteries," as the Church calls them. Terrible are the punishments that sometimes fall on those who act in this manner.

" I depart."

It is related that in a certain church where people did not hear Mass with attention, a terrible event took place. During the first part of Mass they were accustomed to speak to each other, look about them, and pay no attention to the great Sacrifice that was being offered up at the altar.

But on this occasion, as soon as the priest had pronounced the words of consecration, a voice was heard to proceed from the altar. It cried out : " I am going to depart." The people began to tremble, and all looked towards the place whence the voice came. They saw the Sacred Host in the priest's hands as he raised it up for their adoration, and they knew that it was the warning voice of Jesus Himself they had heard.

As they were thus gazing at the Sacred Host, behold, it left the hands of the priest and ascended slowly towards the roof of the church. It stopped about half-way, and again they heard with still more terrible distinctness the same words : " I am going to depart."

They did not cry out for pardon ; even then God

would not have rejected their prayer. So they saw the Sacred Host begin again to ascend till it came to the roof, when a third time they heard the same voice, but now the words were : " I depart."

When these words were spoken our Lord disappeared, and at the same instant the church fell with a terrible crash and buried the guilty congregation in its ruins.

In this way God punished those guilty ones who dared to conduct themselves without due reverence during the most Holy Sacrifice. May it be a warning for those also who read about it, for if God does not always punish in this life those who offend Him, He will most certainly do so hereafter.

VERME : *Instructions.*

VI. VAIN EXCUSES FOR NEGLECTING MASS.

There are so often so many excuses put forward by Catholics for absenting themselves from hearing Mass, that one would think that nothing was so burdensome to them as to assist at it. This shows a great want of faith. Oh, how differently did the Saints act !

BLESSED THOMAS MORE'S ANSWER.

There are some people who do not go to Mass because, as they say, their friends and acquaintances, as well as their occupations, make large demands upon their time.

It is related in the life of Blessed Thomas More that he never omitted to hear Mass, no matter how many or how great his occupations were.

One day while he was hearing Mass, a messenger from the King came to him to say that His Majesty required his immediate presence, to consult him on a matter of the greatest importance.

The holy man sent back this answer to the King ·
" Tell His Majesty to have a little patience, as I am at this moment engaged with a Sovereign Who is higher than he, for I am hearing Mass. As soon as my audience with the King of Heaven is ended, I will at once obey the desire of my earthly King."

He also considered it the highest honour that could be conferred on him to serve the priest at Mass. " I consider it," he used to say, " a very high honour to have it in my power to render this slight service to the greatest of all Sovereigns."

Life of Blessed Thomas More.

ANTONY GINIEN, THE PIOUS LABOURER.

At the beginning of last·century there lived in the parish of Roybon, near the town of St. Marcel-linus, in the South of France, a family belonging to the labouring class, the head of which had already reached a high state of Christian perfection. His name was Antony Ginien.

Although he dwelt at a distance of about five miles from the church, he was always among the first to reach it on Sundays and holidays, that he might hear Holy Mass, and assist at the other offices of the Church.

In the latter years of his life it became impossible for him to travel that distance in the winter-time, on account of his infirmities ; but from the Feast of Easter until All Saints he would rise early in the morning, and, with the aid of two crutches, accomplish the journey leisurely in about four hours. This pious old man died in the month of December, 1809, at the age of seventy-five, leaving to us all an admirable example for our imitation and instruction. *Catéchisme de Rodes.*

VII. ON HEARING THE WORD OF GOD.

Besides hearing Mass on Sundays and holidays, a good Catholic endeavours, as far as lies in his power, to be present at sermons and other devotions in the church. If the priest is bound to preach the Word of God to his flock, it is surely the duty of the flock to listen to it, that they may know their duties and how to fulfil them. " Blessed are they who hear the Word of God," says Jesus Christ.

FATHER LAURENCE'S SERMON.

Father Laurence, of the Society of Jesus, was one day preaching a sermon on the sufferings of Jesus Christ. A large number of idolaters went to hear him, that they might laugh at one who pretended that the crucified Jesus was really God.

But before the end of the sermon a great change came over them. The preacher related in detail all the sufferings of Our Lord—the bloody sweat, the scourging at the pillar, the crowning with thorns, the carrying the cross, and finally the last agony and death ; and he dealt principally on the patience of Jesus under so many cruel torments. He spoke also of His love for us poor sinners that urged Him to die for them ; then of the blessings given to mankind by His death, and the happiness for eternity purchased by His sacred Blood.

The pagans listened attentively to it to the end ; they had gone there to mock, but that simple discourse changed their mocking into wailing, and their laughter into sighs and tears.

The preacher had not yet finished when forty of them, one after the other, cried out : " That is enough, stop ! We cannot any longer listen to these terrible sufferings of the innocent Jesus. We are all anxious to become His disciples. Make us Christians at once."

Immediately they drew forth from their bosoms certain amulets which the bonzes had given them as relics, and threw them away. Then they went to Father Laurence, that they might be baptized. He placed them under instruction, and when he thought they were sufficiently grounded in our holy Faith, he baptized them.

If such was the effect on these poor pagans of a sermon on the sufferings of Our Lord, how much greater ought it to be on one who is a Christian !

Missions in the East, vol. i.

THE WORD OF GOD.

One day, as St. Francis Jerome was preaching at Naples, near the gate of the Church of St. Januarius, it happened that a man was passing by in great haste, as if engaged on some very urgent business. He was an assassin who had been hired to kill a man who had given some provocation to another.

As he was hurrying past, some words that fell from the lips of the preacher struck him, and made him pause to listen as he came opposite the door. He continued to listen, and when he saw the attention of the people, and their tears, and while the words of the Saint were ringing in his ear, he, on the spot, resolved to return home and not to commit the terrible deed he had been hired to accomplish.

When he lay down to rest that night, he could not fall asleep, for the words he had heard in the morning still seemed to sound in his ears. The grace of God was at the same time speaking to his heart, and he took the resolution, when the morning dawned, to change his life and become a Saint.

He kept his word, and as soon as it was light he was to be seen making his way to the church in Rome, called the Gesu, where he made his confession, and began a new life, which ended, after many years of heroic virtue, by dying the death of the Saints.

Such was the blessing that he received from God, because he listened to His Holy Word.

Life of St. Francis Jerome.

CONSTANTINE'S ANSWER TO HIS COURTIERS.

It is related in the history of the Church that the Emperor Constantine the Great was accustomed to hear the Word of God standing, with head uncovered, and in an attitude of great devotion.

One day one of his courtiers asked him why he, so great an Emperor, acted in this manner.

He answered: " It would be unbecoming in me to act otherwise. It is not customary even in this world to receive the orders of one's Sovereign seated ; how, therefore, can I presume to receive the orders of the King of Heaven, the universal Monarch of all men, Princes and people, otherwise than in the humblest of attitudes ? No ; the orders of the King of Heaven must be received by all alike not only in humility and obedience, but also in an attitude of respect and reverence. *Catéchisme populaire*, p. 4.

A HOLY MAN'S PENITENTIAL LIFE.

There was once a great sinner, by name Babylas, who not only committed sins himself, but also caused two companions to fall into great sins.

One day he entered a church through curiosity, or, rather, led thither by the grace of God. The preacher spoke to the people on those words of the Gospel, " Do penance, for the kingdom of Heaven is at hand." So great was the effect of these simple words on his soul that he resolved at once to begin a new life.

As he was leaving the church, he met the two companions whom he had formerly led into sin. On seeing them, he said : " I am going to do penance for my past sinful life."

At first they were astonished at the sudden change which had come over him ; but when they saw that he was really in earnest, they said to him : " Since we have been your companions in wickedness, we will now be your companions in repentance."

So they departed from each other, each to lead a life of penance for their past iniquities. It is not recorded of them how they died, but it may well be imagined that their death was precious in the eyes of God, and that they are now in the possession of the glory of the Saints.

THE AMERICAN FARMER.

Luke Sehort was a rich farmer in America. He had reached the extreme old age of one hundred years, and he had spent that long life in leading a worldly life, and in a total neglect of his religious duties. Even now, when he saw himself standing on the brink of the grave, a truth which he could not hide from himself, he did not even once think of the great God who was so soon to judge him, nor of the eternity he was so soon to enter.

One day, as he was sitting on a large stone in the middle of one of his fields, looking at a rich crop of corn ready for the sickle, his mind wandered into the past, and he began to count the number of harvests he had gathered in since the days of his childhood.

As he was thus musing, the scenes of times long passed away came vividly before him. Suddenly he recalled to mind how that in his early years he had gone one day to the Church, and that he had been much touched by the words that he there heard. It was nearly ninety years before. He could even now remember them ; and he repeated them aloud word by word, as he had heard them on that day. " If anyone does not love our Lord Jesus Christ, let him be anathema." And he remembered, too, that when the preacher had said them, a young man, who was sitting by his side, had fainted. The memory of that event seemed at that moment to be as fresh before his mind as if it had at that instant occurred before his eyes.

" I have not loved God at all," he said to himself ;

" and what will become of me ?   God has continually blessed me during these hundred years I have lived, and I have shown him no gratitude nor love.   And now what can I expect but a curse instead of a blessing from Him whom I have treated so unkindly ?"   This thought made him sad, and he began to tremble.

He next thought of the future, and of the miserable eternity he must so soon enter ; for how could he hope to enter Heaven, which he had altogether forgotten, and for which he had never done any thing ?   " Oh, that I had followed the inspirations God gave when I was listening to that sermon ! Oh, that I had loved God all my lifetime !   But is it now too late ?   Has not God spared me to see this day, and is it not He who has put this thought into my heart ?   Yes, I feel within me a firm confidence that He will not reject me even although it is so late, if I try to love Him for the rest of my days, few as they must be."

He went home, and from that moment led a new life.   God spared him a few years longer, and he spent these years in loving Him with all the fervour of his soul, and thus endeavouring, till his last breath, to repair the past.   He died in the hope of going to see Him in Heaven who had called him at the eleventh hour to serve and love Him.   The sermon he had heard nearly a hundred years before at length brought forth its fruit, and procured for him, let us confidently hope, the eternal joys of Heaven.   PHILOTHEA.

FATHER CHRISTOPHER AND HIS INDIAN CONVERTS.

On a certain Sunday Father Christopher, a missionary full of piety and zeal, was passing along the seashore of one of the islands in Oceania. He was on his way to visit an old man who was dying at a place many miles distant.

As he was passing onwards he was filled with grief and astonishment to see a number of the savages whom he had recently instructed and baptized occupied in mending their boats.

" My children," he said to them, " what are you doing ? Do you not remember that this is the day consecrated to the Great Spirit ? Surely you could find time during the other days of the week to mend your boats, and not offend the Great Spirit who commands his children to do no work on this day, which belongs to Him, but to spend it in prayer and Christian piety.

The only answer they made was that they were working because such was their will.

The Father, seeing them thus so badly disposed, and at the same time being anxious to reach the dying man as soon as possible, continued on his way. On his return home, a few hours afterwards, he passed near the same place, and found that a great fire had broken out, which had consumed all the huts in which these men dwelt, as also the boats they had on that day been repairing.

It was now an easy matter for the good priest to make these savages, lately so regardless of his admonitions, understand the great evil they had done in despising the commandment of the

Great Spirit. He left them covered with confusion, and their souls penetrated with sincere repentance.   *Catéch. de Rodez*, iv. 94.

HE REFUSED TO HEAR THE WORD OF GOD.

Lohner and Mansi relate that there lived in the town to which they belonged a certain man who never went to hear an instruction or sermon. He, indeed, went to hear Mass when there was for him an obligation of doing so ; but as soon as he saw the priest go into the pulpit to preach, he rose up and left the church, to the great scandal of the faithful.

This he did during his whole lifetime. When he died, his relatives brought his body to the church previous to its interment. But just as the Holy Sacrifice of the Mass was about to begin, the people who were present saw a most wonderful thing. Over the high altar there was a large crucifix. As the priest stood at the foot of the altar ready to begin Mass, the hands of the figure of Jesus on the cross seemed to detach themselves from it, and to put its fingers into its ears.

The priest, without even beginning Mass, turned to the people, and said : " You see, my brethren, how God punishes those who neglect to hear His Divine Word. The man whose body lies before you constantly and obstinately refused to hear the word of God, and now God turns a deaf ear to the prayers we were about to offer up for the repose of his soul."

The body was at once carried out to the grave and deposited there amidst the silence of the crowd.

T. LOHNER : *Bibliotheca conctonatoria.*

ST. ANTHONY PREACHES TO THE FISHES.

It is related in the traditions of the Seraphic Order that God, one day, made use of irrational animals to confound the negligence of men in hearing the Word of God. The tradition, which has preserved the history of this miracle for our instruction, is all the more worthy of being believed as God has so often, in all ages, made use of such instruments to confound the pride and indifference of men.

When St. Anthony of Padua went to Rimini to preach the Gospel, he found there a number of heretics who, though they believed in God, had been led astray by the false doctrines which had been preached to them by wolves in sheep's clothing. For a long time he preached among them with great zeal, but without effect, for the people for the most part refused to listen to him, or, if they did, their hearts remained unchanged.

Then, the Saint seeing this, and moved by a secret inspiration from God, went down to the seashore along with the few who had assembled to hear him preach. When he reached the shore he cried out with a loud voice : " O fishes of the ocean, and all you that live in the waters, and in the rivers, come and hear the word of God, for I have come hither to preach it to you, since men endowed with reason refuse to listen to me."

In an instant an immense multitude of fishes of all kinds and sizes appeared, and arranged themselves in order before the servant of God, the smallest in the front and the larger ones behind. They all remained motionless, and listened with respect.

" My little brothers, the fishes," he said to them, " you should, as much as is in your power, thank your great Creator for the blessings He has granted to you. It is God Who has made the great ocean which is your home. It is He Who made the fresh water for some of you, and the salt sea for others. It is He Who has dug for you, deep down in the ocean, caverns, where you can find shelter in the storms that rise up around you. He made for you the waters clear and transparent, that you might be able to search for your food. On the day of your creation He blessed you, and told you to increase and multiply, and that blessing still remains with you.

" Then, when he punished the whole world by destroying all that moved upon the earth in the waters of the Deluge, you alone were spared. Afterwards it was to one of you that He confided the care of His prophet Jonas for three days, and on the third day did make you cast him safe upon the shore, and did this as a sign that His Divine Son would rise from the bowels of the earth on the third day.

" It was also one of your race that was appointed to pay the coin of the tribute for Jesus Christ and His Apostle Peter. And, lastly, you provided food for our Lord Himself after His resurrection from the dead. Praise and bless the Lord your God, therefore, and never cease to do so, according to the words of the Holy Ghost : " Ye whales, and all ye that move in the waters, bless the Lord, praise and exalt Him for ever."

In the meantime, the news of what had taken place spread throughout the city, and all the people ran in haste to the seashore to see with their own eyes this marvellous event. To their utter astonishment they beheld all the fishes listening with every mark of attention to the words of the Saint. Moved by what they saw, not only the Catholics of the city, but even the heretics themselves, begged the Saint to return with them, and they promised to give ear to his words and obey them.

Turning towards them, he stood on that same place, and preached to them with so much zeal that many of them were converted on the spot. When the sermon was ended, he turned towards the fishes, who still remained in the same place as at first, and having given them his blessing, told them that they might depart.

In an instant they bowed their heads to the Saint in sign of respect, and darting into the waters, immediately disappeared.

Life of St. Anthony of Padua.

VIII. On Meditation and Pious Reading.

My child, the Holy Ghost says in the Scriptures : " With desolation is the whole earth made desolate, because there is no one who thinketh in his heart." Reading good books, therefore, and meditating on what they contain, is another means of keeping the Sunday holy.

SERVATUS, THE POOR MAN OF ROME.

St. Gregory the Great relates the following story in one of his books of instruction : " There lived in Rome a poor man whose name was Servatus. He was afflicted with paralysis, and could not walk, nor even turn his body from one side to the other, nor raise his hand to his mouth. He was carried daily by some charitable persons and laid at the gate of the Church of St. Clement, that he might receive an alms from those who went in and out of that church.

" Of the alms that were given him he spent a little for his own support, and the rest he distributed among the pilgrims who came to visit the pious places in the city, many of whom found shelter in his humble home.

" He was accustomed to spend the entire day in meditation on spiritual things, and as he could not read, he used to ask those to whom he gave hospitality to read for him. Thus, by hearing the Word of God read to him, he was able to feed his soul with heavenly doctrine, and people who heard him speak were astonished at his great knowledge and the wisdom of his answers. But the principal fruit of his meditations was the high degree of holiness to which he attained. His patience under his heavy afflictions was invincible ; he was continually heard thanking God for his infirmities, and was always singing hymns of praise to Him.

" When he saw that the hand of death was upon him, he called together some of those who had been most charitable to him, and asked them to read to him some of the Psalms. While they were doing this, he suddenly told them to stop.

" ' Do you not hear the heavenly music ? ' he cried out. And as he was saying these words, he kept his eyes fixed on Heaven, as if he saw something which those around him did not see ; and as he was thus gazing upwards, he died.

"After his death, his humble home was filled with the odour of the sweetest perfumes, so that the bystanders were filled with admiration, and were thereby convinced that the soul of the poor man was already in Heaven, praising God in the company of His holy angels."

WORDS OF A MAN CONDEMNED TO DEATH.

A certain man who had committed the crime of murder was condemned to death.

During the time that elapsed between the sentence and the day fixed for his execution he was constantly visited by a priest, who prepared him to die. This priest also gave him some pious books to read.

One day the unhappy man said to the priest : "O my Father, if I had always had books like these, and if I had since my childhood frequently read them, I should never have come to this terrible end."

THE POOR WOMAN AND THE NUNS.

A certain poor woman, who belonged to the class of those simple souls for whom God has the greatest affection, lived in a convent as a servant to the good religious. She was occupied all day ; but while her hands were working, her mind was meditating, for she used always to be thinking of God and of His blessings to mankind. "I think on them," she used to say with simplicity—"I think on them, one after the other, and I feel very happy in doing so ;

I am always thinking on them. I cannot meditate or pray like the good nuns, but when I see them going to church to pray, I raise up my mind to God in Heaven, and begin again to think on all His benefits to me, and continue my work."

How agreeable was the life of this pious woman in the eyes of God! He, Whose eyes look down upon the humble, and who reads the secrets of hearts, was more pleased with her simple affections than with the long prayers of many who, although they may say them with their lips, have their hearts elsewhere.

Take the resolution, my child, to read every Sunday some pious book which speaks to you of God, and think for a few moments on what you have read, for by doing this you will grow up more piously, and love God more fervently.

IX. What the Third Commandment Forbids.

The Third Commandment forbids all unnecessary work and all profanation of the Lord's Day.

THE SHOEMAKER OF LYONS.

At the commencement of the present century there lived at Lyons a shoemaker whose name was Berthier, who never kept the Sunday holy, but spent it in manual labour in his shop, as he did during the other days of the week. In a house on the opposite side of the street there lived a rich merchant, who was a fervent Christian. When he saw the scandalous conduct of the shoemaker. he was much grieved on account of the sin he was thus committing. One day he went over to his shop and spoke to him of the greatness of his sin, and of the terrible consequences that must follow in the next life if he did not cease working on the day which the Lord called " His own day."

But the shoemaker said that it was necessity that compelled him thus to work. " You, sir," he said, " are a very rich man, and you can afford to remain idle on Sundays. But I am poor, and have a large family to support, and it would be a very great loss to me if I did not work on Sunday ; besides, I am never able to finish on a Saturday night the work ordered during the week, and my customers would be disappointed, and leave me and go somewhere else."

The merchant, shaking his head at these excuses, kindly said to him · " It is very far from my intention that your family should suffer loss, and I now promise you that if you do not work any more on Sundays for the next six months, and go regularly to Holy Mass, I will compensate you for any loss you may sustain. Do you accept my offer ?"

" Very willingly," said the shoemaker, " for it is much easier for me to sit in church than to work, especially since you are so kind as to make me so generous an offer."

They both then shook hands as a sign of their mutual agreement, and separated.

When the six months were ended, the merchant went to the house of the shoemaker, and said to him : " Well, my friend, the six months are ended, and I have come, according to my promise, to com-

pensate you for the losses you have sustained by
going to church and abstaining from work on Sundays, for I see that you have faithfully kept your
promise. Now, tell me how much loss you have
sustained, that I may make it up to you."

" Indeed," replied the other, " I must candidly
state that I have suffered no loss at all, and that,
on the contrary, I have become very much richer
since I began to go to Mass ; and all the claim that
I have on you is that you accept my best thanks for
the advice you gave me. In the beginning, it is
true, I did experience some little inconvenience in
not having my work done on the Saturday night ;
but the thought that you were to compensate me
for any loss I might sustain, and also the promise I
made to you, made me faithful in the due observance
of Sunday, and made my mind easy. I have been
regular in my attendance at church every Sunday
and holiday of obligation, as you yourself well
know, and besides fulfilling the obligation of hearing Mass, I learned many things regarding my salvation of which before I was almost entirely
ignorant ; I have also during that time gone to the
Sacraments, and I now experience a joy and happiness which I never knew before, and my body is
stronger and my arm more vigorous than ever."

" But, my dear friend, how are matters going on
between you and your family, because formerly, as
you well know, there used to be nothing heard in
your house but quarrels and words of evil and
anger ?"

" True indeed," replied the shoemaker, with a
blush on his cheek, " but the case is altered now.

Before, I used to think that my wife was always wrong, and that I was always right, and my anger and my obstinacy were such as to cause scenes the very thought of which now makes me blush ; but now peace and concord reign in my house."

Very much moved at this recital, the gentleman took out his purse and offered him two pounds, saying : " Take this as a remembrance of my affection. When you made the promise, I did not think that my words would have produced such a change ; so I laid past every month a little sum to give to you to make up for the loss which I thought you might sustain. Here, then, is the money which I laid past for you, and I beg of you to accept of it as a token of the delight I feel at your following my counsel. You have now seen from your own experience that God will aid those who endeavour to do to the best of their ability what He requires of them." POWER'S *Catechism.*

THE ZEAL OF NEHEMIAS FOR THE OBSERVANCE OF THE SABBATH.

The holy man Nehemias, who for many years governed the people of God in Judæa, had nothing so much at heart as to impress upon the people their great obligation to observe the Sabbath-day, which so many of them profaned without fear. Thus did he himself speak of it, as recorded in the sacred Scriptures :

" Remember me, O my God, for this thing, and wipe not out my kindnesses, which I have done relating to the house of my God and His ceremonies.

" In those days [it was after the captivity of

Babylon] I saw in Juda some treading the presses on the Sabbath, and carrying sheaves, and lading asses with wine, and grapes, and figs, and all manner of burdens, and bringing them into Jerusalem on the Sabbath-day. And I charged them that they should sell on a day on which it was lawful to sell.

"Some Tyrians also dwelt there, who brought fish and all manners of wares ; and they sold them on the Sabbaths to the children of Juda in Jerusalem. And I rebuked the chief men of Juda, and said to them : ' What is this evil thing that you are doing, profaning the Sabbath-day ? Did not our fathers do these things, and Our Lord brought all this evil upon us and upon this city ? [Jerusalem had been burned to the ground, and the inhabitants had been led into captivity.] And you bring more wrath upon Israel by violating the Sabbath.'

"And it came to pass that when the gates of Jerusalem were at rest on the Sabbath-day, I spoke : and they shut the gates, and I commanded that they should not open them till after the Sabbath : and I set some of my servants at the gates, that none should bring in burdens on the Sabbath-day.

"So the merchants and they that sold all kind of wares stayed without Jerusalem once or twice. And I charged them, and I said to them : ' Why stay you before the wall ? If you do so another time, I will lay hands on you.' And from that day they came no more on the Sabbath. And I spoke to the Levites that they should be purified, and should come to keep the gates and to sanctify the Sabbath-day.

" For this also remember me, O my God, and spare me, according to the multitude of thy tender mercies. Amen."

2 Esdras xiii.

God does not always punish in this life those who offend Him by neglecting to keep the Sunday holy, but reserves the punishment of their sin until the next life. Sometimes, however, he does chastise these by temporal punishments here on earth, either to incite them to repentance, or to serve as a warning to those who may be tempted to follow their bad example.

THE LABOURER OF AUVERGNE.

St. Gregory, the celebrated Bishop of Tours, who lived in the sixth century, relates that a certain labourer of Auvergne, having yoked two oxen to a plough, did not hesitate to go forth to labour in his field on the Sunday, to the great scandal of his neighbours.

While he was thus engaged, God was pleased to punish him. The plough broke in two. Instead of ceasing his sinful labour, he went to look for an axe, and with it began to mend the plough. As he held the instrument in his hands, one of them became suddenly paralyzed, and every effort made to detach the handle from the hand which held it fast was unavailing. In the end, about two years afterwards, the poor man, recognizing in this the hand of God, was inspired to visit the tomb of the holy martyr St. Julian, where he spent the night between Saturday and Sunday in devout prayer to the

Saint to beseech God to have mercy on him and forgive him.

On the following day, in the presence of an immense multitude of the faithful who had come to assist at the Holy Sacrifice, his hand opened of itself, and the handle of the axe he had so long held in it fell to the ground.

This extraordinary example of the punishment inflicted by God on those who neglect to obey His precepts became for all who saw it, or heard of it, the cause of an earnest resolution to observe the sanctification of the Lord's Day with greater and more exact fidelity.

ST. GREGORY OF TOURS : *De Gloria Martyr.*

XXX

THE FOURTH COMMANDMENT—
FIRST PART

I. On the Virtue of Obedience.

THE Fourth Commandment is, " Honour thy father and thy mother." By this precept children are commanded to love, honour, and obey their parents in all that is not sin.

FRANCIS ALDINI, A MODEL OF OBEDIENCE.

It would be almost impossible to find anywhere so beautiful an example of obedience as that which is found in the life of the young Francis Aldini. If his parents chid him for something he had done which did not please them, he heard their words meekly, without saying anything in return, except that he was sorry he had displeased them, and that he would do everything that lay in his power to correct himself for the future.

One day, when his tutor happened to be absent, his father told him to remain in the house till his return. Francis promised to obey, but in the afternoon two of his friends came unexpectedly to call on him, and asked him to accompany them during a short walk they were going to take in the country.

185

Francis, forgetting the order he had received from his father, immediately consented to go with them.

But he had not gone far when he recalled to mind his father's prohibition. " Ah ! what have I done ?" he cried out ; " my father forbade me to go out."

Saying these words, he left his companions ; and, returning to the house, went at once to his father's room, and, going down on his knees before him, told him of the fault, or, rather, the mistake, he had made, and asked him for pardon. His father, charmed with his conduct, not only forgave him, but permitted him to go out with the two friends who were waiting for him, saying to himself : " A son who is so anxious to please his father will always take care to keep out of evil."

This was proved by his son's future career ; for he grew up piously, and gained the esteem and respect of all who knew him.   *Récits Contemp.*

AN OLD LEGEND.

Many years ago there lived in a certain monastery a monk who spent the most of his time in prayer. Every moment he could spare from the duties that were assigned to him he spent in the solitude of his cell. But, knowing that God rewards in Heaven not so much our fervour as our obedience and our fidelity to accomplish the duties of our state of life, he was ever most careful to run immediately, as soon as duty called him, and even left his prayer as soon as he heard the bell calling him to some other duty.

God was pleased to show him how greatly his conduct was pleasing to Him. It was the custom in that monastery for the neighbouring poor to receive alms at the gate at the hour of noon, and each of the monks had to attend to this duty in turns. On the day when it was the turn of this pious Father to go to the gate he was praying in his cell a little before the time appointed.

As he was at prayer, suddenly Our Lord appeared to him in the midst of great glory. The Saint fell down at His feet in adoration, and continued to gaze on His sacred countenance with infinite delight. In the midst of this heavenly vision suddenly the monk heard the bell ring which summoned him to the service of the poor. What would he do ? Would he rise at once and go and fulfil the duties which his Superior had placed upon him, or would he remain to contemplate the glorious vision he saw before him ?

The voice of conscience told him that it was his duty to leave his Lord to go and wait on his Lord's suffering ones. So he rose up at once, and casting one long last look at Jesus, Whom he did not expect to see again, he went to the place where the poor were waiting for him. There he spent many hours in serving them, wondering all the time why there was so much strange joy in his heart, and not daring to think that he would ever behold the vision again. He knew that he had done his duty, and that Jesus would be pleased with him.

When his work was done, he returned to his cell. But what was his joy and surprise to see his beloved Master waiting for him just as he left Him hours before ! Jesus smiled on him, and said to him : " My child, thou hast done well in leaving Me to perform the work I entrusted to you ; if you had not gone, I would have left you, and you would have seen Me no more, but because of your obedience I have waited till your return."

BLESSED SEBASTIAN VALFRE.

The little Sebastian Valfre was a very obedient child. He never required to be told a second time to do anything, because it was his delight to attend to the first wish and to the first word of his parents.

One day he was left by his mother in the kitchen to watch some food which was boiling on the fire ; he attended as faithfully as he could to the orders he had received, but, in spite of all his care, it boiled over, and was spilt upon the floor.

The little boy was very much troubled at what had happened, for, in a poor family like his, this was a great misfortune, and he knew how grieved his mother would feel at the loss. But he never thought of concealing what had happened, or even of making excuses as most children would do. He almost expected that he might be punished ; yet, when his mother came in, he went towards her, saying at once : "O mother, if you like, I am ready to be beaten, but the pot on the fire has all boiled over."

His mother did not punish or even scold her little son, because she was a good woman, who rejoiced to see this proof of Sebastian's truthfulness and obedience.   *From his Life.*

The more readily you obey your parents, my child, the more perfect is your obedience, and the easier will it be for you to become a Saint. Obey your parents whether or not you understand the reason why they have given you the order.

ST. PAUL THE SIMPLE'S OBEDIENCE.

In days long gone by, there lived in the desert with the great St. Antony a holy but simple monk called Paul. Whatever his Superior told him to do, he did at once without ever asking the reason of the command.

St. Antony, knowing that obedience is one of the virtues most pleasing to God, and seeing his disciple anxious to practise it, resolved to exercise him continually in it, that he might gain more and more merit for Heaven.

Sometimes he told him to take a pitcher, go to the river, and fill it with water, then bring it to him. When this was done, he poured it on the ground and told him to go for more. Paul did this with the greatest pleasure, and without showing any sign of being annoyed at what his Superior had done.

At other times he told him to make a basket, as the monks of those days were in the habit of doing. Paul made it with the greatest care, and brought it to St. Antony. As soon as he looked at it, he told his disciple to take it all to pieces, and make it over again. Paul did so, joyfully, without saying a word.

Again, St. Antony ordered him to make a coat out of some cloth that had been given him. Paul made the coat very neatly and carefully, and brought it to the Saint, who said to him : " My son, the coat is well made, but just go back to your cell, and take out every stitch you have put in one by one, and make it over again." Paul did so at once without murmuring.

It was in this way that he reached the great glory he is now enjoying in Heaven.

Lives of the Fathers of the Desert.

THE FOUR DEGREES OF GLORY.

One of the ancient Fathers in the desert had a vision of Heaven. He saw there, as it were, four different companies of Saints placed one above the other in glory.

The lowest group was composed of those who, while on earth, had been afflicted with sickness and bodily infirmities, and had borne them patiently for God's sake. The second group consisted of those who had in this life been kind to strangers and the poor, and had spent their lives in acts of charity towards their neighbour. In the third group were those holy solitaries who for Christ's sake had left the world to seek only the kingdom of God by a life of prayer and penance. All these were enjoying great happiness in God's holy presence.

But the fourth group was still more glorious ; and those who composed it seemed to possess even a greater happiness than the others.

The solitary asked the angel who showed him these things who those were who formed that glorious company.

" Those whom you see so high up and so beautiful," answered the angel, " are those who, when in the world, had been obedient. The others served God well, therefore they are now enjoying the reward of their fidelity. But in their good works there was much that was agreeable to themselves. But those who were obedient renounced their own will to submit themselves to the will of others whom God had placed over them, and for this God has bestowed on them a higher degree of glory."

Learn, then, from this example how agreeable to God is an obedient child.

"AM I LIKE JESUS?"

A pious boy once received a little picture representing the holy Child Jesus. Every day he looked at the picture, for it was a very beautiful one, and every day, too, he tried to resemble the Divine Child by leading a holy life.

"Have I been like the holy Child Jesus to-day?" he used to ask himself every night before going to rest. "Was I obedient like Him? Did I say my prayers as piously as He did? Did I try to serve God and my neighbours as He did? Do I increase in wisdom, age, and grace as He did?"

In this way the boy grew up until he reached manhood, trying every day to resemble the Divine Child Jesus in all his actions, and he became a model of virtue to all around him, and a great Saint. Could not you also follow his example?

HE DID NOT DO HIS MOTHER'S BIDDING.

Not very long ago a little boy was sent by his parents for his education to one of the principal schools of Paris. Before leaving home his mother took him to her side and said to him : " My dear child, you are going to leave me for the first time in your life to live among strangers. I will no longer be able to watch over you as I have done until now, and I am afraid lest perhaps you forget, in the midst of the gay city, the lessons I have given you."

At these words the boy looked up with affection into his mother's face, and, with tears in his eyes, threw his arms round her neck.

His mother continued : " Promise me, my own dear child, to learn well your catechism, to say devoutly your prayers every day, and to keep away from any companion who speaks irreverently of God, or neglects his prayers or religious duties."

The boy promised that he would be faithful to his mother's request, and it may be added with truth that no promise was ever more earnestly made.

Very soon after he entered college, he formed the acquaintance of two boys of his own age, who seemed to be very kind and pleasant, but whose conduct was far from being good. They did not show themselves in their true colours to their new companion at first, but as soon as they had gained his confidence, they little by little led him to follow their example. He very soon neglected to say his prayers and to learn his Catechism, lost his innocence, and became even worse than his two companions who had led him astray. His masters were unable to restrain him, and even his companions shunned him.

In a short time he became so stubborn and slothful that those over him were obliged to have recourse to punishment, which, however, instead of withdrawing him from his evil ways, seemed only to make him worse than before. On one occasion, when he had been guilty of some more serious fault, he was shut up alone in a room for several hours, and ordered to study while his companions were at play. When the time had expired, the Superior went to release him. On approaching the door, he was surprised to hear no sound proceeding from the room, and on opening it, was terror-stricken to find the boy hanging by the neck from the roof, and already dead.

Such was the terrible end of one who neglected to follow the instructions of his mother, who gave up his prayers, and went with companions who led an evil life. O my child, say from your heart, " My God, keep me from following such a terrible example."

X   HOW A LAZY BOY BECAME A GREAT SAINT.

Saint Anscairius lost his mother when he was only five years old. He was sent to a convent school, where he had every opportunity of knowing how to love and serve God ; but as he was a lazy boy, he would not learn his lessons, nor obey the teachers who had charge of him. He was too fond of play, and spent his time in amusing himself, and in distracting his companions instead of learning his lessons.

He might have grown up to manhood in this way, if God had not checked him by means of a dream. It is true we must not believe in dreams, but sometimes even dreams may teach us a good lesson.

One day at school he fell asleep over his books, and as he slept, he dreamed that he was going through a field which was soft and marshy, and that he could scarcely walk, because at every step he took his feet sank deeper and deeper into the mire, and became all covered with mud.

Along the side of the field there was a splendid road, with gardens on one side of it, full of beautiful trees and sweet-smelling flowers. Coming along this road, he thought he saw Our Blessed Lady, surrounded by a multitude of holy women dressed in white, and amongst them he beheld his own dear mother.

His heart was filled with joy when he saw her, and he tried to run at once and throw himself into her arms ; but he could not move from the spot where he stood, because his feet were fixed so firmly in the soft ground. He stretched out his arms towards her, and tried to extricate himself, but all his efforts were in vain.

Our Blessed Lady then said to him : " My child, if you wish to come to me, and to be with your good mother in Heaven, you must become a better boy than you are ; for you will never reach us in Heaven if you continue to be lazy and disobedient. You must henceforth be diligent and pious, and you must do every thing your Superiors tell you to do, for in doing that you will serve God, and those who serve God on earth will one day see Him in Heaven."

When Anscairius awoke he saw that he had been dreaming, but the dream seemed to be always before his mind. From that day he became a better boy. In a very short time he was at the head of his class, and none of his companions were ever able to get above him.

His Superiors wondered how this sudden change

had been brought about, and how one who had given them so much trouble had become so good and obedient all at once. But the boy kept his secret to himself, and told no one. It was only long afterwards, when he became an apostle among the Danes, that people knew of the dream, and of the firm resolution he had taken in consequence of it to become a faithful child of God, and to spend all his life in serving Him.

Anscairius is now a Saint in Paradise because he became a pious and obedient boy in school. If we imitate the good example he has given us, we shall also one day share with him his eternal happiness.

Lives of the Saints.

II. We must Honour our Parents.

My child, you must not only obey your parents, but you must also honour them, because it is God Himself Who has placed them over you, and they occupy His place with regard to you. And this you must do not only when they are kind and gentle towards you, but also when they may treat you harshly or even with severity.

KING FERDINAND AND HIS SON ALPHONSUS.

Ferdinand II., who reigned in Leon about the year 1157, had several children, amongst whom was Alphonsus VI., who succeeded him. Ferdinand lived till a good old age, and towards the end of his life was weighed down with many infirmities.

Alphonsus acted towards his father the part of a most dutiful son, never leaving him except when the duties of the regency, which had fallen on him, caused him to be absent. On his part, Ferdinand on every occasion showed him the most profound gratitude in return for his affectionate attention. He carefully concealed from him many of the pains his infirmities caused him to endure, that he might spare him as much grief as he could, and never allowed any occasion to pass without publicly giving marks of his love and esteem for him.

One day he learned that Alphonsus was returning home triumphant, after having overcome the Moors in battle. In order that he might be the first to offer him his congratulations, he caused himself to be carried in a chair to meet him.

As soon as Alphonsus perceived his father coming, he dismounted from his war-horse, and ran on foot to the place where his father sat. Ferdinand endeavoured, by every means, to persuade him to remount, saying to him that it did not behove him to walk on foot while the knights who accompanied him were on horseback.

Alphonsus said to him in answer · " It is true, father ; but, then, they are not your sons ;" and he continued to walk by his side.

On their arrival at the palace, he placed his arms around his father and lifted him from the litter, and himself bore him into the castle, at the same time bestowing on him marks of the tenderest affection. " My father," he said, " you indeed may know how great is the affection with which you love me, but you can never know how great is the love I bear for you. Not only did it make me accompany you on foot, but it made me envious of your servants who carried you. Several times was I on the point of making them stop, that I might take you on my shoulders and bear you home.

When his cherished father died, Alphonsus followed his remains to the tomb, shedding genuine tears of sorrow, arrayed in sombre garments, and his eyes cast upon the ground.

History of Alphonsus VI., Twelfth Century.

THE ANSWER THAT LITTLE LOUIS GAVE.

The mother of a little boy, whose name was Louis Bauvais, one day scolded him with much harshness for a fault which he had not been guilty of. When she had gone out of the room, one of the servants, who had witnessed the whole affair, said to the boy : " Why did you allow your mother to treat you in that harsh manner, especially since you were not guilty ? It is quite clear that your mother does not care for you."

Louis did not allow himself to fall into the snare that has so often entrapped little children. He answered · " I will never allow you to say one word against my mother. If she has punished me, and spoken harshly to me to-day, it is because she thought that I deserved it, and that it was for my good."

Souvenirs of Pious Youths.

" FOR THE CHILD'S CORRECTION."

The parents of St. Joseph of Cupertino were very poor, but in their poverty they were very pious. His mother loved her child, as pious mothers should always do, by gently attracting him to virtue, and by punishing him for every fault, even the smallest that he committed.

These frequent punishments did not cause him to utter a complaint, nor to lessen the love he had for his mother ; and when the punishment was over, he was accustomed to say : " God permits this, to root out of my heart my great inclination to anger." Moreover, he used to ask her forgiveness every time that he had done anything that displeased her.

It was in this way that he laid the foundation of that sanctity for which he was in after-life so renowned.   *Les S. Legendes.*

III. WE MUST NEVER BE ASHAMED OF OUR PARENTS.

We must never be ashamed of our parents. Sometimes poverty is their lot in life ; such has been for them the holy will of God. If a child has, by God's goodness and his own natural talents, risen higher in the world than the position in which he was born, he must always remember that that does not dispense him from the duty of honouring and obeying his parents who may be still poor and humble.

ONE WHO WAS ASHAMED OF HIS FATHER.

During the course of last century, there was a celebrated poet who was the son of a poor man, and who had risen to the high renown he had obtained because his father had laboured hard by the sweat of his brow to give him a good education.

When he was at the height of his renown, it happened that a certain nobleman desired to introduce him into the highest society of Paris. For this purpose he invited him to his mansion, and when the guests were assembled, the young poet found himself among the chief of the aristocracy of the capital.

The humble father of the poet, hearing of the great honour that was to be bestowed on his son asked to be permitted to be present on the occasion. This permission was willingly granted.

While the poet was declaiming his verses, his father's heart was filled with the most profound emotion, and with pardonable pride, as he heard the applause of the audience. When the poem was concluded, the room in which they were assembled rang with the shouts of admiration that burst forth from their lips. In the midst of it, the old man rose up at the further end of the hall, and, approaching his son, cried out : " Ah, my son, my son, how happy you have made me this day !"

But the youth, instead of coming forward like a dutiful son, and welcoming his father, turned away his head, as if he did not know who he was, his face at the same time becoming scarlet with shame as he saw his father standing before him, clothed in plain garments in the midst of such a brilliant assembly.

In an instant the audience took in the meaning of what they saw. Their shouts of applause immediately ceased, and cries of indignation took their place. They, with one accord, turned away in disgust from the undutiful son, saying : " What a pity it is that one who is gifted with such great talents should be such a bad son !"

POUSSIN : *Catéch. en Histoires.*

POPE BENEDICT XI. AND HIS MOTHER.

The illustrious Pope Benedict XI. was the son of a humble shepherd.   When he was raised to the pontifical throne, word was spread through Rome that his mother had come to visit him, and the whole city went out to meet her in honour of her son, who was the Pope.   The good woman was magnificently dressed in clothing far above her humble condition in life, and looked more like a princess than the wife of a poor shepherd.

When she was introduced into the presence of the Pope, and he was told that his mother had come to see him, he looked at her, and, without showing any sign of recognition, said : " That lady cannot be my mother ; my mother was too poor to purchase such a magnificent costume."

The poor woman was obliged to go out without even speaking to the Pope.   And when she had laid aside her rich robes, and put on the humble dress belonging to her lowly station, she again appeared before him.

No sooner had she entered than the Pope, at once rising from his throne, left his Cardinals and went to meet her.   When he drew near to her, he threw his arms around her and wept, as he said : " Ah, this is my mother now !   There is no one in the world who could love his mother as much as I do mine."

This beautiful example is handed down to us to show that in whatever condition in life our parents are, it is our duty to honour them.

IV. We must Pray for our Parents' Welfare.

The great duty of a good child is to pray for his parents, not only when they are good and pious, but also when they are not pleasing God. How many parents are daily kept from evil by the prayers of their little ones ; and how many, also, who have gone astray have been brought back to the path of piety because their children have prayed fervently for them !

CHARLES AND LINA.

Charles and Lina were the children of virtuous parents, who had taught them from their tenderest infancy to love God and always please Him. As was natural, they also had the greatest love for their father and mother, and showed this love by their obedience to every order they received from them.

Now it happened that they had also a great love for their lessons. They were so anxious to learn that they would often leave their breakfast half done that they might have more time for them.

But a change suddenly came over them. Instead of going at once to their lessons after breakfast, they went into the garden, and it was only after they had been there for some time that they began to study them. At first their parents were afraid lest they had become careless about them. Their father often asked them what they were doing every morning in the garden, but the only answer they made was to hang down their heads and say nothing.

Their mother made up her mind one day to watch them ; so, as soon as they went into the garden, she followed them at a little distance, so as not to be seen by them. She saw them go towards a shady place among the trees, where there was a little summer-house, into which they entered. She watched them from a little distance, and was surprised and gratified to see them fall on their knees and begin to pray. And as they prayed aloud, thinking that no one was near them, she was able to hear all they said.

Charles said aloud the following prayer, and Lina repeated it after him word for word · " O dearest Jesus Who, when on earth, didst love Thine own blessed Mother Mary, remember that we have a mother, too, whom we love, and a dear father also. Now, we have come here to ask Thee to make them live a very long time with us, and to make them always happy, and to make us good children, that we may never give them any cause to be unhappy. Amen."

The mother at once escaped from her hiding-place, and ran in tears of joy to tell her husband what she had heard and seen. They were both brimful of happiness. " Oh, what a pleasure it is to see these children so good !" they said. " We are indeed amply rewarded this day for all the trouble we have spent upon them."   SCHMIDT : *Catechism.*

THE DYING FATHER AND HIS LITTLE CHILD.

There was once a little girl whose father lay at home very ill. She was only eight years old, but she had gone to Sunday-school from the time she began to walk, and had always paid great attention to the instructions that were given there.

When she saw that her father was so ill, she was

filled with grief on account of her great love for him ; and the thought that he might soon die made her cry very bitterly.

But she was sad from another reason also. She knew that her father had been leading a careless life, and had not been to the Sacraments for years, and she knew that if he did not repent before he died, she could never see him in Heaven.

Now, although the doctor had told his friends that he was in great danger of death, none of them had the courage to tell him about it. When his little daughter saw this, she was more grieved than ever, and, as she sat weeping at the thought of losing him, she made up her mind to go to him herself and tell him. So she went to his room, climbed up on his bed, and put her arms round his neck.

The dying man, seeing his child there sobbing and crying, asked her what was the matter.

" O papa," she said, " you are very ill ; I heard the doctor say that you could not get better. O papa, what shall I do without you ?"

" My dear little girl, do not cry in that way. I shall soon be well again ; I shall not die."

" But, papa, if you do not get better, and if you really die, oh, it will be a terrible thing, for I shall never see you in Heaven !"

" What puts that into your head, child ?"

" I learned it at Sunday-school ; for the Catechism says that if a person has been neglecting his duties, and dies without repenting, he cannot get to Heaven ; and you know, dear papa, that you have not been to the Sacraments for a very long time, and it is that that makes me so sad. For, O papa, I do love you so much, and I want to see you one day in Heaven !"

Tears came into the eyes of the dying man. " Run, my own dear child," he cried out—" run as fast as you can and bring the priest ; tell him that your father is dying, and desires to receive the last Sacraments."

The little girl ran immediately, and in a short time the priest stood at his bedside. The dying man made his Confession, and received the last Sacraments with the greatest devotion. He did not die for some time afterwards, but until his last hour came he never ceased to say to those who came to see him : " I have to thank God for the blessing He gave me in sending me that dear little child. If it had not been for her, I should very likely have died in my sins. and have been lost for ever. As it is, I now die resigned to God's holy will, and full of hope in His mercy."

When the end came, his little daughter wept much for him, but this time there was much joy in the midst of her sorrow, for she knew that her dear father was with God in Heaven, and that she would one day meet him there. *L'Ami de la Jeunesse.*

THE RICH MERCHANT'S DAUGHTER.

There was a rich merchant in Paris who led a very worldly life, and entirely neglected his religious duties. He lost his wife a few years after his marriage, leaving him two daughters As soon as they were of an age to be sent to school, he sent them to a convent to be educated by the nuns.

In the convent they received an education which

would fit them for the position of life they were to occupy in the world ; but they also received that which is of infinitely greater importance, a thorough Christian training.

When the elder daughter was sixteen years of age, her father took her home to attend to his household affairs. In this new position she remained as faithful to her religious duties as she had been when in the convent ; but she had to conceal many of her practices of devotion from her father, lest he might be angry with her.

One morning her father happened to go out very early, and met his daughter coming along the street. " Where have you been so early in the morning ?" he said to her in a harsh tone.

" My dear father, I was at Holy Mass, where I prayed much for you."

" And you were at Communion, too, I suppose ?" he said in anger.

" Yes, father, I have had that happiness."

" Do you go often to Communion ?" he said, in a still more angry voice.

" Yes, my dearest father, I go very often ; for it is there that I get strength and courage to accomplish my daily duties at home, and to please you, as I am endeavouring to do."

At this answer her father hung down his head and said nothing. When he raised it up again, there were tears in his eyes, and he said, in a voice choked with emotion : " Oh, what a happiness it is for me to have a daughter like you ! Go to Mass and to your Communion as often as you like, my child, and continue to pray for me."

That man did not at once become a fervent Christian, but the prayers of his good daughter soon accomplished the change. How many children might obtain the conversion of their parents, whose lives may not be what God wishes them to be, if they would only pray fervently for them !

Hortus Pastorum.

V. How to Become a Saint at Home.

Sometimes we hear pious children say that they would be Saints if only they were in a convent or monastery, where everything around them would speak to them of God, but that it is impossible for them to be so at home in the midst of the noise and bustle of the world. My child, this is a great mistake ; it is as easy, and sometimes easier, to become a Saint at home than in the cloister. We can all become Saints in the place where God has put us, if we only try.

A SAINT IN HER MOTHER'S HOUSE.

A young lady had been sent by her parents to a convent for her education. The peaceful and holy life of the religious inspired her with a great desire of forsaking the world, and of becoming, like them, the Spouse of Jesus Christ. But when she mentioned it to her parents, they refused to allow her, and at once took her away from the convent, that she might stay at home with themselves.

The child obeyed them, although she shed many tears as she left that house in which she had been so happy.

" O my God," she said, when once more in her parents' home, " since I cannot at present be a religious in a convent, I will be one here in my own house."

From that moment she began to lead the life of a nun. She divided her time between work and prayer. She heard Mass daily, made her meditation, and her visit to the Blessed Sacrament every day, said the Rosary, and read spiritual books, as she had seen the Sisters do in the convent.

But her mother, who watched all she did, saw that these things only made her more intent on following out the vocation to which she felt herself called. So, to force her to change her resolution, she gave her so much work to do that the young woman had but little time left for her works of piety.

But she had learned in the convent that obedience is a virtue most agreeable to God ; so she took the resolution to renounce her own will, and be obedient in all things to her mother for the present, hoping that God would afterwards call her to Himself in the religious life.

So for many years she lived with her mother, and was obedient to her in everything. She did not spend much time in the church, nor did she say long prayers, because the work her mother gave her left her but little time for this. But every hour of the day she raised up her mind to God by some fervent aspirations, and offered up all her actions to Him.

In the end, God moved the hearts of her parents. She obtained their consent to consecrate herself to God in a Religious Order, where she became famous

for the miracles God performed by her hands. After
her death the Church enrolled her name in the cata-
logue of her Saints.   *Heureuse Année.*

WHAT A LITTLE BOY'S PRAYER CAN DO.

A little boy had just made his first Communion.
Jesus had on that happy day spoken to his young
heart, and the boy promised he would always love
Him. One thing only grieved him : his father and
his mother never went to Mass. He had asked them
and begged of them to go, but all in vain.

But a thought came into his mind : he had heard
in the instructions given preparatory to his first
Communion of the power of prayer with God : he
would pray for them. On two mornings every week
he went to hear Holy Mass, and offered it up for their
conversion. On one day it was for his father, on
the other for his mother.

His mother soon observed that he went out at a
certain hour regularly on these two mornings every
week. She would watch him. One day she followed
him without being seen, to see where he went. She
followed him into the church, and saw him kneel
with the reverence of an angel, praying with the
greatest fervour. She waited for him at the door
of the church when he was coming out. She thought
she saw the trace of tears upon his cheeks, and she
eagerly asked him the cause of them.

He threw his arms around her neck and made this
simple answer : " Yesterday it was for my father ;
to-day it is for you, mother."

The rest can be easily understood. Faith had

not yet been extinguished in these two hearts, although they had wandered from the path of duty ; and on the following Sunday, they—the father and the mother—knelt to hear Holy Mass at the side of their devoted child. *L'Apostolat de la Prière*, 46.

THE MODEL HOUSEHOLD.

A venerable priest who was preaching a mission in one of the towns of Picardy, in France, relates that the parish priest of that place, one day pointing out to him a little dwelling-house situated at a very little distance from his own, said to him : " Do you see that house over the way ? Well, I prefer it to all the rich farms that are in the district, and even to the splendid château jtself."

" And who is it that dwells in that house, which you seem to commend so much ?"

" It is occupied by an excellent man, with his pious wife and family, whom God has blessed in a most particular manner. When the father and mother were married, they were exceedingly poor— five shillings seemed to be all they possessed—and for some time they had to endure many hardships. In a short time, by strict economy, and, above all by their industry and edifying conduct, they procured for themselves the support and good-will of their neighbours. They were enabled in a short time to open a little store, where they sold provisions. At first their income was exceedingly small, but by their perseverance, honesty, and their engaging manners, it began marvellously to increase.

" Children were born to them in due course. At

the present moment they are eight in number, all healthy, well educated for their position in life, and, like their parents, industrious, gay, and happy. Now that family, though yet in humble circumstances, live comfortably, for each of the children has been taught a trade, which adds to the little income of their home, where they all dwell together. Their life is a laborious one, but one also of regularity, and imbued with that Christian virtue which alone can insure temporal and eternal happiness. By their prudence, also, they are daily laying aside part of their earnings, that they may not suffer in the day of need."

The missionary here asked · " To what do you mainly attribute that prosperity and that happiness, so rarely to be found amongst people of their condition ?"

" Without doubt to the blessing which God has visibly bestowed on that home, which is, as you see, truly Christian," said the priest. " The father and the mother are of all my parishioners the most exact in sanctifying the Sunday, and in accomplishing all the commandments of the Church. They are charitable towards the poor, and their hearts are always open to all those who are in affliction. Their eight children, without even one exception, formed on their model, and imitating their example, fulfil their duties with the same exactness. They carefully keep away from all occasions dangerous to their innocence ; they are models to all the young people of the place, the edification of my parish, and the joy of their parents."

The Father missionary, hearing these words, felt a great desire to visit that home so singularly blessed.

After his first visit he returned to the parish priest, and said : " Yes, you did not exaggerate in the smallest degree the excellence of that truly Christian home. There was in that home an atmosphere of simplicity and joyful serenity ; happiness was painted on the countenances of every one of the inmates. What respect, what submission and obedience, on the part of the children ! What anxiety to anticipate even the very wishes of their parents ! And on the part of the parents themselves what gentleness, what affection, what sweet firmness, with regard to their children ! What tidiness, what order, in their modest house ! What assiduity, what diligence, in their work ! What heavenly charity, what union, between father and mother, between brothers and sisters ! That pious family is truly an image of the Holy Family of Nazareth.

" God, His spirit, His love, reigns there in the hearts of each and all of them. It is truly Heaven on earth—a home that truly foreshadows the happiness of the eternal home of Paradise."

VI. We must Assist our Parents in their Needs.

It is the duty of a good child to assist his parents both in their spiritual and temporal necessities. If **you see your parents neglecting their religious duties,**

"BE KIND TO YOUR MOTHER."

Frederick, King of Prussia, one day rang his bell, and, no one answering, he opened the door and found his page fast asleep in his elbow-chair.

He advanced towards him, and was about to waken him, when he perceived a letter hanging out of his pocket.

Curiosity prompted him to know what it contained ; so he took it out and read it. It was a letter from the young man's mother, in which she thanked him for having sent her part of his money to relieve her misery, and telling him that God would reward him for his filial affection.

The King, after reading it, went softly to his chamber, took out a purse full of money, and slipped it, along with the letter, into the page's pocket. Returning to his chamber, he rang the bell so loudly that it awoke the page, who instantly made his appearance.

" You have had a sound sleep," said the King.

The page was at a loss how to excuse himself, and putting his hand into his pocket by chance, to his utter astonishment found there the purse. He took it out, and turned pale when he saw what it was.

" What is that ?" said the King ; " what is the matter ?"

" Ah, sire," said the young man, throwing himself on his knees, " someone is trying to ruin me. I know nothing of this money that I have just found in my pocket, nor do I know how it has been put there."

" My young friend," said Frederick, " God often does great things for us even in our sleep. Send that to your mother, salute her on my part, and assure her that I will take care of both her and you."

Ave Maria.

A LITTLE CHILD CONVERTS HIS FATHER.

It is the great Louis Veuillot himself who has told us the following story :

" I was, from my childhood, brought up as carelessly as it was possible with regard to my religion—not only in ignorance of the truths of our Holy Faith, but without having any desire to learn them, or having any respect for them ; on the contrary, when my education at school was ended, I came forth to the world, my mind filled with ideas against Our Lord and against His Church. Then my life was similar to .that of the young men of Paris ; I was, moreover, a true citizen of the Montmartre District, very busy with my worldly concerns, and spending in amusements and in political arguments all the time that was not occupied with these temporal affairs.

" Then I married. The goodness of God for me caused me to be united to a woman whose mind was far above earthly things, and endowed with a true spirit of piety, while at the same time she possessed what at the moment I esteemed more precious—beauty, a profound intelligence, and a considerable fortune. Brought up as I had been, she differed much from me. She was much superior to me ; she was imbued with a deep feeling of religion. This became more pronounced when she became a mother, and after the birth of our first child she became more and more impressed with her new responsibilities, and even more deeply imbued with fervour, and the sense of the duties which motherhood imposed upon her.

" When now I think on these things of the past, I am moved with feelings of gratitude towards God ; but then I did not heed them, nor even think of them. If my wife had been like myself, I believe that I would never even have thought of having my children baptized. These little ones grew up around me, and when the older ones had reached the age for making their First Communion, I paid no attention to the matter. My wife, in whom I had the most implicit confidence, looked after all these things.

" The time arrived for the youngest of them to make his First Communion. This dear boy had a wayward turn of mind, and was much given to anger without any provocation. I loved him, indeed, as much as any of the others, although I found myself under the necessity of frequently punishing him. My wife had often said to me : ' Just have a little patience ; he will change at the time of his First Communion.' These words, especially when the time was fixed for their fulfilment, seemed to me very unlikely.

" Nevertheless, the boy began to attend the classes in preparation for this great event, and I could not but observe a great change for the better in his conduct. This was evident, and, above all, this new feeling increased daily. I watched him now more attentively. I saw that daily he became more careful to battle against his faults ; he became more gentle, more respectful, more affectionate. This astonished me, for reason left to itself could never have produced in the heart of anyone such a rapid and persevering change ; and so it came to pass that this child had suddenly become to me more dear than all the others.

" At the same time I thought much on this wonderful change, and I myself went to hear the instructions given to the children. While listening to them, I could not avoid recalling to my mind what I had learned in my studies at school, and I compared them with the simple instructions on the Catholic Faith. The problems of good and evil which, in the past, I had avoided thinking of, seeing that I was unable to solve them, forced themselves now upon my mind in ail their terrible light.

" I questioned my child on this subject, and his answers were so clear and convincing that they quite overwhelmed me. It then appeared to me that any answers to them would be useless, if not sinful. My wife saw clearly what was passing in my mind, but she said nothing ; only I saw that she prayed longer, and with greater fervour.

" I passed sleepless nights. I could not shut out from my mind in the darkness and the stillness around me how different was my life from the innocent lives of those two objects of my affection, my wife and my son, and how different, also, was the love that burned in their hearts from that which was in mine ; and I said to myself : ' There is something in me which they love and which I do not love, either in them or in myself : it is my soul.'

" At length the great week of the First Communion

arrived. It was not only an increasing affection which the conduct of my boy raised within me, there was another feeling which I could not express, which created a strange, almost humiliating, sentiment in my mind, and which sometimes produced a feeling of irritation. I felt a kind of respect even for him. I felt, also, that there was something within him that made him superior to me, and I felt, moreover, that I dared not give utterance in his presence to certain ideas which my state of mind caused to arise within me. I did not want that he should be the one to convince me that they were wrong, and I thought it would be sinful to expose his innocent soul to be placed in the danger of being impressed by them.

" There were now only five or six days more to pass before the greatest event of his life would take place. One morning, on his return from Mass, the boy came to my room, where I was alone.

" ' Papa,' he said to me, ' the day of my First Communion is at hand, and I cannot approach the altar without having asked pardon for all the faults I have committed, and all the sorrow I have caused you, and without receiving your blessing. Think, now, on all the evil you have seen me do, that you may reproach me with it, so that I may obtain your forgiveness for everything, and I will promise never to do any evil again.'

" ' My dear child,' I replied, ' a father forgives everything, even in a child that has not been so good as he ought to have been ; but I have the happiness of telling you to-day that I have nothing to forgive in you. I am very well pleased with you.

Continue, then, to work, and to love the good God, and to fulfil all your duties faithfully, and you will make your mother and me very happy.'

" ' O papa,' he answered, ' the good God who loves you so much will help me to be always your consolation, as you ask me. You will pray much for me, papa ?'

" ' Yes, I promise, my dear child.'

" He then looked on me for a few minutes with tears in his eyes, and threw his arms around my neck. I also at the moment was full of emotion.

" ' Papa,' he continued.

" ' Well, my child ?'

" ' Papa, I have something to ask of you.'

" I knew this, and, what is more, I knew well what he was going to ask. Must I acknowledge my weakness ? I began to be afraid ; I was even so cowardly as to profit by his short hesitation in putting forward his request.

" I said to him : ' Go away, my boy ; I have something very important to do at present. This evening or to-morrow morning you will tell me what you want, and if your mother thinks that it would be good for you, I will grant your request.'

" The boy now lost courage at hearing these words, and having again embraced me, he went away, sad and dejected, into the little room where he slept, which was near that of his mother. I felt then a great remorse at having treated him in this manner, and, above all, for having yielded in such a cowardly manner to the temptation of sending him away so **abruptly.**

" **I could not find any peace. I arose and followed**

him on tip-toe to his little bedchamber, so that I might in some way give him consolation for the sorrow I had caused him. The door was a little open, and I was able to watch him unobserved. He was on his knees before a picture of Our Blessed Lady, praying with all the fervour of his soul. Oh, I can assure you that at that moment I could understand how the apparition of an angel can affect the soul.

" I went back to my room, and placed my head in my hands upon the table before which I sat, and felt that I could weep with joy and sorrow. I remained in this position for a few moments. When I raised up my eyes, my little boy was at my side, his countenance full of an expression of fear, of resolution, and of love.

" ' Papa,' he began with firmness, ' the request I am going to make is for something that cannot be delayed, and mamma will be pleased if you grant it. It is this : that on the day of my First Communion you will come to the Holy Table with her and me. O papa, do not refuse to come. Do this for the love of the good God Who loves you so much.'

" Ah ! I could not hold out any longer. God was calling on me, forcing me as it were to go ; I could not refuse. I pressed the child against my heart, and I said : ' Yes, yes, my dearest boy. Yes, I will do so, and whenever you like—to-day even. You will yourself take me by the hand, and you will lead me to your confessor, and you will say to him : " See, I have brought my father to you." ' "

Louis Veuillot.

VII. We must Honour and Obey our Teachers.

St. Paul teaches us to be obedient, not only to our parents, but also to our lawful superiors, and to those who are chosen to be our teachers ; in obeying them, therefore, we are obeying God, in whose place they are.

THE EMPEROR THEODOSIUS AND HIS WIFE FLACCILLA.

The Emperor Theodosius the Great and his pious spouse Flaccilla had so much at heart the education of their children that, not being able to find in their own dominions one whom they considered suitable for this great work, they wrote to the Emperor of the West, praying him to approach the Sovereign Pontiff, and ask him to send someone to them whom he could recommend as a fit preceptor.

The Pope readily granted their request, and sent them St. Arsenius, who was as distinguished for his learning as for his virtue.

Full of gratitude to the holy man, Theodosius took care that his children should treat their preceptor with the greatest respect, not only on account of his virtues, but because of the duties he had to perform towards them.

One day he went into the room where they and their master were assembled. He perceived that they were seated at their tasks, while Arsenius was standing.

" This must not be," he said, in a tone of disappointment ; " it is not right that the pupils should be sitting down and their teacher standing. From this moment you must stand up while receiving your lessons, and he, your preceptor, shall be seated before you."

This order he commanded to be rigidly enforced, that they, although of royal dignity, might ever remember that he, their master, was then their superior. St. Paul had said : " As long as the heir is a child, he differeth nothing from a servant, though he be lord of all ; but is under tutors and governors until the time appointed by the father " (Gal. iv. 1, 2).

VIII. On the Duty of Servants.

My child, God has not placed us all in the same position in life : some are masters and mistresses, and others are their servants, and subject to their authority. It is His Holy Will that those who are in the service of others should be obedient to them, just as they would be to Himself, if they saw Him in their place, or if He gave them the commands they receive.

THE STORY OF ST. ZITA.

There is a great Saint in Heaven whose name is known everywhere on earth on account of her great perfection and holiness : she is called St. Zita.

Who was she ? Was she a queen ? No. Was she a nun ? No. Was she a noble lady with plenty of time to say her prayers ? No. Who, then, was this great St. Zita ? She was only a lowly servant in a gentleman's house. Read attentively the story of her life, and you will see how she, a poor servant girl, served God perfectly, that you also, by imitating her, may become perfect.

She was the daughter of very poor but pious parents, who taught her, when she was quite a little girl, to love and serve God.

When they wanted her to do anything, they always said to her : " God wishes it ; it is the will of God," and she did it at once ; and when they wished her not to do something, they said : " My child, God will be displeased if you do that ;" and that was enough, she did not do it.

As she began to grow up, she could not under stand how people could offend God, seeing, on the one hand, that He is so good and so kind, and, on the other, that He punishes sin so much.

As soon as she was old enough to go to work, her parents sent her to try and obtain something to enable them to live. She was just twelve years old when she was engaged to be a servant in a gentleman's family. In this situation she had a great deal of hard and disagreeable work to do, but she did not complain of this, because she did it all for God. She had scarcely any time for prayer, because she had to get up so early in the morning and work all day till late at night ; but her morning and evening prayers, short though they were, were always well said, and often during her work she thought of God, and said some short ejaculations.

She was most punctual to do whatever her master and mistress told her, for whenever she got an order from them to do something, she thought it was God Himself who spoke to her, and she said in her own mind : " Yes, dear Lord, I will do it at once for the love of Thee."

She was sometimes scolded, poor girl ! because she did on some occasions make slight mistakes at her work, but she never complained ; on the contrary, she would go on her knees at once and humbly ask pardon.

There were a great many servants in the house, and they hated her, because she would not do as they did, for they were very careless. One of them especially was full of envy against her, and did everything she could to torment her. If anything was lost or went astray, Zita was sure to be blamed for it. If any command of the master or mistress was not duly fulfilled, the blame was all put on Zita. If anything was done well, it was because Zita had no hand in it. All bad things were due to Zita ! Zita never could do anything right.

Poor Zita ! many a bitter tear did she shed when alone at night lying on her humble bed ; still, she never complained, but tried to bear all patiently for the sake of God. And God gave courage to His persecuted child to bear her cross ; so that, instead of leaving the place and looking for another, she stayed where she was, because she knew that each one of these crosses and trials would bring her a very great reward in Heaven.

But what grieved the poor child most was the wrong opinion her employers had about her. At first they both liked her very much, but, being deceived by the falsehoods of the other servants, they began to lose all regard for her. She got from them cross faces, hard words, bitter rebukes, and severe threats ; and these were all the more afflicting because she knew well she did not deserve them.

But God was watching over her with the love of an affectionate Father, and in His own good time He made known her innocence.

It happened that the servant who had been most cruel and unjust to her fell sick. During her illness Zita attended on her as if she had been her greatest and dearest friend. Such conduct could not fail to soften her hard heart. So one day, full of repentance, she sent for her mistress, and confessed to her how wicked she had been in saying so much evil about Zita, who was so good and pious.

" O my mistress," she exclaimed, " Zita is an angel, and I have been her enemy. It was envy and jealousy that blinded me, and I told lies about her. O my mistress, forgive me ; and you too, Zita, forgive me for the evil I have done to you."

But Zita had prostrated herself at the foot of the bed, praying for the dying woman, now so penitent. Rising from her knees, she embraced her, as a sign that she freely pardoned her, and she remained at her bedside all the time she lived, and when her last hour came the servant died in her arms.

After this event Zita was raised to a higher position in the household. Having discovered her integrity, and desirous to make amends for their past harshness towards her, they placed her above all the other servants. This did not make her proud ; she thanked God for it, because it was His Holy Will, and because it gave her more opportunity for helping the needy and the poor, and allowed her more time for her devotions.

She remained in that same family for fifty years, and then she died. The following is the account of her holy death as told us by her historians :

" On Wednesday, April 27, 1272, a bright star appeared above the town of Lucca (where Zita dwelt). It was so bright that it seemed to be like the sun at midday. The people of the town were astonished at this wonder, and their astonishment was increased when they saw all the children running through the streets and crying out as if inspired : ' Come to the church ! come to the church, for Zita the Saint is dead !' It was at this very hour that she died.

" For after five days of low fever, surrounded by some devout women who had attended her, and fortified by the Holy Sacraments of the Church, she calmly closed her eyes, and her holy soul went to receive the crown of glory in Heaven. She was buried with great solemnity ; the church was crowded with people of every class and condition. The streets through which the funeral passed were crowded by the people who wished to see once more the remains of the pious housemaid. And as years rolled on pilgrims came to kneel at her grave to beg her intercession, and God, to show the sanctity of his humble servant, worked many miracles ; for the dumb spoke, the blind saw, the deaf heard, and those in affliction found consolation at her tomb."

Like St. Zita, let us humbly and diligently do our daily work for God, and the same reward that she obtained in Heaven will be given also to us.

Life of St. Zita.

XXXI

THE FOURTH COMMANDMENT— SECOND PART

I. PARENTS MUST SET A GOOD EXAMPLE TO THEIR CHILDREN.

ALTHOUGH the Fourth Commandment treats chiefly of the duties of children towards their parents, it has also for its object to teach parents their duties towards their children, since God has made them the guardians and the models of His little ones.

The principal duties of parents towards their children are the following : they must love their children ; they must bring them up in a Christian manner ; they must provide for their temporal wants, instruct them, correct them, and above all things else, set them a good example.

REMARKABLE WORDS OF CARDINAL WISEMAN.

" If parents, mothers in particular," writes Cardinal Wiseman, " knew how to train their chil dren from the cradle for God ; if, instead of fondling their infant humours and caressing their very passions and caprices, they turned the first dawn of their reason to the knowledge and consideration of the Divine goodness, and shaped their lips to utter as first sounds the two sweetest names in human speech, " Jesus and Mary," many who now have to weep over the follies and vices of their offspring might be thanking God instead, for having blessed their family with a Saint."

The Lamp of the Sanctuary.

JESUS AND THE LITTLE CHILDREN.

" At that hour the disciples came to Jesus, saying : ' Who thinkest Thou is the greater in the Kingdom of Heaven ?'

" And Jesus, calling unto Him a little child, set him in the midst of them, and said : ' Amen, I say to you, Unless you be converted, and become as little children, you shall not enter into the Kingdom of Heaven. Whosoever, therefore, shall humble himself as this little child, he is the greater in the Kingdom of Heaven. And he that shall receive one such little child in My name, receiveth Me. But he that shall scandalize one of these little ones that believe in Me, it were better for him that a millstone should be hanged about his neck, and that he should be drowned in the depth of the sea."

St. Matthew xviii. 1 *et seq.*

To you, O parents, has God in His wisdom confided these little children who are so dear to Him. What an honour, but at the same time, what a responsibility !

MOTHERS BRING THEIR LITTLE ONES TO JESUS.

" And they brought to Him young children, that He might touch them. And the disciples rebuked them that brought them. Whom when Jesus saw, He was much displeased, and saith to them : ' Suffer the little children to come unto Me, and forbid them not ; for of such is the Kingdom of Heaven.' And embracing them, and laying His hands upon them, He blessed them " (St. Mark x. 13, 14, 16).

Oh, how much is it to be desired that mothers in our own days would bring their little children to Jesus in His holy tabernacle that they might receive His blessing ! And how happy would the children themselves, begotten of pious parents, be, if, by hearing from their lips from their earliest years of the love and of the sufferings of Jesus for them, they would in return learn to love Him as He deserves— Him who, when on earth did say : " Suffer the little children to come unto Me " !

BELOVED OF GOD AND OF MAN.

A child born of Catholic and pious parents in a land of faith is like guileless Adam in the groves of Paradise. Oh, how solemn a thing it is to keep company with little children, so lately arrived, as it were, out of another world, and from God's neighbourhood, who are now in that wonderful state wherein we were once, and did not, alas ! comprehend it till it had slipped away from us.

Marina de Escobar, when only three years of age, used to be heard repeating : " I love God more than my father, and mother, and aunt, and all things else ;" and she used to place herself in secret corners of the house, or field, and say that she would find God, who was her life, in solitude.

" I remember," said the same saintly woman,

" that when I was a little girl, and did not know what was meant by mental prayer, I used to consider with great emotion the mysteries of the life of Christ."

Again she thus speaks of what she sometimes did in her childhood. " It used to happen sometimes, that while walking in the streets, and meeting little boys, I could not restrain the desire I felt of accosting them, through a desire of inducing them to love God ; and I used to interrogate them, saying : ' Little one, do you know the angelical salutation and Our Lord's prayer ?' and when they used to reply that they knew them well, I would add : ' Pray thus, my pupils, daily, and beseech the Blessed Virgin that God may make you His servants, and give you a great love for Himself.' They used to look at me while I spoke, and say : ' So we will do, lady.' "

The greatest Saints of God, following in the footsteps of Jesus Christ, have always placed the little children before us as our models on our way to Heaven.

" You know," said St. Thomas of Villanova," the manners of boys, the characteristics of children, that these are innocence, simplicity, purity, truth, and humility. They have no shameful concupiscence, no ambition, no care for riches, no anxious solitudes, neither malice nor fraud nor suspicion nor hatred. Truly, it would be good for them to continue thus until Christ shall come."

" Children know the secrets, not of cities, not of human society, but of God ; their fair eyes are full of infinite sweetness ; their little hands, joyous and blessed, have not committed evil ; their young feet have never touched our defilement ; their sacred heads wear an aureole of light ; their smiles, their voices proclaim their twofold purity."

When St. Peter Nolasco was a little boy of eight years, he had such love for Blessed Mary, that in all the palaces of the Viscountess of Narbonne, his aunt, where he was educated by the monk Gaufred, he made little altars, on which he placed her image.

How the young maiden Geneviève was sweetly moved, when the holy Germain of Auxerre—being on his journey to the sea with St. Loup, Bishop of Troyes, travelling on foot—on coming to Nanterre, singled her out of the crowd of children, kissed her forehead, saying to her parents, happy was the day of her birth, for it was a festival, not only in their hearts and in their house, but also in Heaven ; and then, giving her a medal, bestowed upon her his parting benediction !

St. Peter of Alcantara, when a child, being missed from home at dinner-time, his parents sent to look for him, and he was found in the church absorbed in contemplation.

St. Martin was only ten years old when he fled to the church against the wish of his parents, who were pagans, to become a catechumen.

Le Febvre, one of the first companions of St. Ignatius of Loyola, when a child of six years, used to mount on a great stone, and preach on the mysteries of faith, on festivals, to the country people, who listened to him with admiration.

Marina de Escobar beheld in a vision among spirits glorified, Marina Hermandez of Valladolid, who died in her fifth year, saying with her last breath : " I am going to Heaven to bless and to praise God in the choir of angels." "Ah, my little darling, how well I know you !" she exclaimed now, on seeing her in ecstasy ; to whom the child replied : " Dear aunt, my occupation here is what I said it would be as I expired."

In his last years the venerable John Gerson could not even endure any society but that of children. He lived with and taught them, or rather he sought to receive instruction himself from these innocent friends of the Saviour. He counted on their intercession, and assembled them on the eve of his death to beg that they would pray for him, saying · " Lord have pity on your poor servant John Gerson."

St. Catherine, of Sienna, when a child, in order to imitate the life of hermits, resolved to withdraw to the desert. Leaving that lovely city by the gate which now bears the name of St. Mark, she walked on till she had lost sight of all the houses. Here, she thought, must be the desert she was in search of. To complete her joy she observed a little cave at the side of a mount, and here she resolved to commence her life of solitude.

In the time of Vincent of Beauvais, who relates the circumstance, there was in Thorouth, a town in Flanders, a boy named Achas, who was so moved by seeing some Franciscan Friars in his father's house, that he begged and obtained permission to be clad thenceforth in a little habit like theirs ; and so wonderfully did he evince the spirit of that holy rule in all his actions, imitating the friars even in preaching to other children, and giving salutary admonitions to all, not excepting his own parents, that strangers used to come from afar to see him. It was impossible to describe his gravity and sanctity; and this ministry he discharged during two years, till, at the age of seven, he passed to a better life.

We need no longer be surprised at the terrible words uttered by Our Divine Lord Jesus, who loved the little children so well, against those who should give scandal to a little child · " He that shall scandalize one of these little ones that believe in Me, it were better for him that a millstone should be hanged about his neck, and that he should be drowned in the depth of the sea " (St. Matt. xviii. 6).

Compitum, Book I., chap. ii.

THE BISHOP AND THE CHILD.

Monsigneur du Tillet, Bishop of Orange, was one day walking along the streets of that city, when he heard the shrill cries of a young child, issuing from the furthermost end of a little shop, the door of which he was passing.

Moved with a feeling of compassion, he entered the house, to learn the cause of the noise that had reached him, and he found, lying in a cradle, a little child, whose mother had gone out for a short time, and had left him alone till her return.

The good Bishop drew near to the child, and spoke to him in accents of tender affection, caressed him, and did all in his power to console him ; but, notwithstanding his most earnest endeavours, the child continued to cry as loudly as ever. The Bishop then seating himself near him, began to rock the cradle in which he lay.

The boy's mother returned a few moments afterwards, and was surprised to see a stranger thus occupied. Her amazement was only increased when, approaching nearer, she saw his purple cassock and pectoral cross, and knew that it was the Bishop himself who was there.

" Oh, my lord," she exclaimed, " is it possible that it can be you yourself who are sitting there rocking the cradle, as if you were a servant ?"

" And why should I not do so ?" said the Bishop. " As I was passing down the street I heard the child cry, and I imagined that something must have happened to cause him pain, so I came in to see if I could in any way appease him. My only regret is that I was not able to do so as soon, or as much, as I wished. But you are his mother, and your maternal tenderness will soon discover a means of accomplishing what I was unable to do. Take great care, then, of this little angel," added the Bishop, again caressing him, " and while being assiduous in attending to his temporal wants, be careful, above all other things, to inspire into his soul, especially when you perceive his reason developing, a tender love of God, and a great fear of ever offending him, for this only is what will hereafter bring happiness to him and to yourself."

Then, after saying to her these words, and bestowing his benediction on her and on the child, the good Bishop resumed his journey, leaving the mother full of gratitude and admiration.   *Anecdotes Chrétiennes.*

II. Parents must set a Good Example.

EXAMPLE THE BEST LESSON.

There was once a father whose life was far from being so edifying as it ought to have been. He had a large family, and although he himself had but little piety, his greatest desire was to see his children virtuous and good.

So he one day asked a friend, whom he much esteemed for his wisdom and experience, what he would consider the best means of attaining this object.

He answered him · " I know only of one ; and that is, to set them a good example. Children often forget what is said to them, but for the most part they willingly do what they see others doing."

EFFECT OF A FATHER'S EXAMPLE.

There was once a pious mother who had a son whom she taught to love God. From his earliest years he followed the holy counsels she gave him, and grew up a model to all the young men around him. He went very frequently to the Sacraments, and there was every appearance that he would live and die a Saint.

Things went on in this hopeful way till he had reached his seventeenth year. All at once a change came over him. His piety seemed to melt slowly away, and he no longer went to the Sacraments as he used to do. This change in his conduct was soon observed by the watchful eye of his good mother, and she sought diligently to know what could have been the cause of it. For a long time she sought in vain. He never went with bad companions, who so often are the cause of the ruin of souls, and she never saw him read any of those books which destroy the faith of so many young men.

One day, when she had wept more than usual over the carelessness of her dear boy, she went to see him in his room. " My dear child," she said to him, " you must tell me what is the cause of the great change that I have observed in you ; you are not the same pious boy that you used to be, and you never go to the Sacraments now. You must tell me all about it."

But the son did not speak. He hung down his head, and his face grew crimson with shame.

His mother became more and more alarmed, and pressed him by the most endearing words not to hide anything from her.

" My mother," he began, " since you have asked me in this way, I will not hide anything from you ; I will tell you all. The beautiful lessons you gave me in my childhood, and especially your holy example, made me love my religion ; I loved it dearly, and I found in the practice of it, as you taught me, my own dear mother, my greatest delight. But now I have grown up, and I have begun to reflect. Look at my father ; see how the world honours and esteems him, and seeks his company. Oh, how much I would like to resemble him ! Yet he does not practise his religion, and he is not without instruction, and he is too upright to go against his conscience. Surely I cannot do wrong in acting as he does. Now, dearest mother, I have told you all, and if you see my conduct different from what it was before, it is because I am trying to be like my father, and to be esteemed and honoured as he is."

The poor afflicted mother left her son, and flew at once to the room where her husband was. As soon as she entered, she fell at his feet, crying out : " O my husband, your son, your son——" and she fainted in his arms.

Her husband, terrified at what had happened, used every remedy to restore her to consciousness. When this was accomplished, she sat down by his side, and in the midst of tears and sobs, told him all that her son had just said to her.

As she was speaking he began to tremble violently, and, when she had ended, he said : " Come with me ; I have ruined my boy, but I may yet save him." Saying these words, he went down to his son's room.

" My child," he said, " it is indeed a hard thing for a father to go on his knees to his own son, but I will do it. Yes, my child, I am guilty—guilty of a great sin. Your mother has told me all. But, my dear boy, I have not lost my Faith ; it is still in my soul. It is that cursed human respect that has made me ashamed to profess my Faith openly ; I never for an instant thought that my conduct would ever have any influence on you, but that your good mother's example and her lessons would have a lasting effect on you. Thanks be to God, it is not too late. Forgive me, my child, for the bad example I have given you ; I too, for the time to come, will be like your mother ; I too will, for the time to come, go to the Sacraments as she does, and thus the past will be redeemed. . . . Who is your confessor ?

He shall also be mine. Let us go to him together, you to confess your weakness, and I to confess my crime."

This was done, and ever afterwards there was fervour in that family, which had nearly suffered shipwreck on account of the father's sin. Would that every father would read this example, and always keep it in his mind!   *Father Guyon.*

LEON DUPONT AND HIS DAUGHTER.

Henrietta, the daughter of Mr. Dupont, was born in the year 1832 ; her happy death took place in 1847, and this is the account that has been left of it.

This young girl, aged only fifteen, was all that the most loving heart of a father could desire : she united to the gifts of nature the most angelic piety, and was a living picture of her mother, beautiful and tall, though delicate in health. Gifted with an intelligence beyond her years, she enchanted all who approached her by the nobleness of her mind and her candid graces.

Her father loved her, but with the affection of a Christian parent. One day during a visit to Paris, Henrietta showed all at once a desire for those worldly spectacles she saw there, and expressed her regret at having been hitherto deprived of them. It had been in that pious heart only a passing cloud, but the watchful eye of the father had perceived it, and he became afraid.

" My God," said he in his prayer, " if Thou fore-seest that she should one day wander from the right path, I consent that Thou shouldst take her, rather than see her abandon herself to the vanities of the world."

It seemed as though God had accepted this heroic offering, made with the faith of Abraham, for shortly afterwards the young lady was suddenly seized with typhoid fever, which neither the tender attention of those who nursed her, nor the skill of physicians was able to master. In five days she died.

During these days of agony Mr. Dupont showed himself the generous and faithful Christian ; he offered anew his daughter to God, liking better to give her to Him than see her exposed to the dangers of the world. When all hope of her recovery had vanished, he prepared her himself for her passage into eternity, exhorting her to the last moment, speaking to her of Heaven with a pious enthusiasm, making her the bearer, by a kind of paternal authority before God, of his orders and recommendations in the name of his friends, and of the persons of his household.

Dr. Bretonneau, who had attended her during her illness was present when she breathed her last. Her father, turning towards him with a celestial expression on his countenance which no earthly words could describe, said : " Doctor, my daughter has just seen God," and he recited the *Magnificat.*

Ave Maria, xiii. 105.

" BECAUSE I SAW MY MOTHER DO IT."

It was from his pious mother that St. Aloysius learned to pronounce the holy Names of Jesus and Mary as soon as he was able to speak, and to make the sign of the Cross.

When he was about five years old he was often
to be seen kneeling in some lonely place in his
father's house saying his prayers with great devotion.
And when he was asked why he did this, he used to
answer : " Because I saw my mother do it."

He loved the most holy Mother of God very
tenderly, and was accustomed to say special prayers
in her honour every morning and evening, and often
during the day.   He also would often speak to
others about her, and reverenced the holy images
and pictures that represented her ; but above all
things else he always tried to do that which he
thought would please her most.

St. Aloysius became a great Saint ; but under
God he owed his sanctity to the beautiful example
and exhortations of his pious mother.

From his Life.

THE GOOD MOTHER.

Mrs. Vianney, the mother of the venerable Curé
of Ars, always kept before her mind that her children
belonged to God more than to herself, and that they
were all His children'; hence she taught them from
their very infancy how to love and serve Him, their
Heavenly Father.

Every morning she herself went to the room where
they slept to awaken them, that she might see that
they offered their hearts to God, and be sure that
the first thought and the first action of the day were
for Him.

" You were very happy " said one of his friends
to him, in after-years, " to have had so early a love
of prayer."

He answered · " After God, it was the work of my dear mother ; she was so good. Virtue passes from the heart of a mother to the hearts of her children, who do willingly what they see her do."

Life of Blessed John B. Vianney.

" MY MOTHER, I ALSO WANT TO BECOME A SAINT."

The mother of St. Francis of Sales endeavoured to infuse into the young soul of her son a true and solid piety which would manifest itself by good works.

Whenever she went to the church, or went forth to visit the poor and the sick, she took care that the little boy Francis should always accompany her. It was in this way he learned to love both God and man.

When she read to him the lives of the Saints, which she did every day, she always pointed out to him the way in which he, young as he was, could imitate them.

Often as she was reading to him about them, and telling him how faithfully and courageously they served God, he would say to her : " My mother, I also want to be a Saint." It was on hearing these words so often fall from his lips that her maternal heart became full of tender emotion, and she would answer him : " My dear child, if you sincerely desire to be a Saint, God will give you the grace necessary to become one." *Life of St. Francis of Sales.*

THE MOTHER OF ST. CLAIR, ABBOT.

The mother of St. Clair was very pious. She had **no other child but himself, and she resolved to spend** her whole life in bringing him up a child of God, for she knew that God had entrusted him to her care for this end only.

And knowing the effect of good example, especially in a mother, she not only taught him by her words but also by her actions. She used every day to visit the church of the district in which she lived, and always took her little boy with her, even when he was too young to understand what prayer meant. But as he saw her kneel down and join her hands together, he learned to do the same, and as he became older he would say with devotion the little prayers she had taught him. Thus prayer grew in his young heart as he grew in age, and when he reached the years of manhood, and when his mother was taken away from him to receive the reward of her labours in Heaven, he was already a great Saint. After many years of labour, he himself died the death of the Saints, and went to enjoy in Heaven the eternal reward of the Saints in company with his mother, who had first taught him to love God by word and example.

Would that every Christian mother would remember the great influence her example has upon her children for good or for evil, that she may for ever keep before her mind the importance of always following up her instruction by her good conduct.

Lives of the Saints.

MARSHAL SUCHET.

The great Marshal Suchet one day went into the Church of Our Lady at Lyons. His name at that time was a household word among the French people. When the people in the church saw him coming in, they eagerly made way for him to pass.

Going up to one of the priests of the church, he said to him · " Reverend Father, when I was a very little child, my good and pious mother used to bring me into this church, and to lead me to Our Lady's altar, where she made me kneel and pray. I used to join my hands together, and look up into the face of the holy image, and pray with great fervour. Ah, these were happy days ! the memory of them is very dear to me ; I have never forgotten them."

After giving the good Father an alms, that he might offer up the holy sacrifice for his intention, he went over to the altar, and, humbly kneeling where he had so often knelt when he was a child, prayed for a long time with edifying fervour.

III. Parents must Instruct their Children.

Parents must not confine themselves to the giving of good example to their little ones ; they must also teach them by their words how to please God and fulfil their duties towards Him.

" yves, you must be a saint."

There lived about the middle of the thirteenth century, in the little village of Kermartin, in Brittany, two pious Christians, Helor and Azoua, his wife. God blessed their union by giving them a son, whom they called Yves, and whom they resolved to bring up in piety and the knowledge of God's holy law. The mother especially watched over him day by day with **religious care, and from the first moment that he** was capable of learning anything, she ceased not to say to him, over and over again, these words · " Yves, you must be a Saint."

The child, hearing these words so often, said to her one day : " Mother, what is a Saint ?"

" A Saint, my child, is one whom God has made to be for ever with Himself in Heaven. A Saint is one who loves God above all things, and His Son Jesus Christ ; one who keeps all the commandments of God, and who is willing to bear his cross in this world, that he may be with Jesus Christ in Heaven."

The child used to listen to these lessons of his mother with his hands joined and his eyes fixed on hers, as if drinking in every word she said, and when she had ended, he used to say to her : " My mother, I must be a Saint ; I will love God with my whole heart, and all my lifetime I will try to please Him."

His father's lessons were also full of heavenly wisdom : " My child, your mother has taught you how to love God ; I will teach you how to love your neighbour for God's sake." And he would take his little boy with him in his missioms of charity towards his neighbour, and show him those outward deeds of virtue that mark the Christian before men, and make him glorify his Father, Who is in Heaven. And thus the holy child grew up a Saint.

But the time came when he had to leave his father's house, and could no longer be under the watchful eyes of his mother. He was sent to Paris to one of the great schools there, to cultivate those talents which he had received from God.

In that city he was surrounded by those who thought only of gratifying their evil inclinations, and who forgot that God made them for the eternal joys of Heaven. In the midst of all these temptations and dangers the young Yves remained pure as an angel. He made use of those arms which God has placed in the hands of every Christian, and which make him invincible if he only makes use of them— viz., prayer, vigilance, and going frequently to the holy Sacraments. Those words he used to hear so often from the lips of his good mother also sustained him in the combat : " Yves, my child, you must be a Saint."

When his studies had come to an end, he left the college as pure as when he had entered it, his soul adorned with virtues and merits, and his mind full of knowledge both secular and religious.

It was a joyful day for his parents when he returned to them ; they began already to reap the harvest of the good seed they had so carefully sown in his tender soul when an infant at their feet.

It is not necessary here to follow the career of this youthful Saint ; it continued and ended as it had begun, and he died, after a long and happy life, renowned and beloved. Whenever anyone spoke to him of the holy life he led, and of the great virtues of which he gave so beautiful an example, he used always to answer : " If there is any good in me, I owe it all to my mother's exhortations and to my father's holy words ; from the first moment that I was capable of knowing anything, my mother used to say to me: 'Yves, you must be a Saint.' These words have been for me my safety in dangers, my courage in trials, and the guiding star of my whole life."

God grant that every parent who may hear these

16—2

words may repeat them over and over again to their little ones, that they one day may become Saints in Heaven along with Saint Yves. *From his Life.*

THE BABY WHO COULD SAY HIS CATECHISM.

A little boy was one day sitting by the roadside amusing himself while his mother was working in an adjoining field.

A priest who was walking along the road saw the child. Something in the eyes of the boy attracted his attention, and he stopped to speak to him.

" Can you make the sign of the Cross, my child ?" said the priest in a kind voice.

The child looked up into his face and smiled, but did not answer him ; just as if he would have said : " Is that all you think I can do ?"

The mother, who was near enough to hear the question which the priest had asked, came forward and said : " Reverend Father, he knows much more than that ; be pleased to ask him some of the easier questions of the Catechism, and you will see that he is already able to answer them very well."

The priest then asked him such questions as these : " Who made you ?" " Why were you made ?" " Who is God ?" " Who is Jesus Christ ?" The child answered them all correctly, without the least hesitation, so that the good Father was astonished at the answers he gave—answers which his little lips could scarcely pronounce.

" How old is your child ?" said he, addressing the mother.

" He will soon be three years old," she replied.

" Only three years old ! and he knows so much

already ! How have you been able to teach so young an infant so many things ? Why, he can scarcely say the words as yet, and he knows the answers as correctly, and even more so, than many grown-up persons who think themselves so learned."

" Father," she replied, " it was very easily done, and, if you please, I will tell you how I did it. You have often told us in your sermons that it is our duty as parents to instruct our children, and to tell them who God is, and their duties towards Him. Well, I knew that the sooner I began the easier it would be for me to fulfil it. So when he was quite an infant at the breast, and now, when he sits on my knee, or stands by my side, or when I dress him and give him his food, I say over and over again these questions and answers ; and it is because he hears me saying them so often that he himself tries to say them, and by frequently saying them along with me, he has come to know them."

" Ah, my good woman," said the priest, " your reward for this will be very great in Heaven. The duty which you are so carefully fulfilling is one very often neglected, and the consequence is that the age of childhood passes by without the child being taught these truths. These early lessons which you are giving your little one cannot fail to bring forth fruit in due season ; and although he may not at present understand them, the day will soon come, if God spares him, when he will be able to do so, and I am sure he will all his life-time thank God for having given him so good a mother. May God bless you both !" And the priest continued on **his way.** *Catéchisme de Persévérance.*

IV. Parents must themselves be Pious.

True Christian piety flows from the hearts of the father and the mother into that of the child. Christian parents must themselves be truly pious, if they desire to see their little ones grow up in piety.

" do not deny jesus christ."

St. Leonidas was in prison for the Faith. He had gloriously confessed Jesus Christ before the judge, and was condemned to die.

He had a large family, but he loved his eldest son Origen more than the rest of his children. The thought of leaving this dear child, who was only fourteen years old, was a terrible one to his loving heart.

Origen, fearing that his love for him might make his father waver, and perhaps even deny his Faith that he might be spared to him, wrote him the following letter : " O my father, I on my knees beseech you to remain constant to the end. Let not your tender affection for me ever make you deny Jesus Christ. I will fill your place with my mother and my six brothers, and if you have the happiness of dying for the sake of Jesus Christ, oh, I shall very willingly beg from door to door for bread to support them ! But oh, my father, I again beg of you, do not deny Jesus Christ."

Life of Origen.

O Christian parents, train up your children from their very infancy in the knowledge of God and of their holy Faith, and, like the little Origen, when they grow up, and when the time of trial comes, the good seed you have sown in their young breasts will bring forth its fruit.

" MOTHER, I AM SO THIRSTY."

A little boy, only seven years old, went up to Asclepiades, the governor of the city in which he lived, and told him boldly that he was a Christian.

The governor did not for some time pay any heed to the boy, seeing that he was so young ; but the child continued to say : " I am a Christian ; I believe in God the Father Almighty, Creator of Heaven and Earth, and in Jesus Christ, His only Son Our Lord."

The judge at last grew impatient, and, sending for the boy's mother, ordered him to be severely scourged in her presence.

The men did as they were ordered, and tore his little body in such a cruel way that the blood ran down from his wounds upon the ground. Tears filled the eyes of the people who came together to see what was going on, and they asked the mother to tell her child to renounce his Faith, that they might cease to beat him.

But that holy mother said : " No, he is suffering for the cause of God, Who gave him to me, and I would not lift up my finger even to keep him back when God calls him to suffer for His sake."

" O mother, mother !" cried the child, in accents which must have pierced her very heart — " O mother, I am so thirsty !"

But his heroic mother answered : " Patience, dearest, patience, and in a few moments you will reach the Fountain of Life, Jesus Christ Himself,

Who will give you to drink of that living water which is in Heaven, and you will never thirst again."

The pagans who heard these words and saw the sufferings of the child were filled with admiration, and the governor, fearing that a tumult might arise, gave orders that the boy's head should at once be cut off.

Then his mother ran up to him, and, taking him into her arms, pressed him once more to her bosom, and lovingly kissed him. " O my own boy, farewell ; we shall meet again in Heaven."

When she said these words, she handed him back again joyfully to the cruel executioners, saying to them · " Take him and do your worst with him, for he is not afraid to die, since death will open for him the Kingdom of Heaven. Precious in the sight of the Lord is the death of His Saints."

They very soon beheaded him, and he ended his innocent life on earth to begin an eternal life of joy in Paradise. PRUDENTIUS : *Corona Martyrum.*

V. CHILDREN A GIFT GIVEN TO PARENTS BY GOD.

A pious father and mother will not fail to receive their children as a gift from the hands of God, and will take care to consecrate them to God from the day of their birth, and will train them up in the fear of God.

ST. ELIZABETH AND HER INFANT CHILDREN.

In the life of St. Elizabeth of Hungary we read that as soon as she was able to go out, after the birth of her children, she took her new-born infant in her arms, went out secretly from the castle, clad in a plain woollen robe and barefooted, and directed her steps towards the Church of St. Catherine, outside the walls of Eisenach.

When she arrived at the church, she laid her child upon the altar, with a lighted taper and a lamb, saying : " Lord Jesus Christ, to you and to your dear mother Mary I offer this cherished fruit of my womb. Behold, my Lord and my God, I give it with all my heart, such as Thou hast given it to me— to Thee Who art the Sovereign and the most loving Father of the child and the mother. The only prayer I make Thee to-day, and the only grace I dare to request, is that it may please Thee to receive this little child, all bathed in my tears, into the number of Thy servants and Thy friends, and to give it Thy holy benediction."

MONTALEMBERT : *Life of St. Elizabeth of Hungary.*

THE MOTHER OF ST. ALOYSIUS.

There was great joy in the Castle of Castiglione on March 9, 1568, for on that day was born to its noble lord, Don Ferrante di Gonzaga, a son and heir to his vast domains.

Donna Marta, his mother, had often asked God to give her a son, who might serve Him perfectly on earth, and one day be a Saint in Heaven. She had now received an answer to the first part of her prayer; the second was also in due time to be granted.

The little boy was baptized as soon as he was born, and received the name of Aloysius. When his mother took him into her arms immediately after his baptism, she made over him the sign of the Cross, and placed him under the protection of the Immaculate Mother of God, that he might be her child for ever.   From that moment she looked on him as a little angel confided by God to her care.   Every day she used to bend over him as he lay in his cradle and whisper into his ear the holy names of Jesus and Mary; then, taking his infant hand within her own, she would sign him with the sign of the Cross.

Great was her joy one day, as she was thus bending over him, to see him smile on her as he looked up into her face, and to hear him utter the holy names that she had so often whispered to him.   They were his first words.   *Life of St. Aloysius.*

VI. Parents and their Children Leaving Home.

There is a time in particular that should be for every parent one of great anxiety—namely, the time when the child has to leave home to live among strangers.   That should be a time of more than usual fervent prayer, and of special instruction.

A mother's parting advice.

A pious mother who had brought up her son with great care, seeing him about to leave her to enter the world, in order that he might earn for himself a livelihood, desired to give him a lesson which he might never forget.   For two days before the time of his departure, she gave him nothing to eat but sweet food and other dainties.   At first the young man was pleased with it, and thought that his mother had given it to him as a mark of her affection, since he was so soon to be separated from her. But when the evening of the first day had come, he asked her to give him some solid food, as he had already begun to become dissatisfied with the sweet food she had given him. But she told him that he must be content with what she had placed before him.

The next day, as he received the same kind of food, he became so disgusted with it that he could not even look at it, and he begged his mother not to allow him to perish with hunger, but to give him some plain bread.

His mother said to him · " My dear child, I had a special object in placing before you all these sweet and dainty dishes. You are about to leave me to enter a world that is full of wickedness. It will put before your eyes many things which at first sight appear pleasing enough—glory, honour, riches, and pleasures. They dazzle the eye, but they can never satisfy the heart. They may be very pleasant for a moment, but they bring along with them in their train only remorse and unhappiness.

" O my child," she continued, " do not allow yourself to be deceived by them. Yesterday I saw with what avidity you at first ate the sweet pastry I had prepared for you. To-day, on the contrary, you are filled with disgust at even the very look of it. So is it with those who allow themselves to be deceived when they first enter the world. They so often fly at once to its pleasures, which very soon bring them much bitterness. Be warned, therefore, in time, my child, and as soon as you are tempted by these things of which I have spoken to you, thrust them aside, and be content with the plain food of a

Christian—that is, bearing patiently with all your crosses here on earth, that you may obtain an eternal reward in Heaven."

Lettres Édif.

VII. PARENTS AND THE DEATH OF THEIR LITTLE ONES.

When God calls any of your little ones to Himself, what a happiness it is for them, and what a consolation it is for yourself, if you have brought them up in the fear and love of God! There is no joy in this world that can in any way be compared to it.

ST. BRIDGET'S DAUGHTER.

One of the daughters of St. Bridget became a nun in the convent of Risaberg, and died there a holy death. When the messenger came to Bridget to tell her that her daughter was dead, instead of being plunged into grief, she broke forth into hymns of praise, saying : " O my Lord Jesus Christ ! O my Love ! Be Thou blessed for ever, because Thou hast been pleased to call my beloved child to Thyself in Heaven before she was hurt by the sins of the world."

Then, rising up, she went to the church, where, falling on her knees before the altar, she began to weep and to sigh so loudly that many who were in the church heard her, and said to each other : " See how that woman is weeping for her daughter who is dead."

At the same time Jesus appeared to her and said : " Woman, why weepest thou ?"

" O my Lord, I weep, not because my beloved daughter is dead, but because I did not teach her sufficiently to obey Thy commandments, and because I did not give her so good an example as I ought, and did not correct her faults."

Jesus answered : " A mother who weeps for her daughter's faults, and who has done her best to teach her how to please Me, is a true mother and worthy of the name of mother ; and the daughter of such a mother is truly the child of God. But the mother who takes pleasure in seeing her child live and act as those do who live for the world, and not for God, and who is careless in teaching her child to be pious, but seeks to make her appear great in the eyes of the world, is not that child's true mother. Therefore, on account of your love for Me, and your great anxiety concerning her, your daughter has, after a short life, gone to receive the crown of glory in Heaven."

Life of St. Bridget.

VIII. PARENTS MUST PRAY FOR THEIR CHILDREN.

THE POWER OF A MOTHER'S PRAYERS AND TEARS WITH GOD.

Fathers and mothers, pray for the children God has given you, and you will save their souls.

St. Augustine was born in the year 354, in the little town of Tagaste, in Algeria.

His mother, St. Monica, brought him up in the fear of God ; but he was carried away by the passions of youth in the pursuit of the pleasures of life, and with an insatiable desire for the acquisition of science.

At twenty-eight years of age he had already acquired all the learning which at that time could be gained, and was considered by his masters to be the first among their pupils. He lived in the world as other young men of his condition lived, and when at times the voice of God spoke to him in his heart, and urged him to lead a life more worthy of a man and a Christian, he would for a time try to do better, and even prayed to God to raise him up from the gulf of sin into which he had fallen, and to create within him a pure heart. But, overcome by the thought of the austere life this would involve, he had not the courage to embrace it, and would say to God · " Yes ; but later on, later on."

In the meantime St. Monica, who had given him his temporal life, wished to procure for him a much greater blessing — his life with God in eternity. Augustine turned a deaf ear to his mother's entreaties, and in order to escape from her further admonitions, he resolved to join the heresy of the Manicheans.

From that time forward the mother and the son avoided all reference to religion in their intercourse with one another—Augustine, through respect for his mother, whom he loved and revered, and Monica, on her part, because she expected a better result from fervent prayer than from frequent controversy.

" During that sad time when I was walking in the mire of my evil ways, and among the weeds of heresy," afterwards wrote St. Augustine, " that pious and chaste widow, full of hope, and assiduous in her prayers and tears, ceased not to implore Thy mercy in my behalf. And, O my God, Thou wert graciously pleased to listen to her, although as yet the hour had not come for dispelling the darkness with which I was then enveloped."

But if his saintly mother in her humility refrained from all discussion on her own part, she endeavoured to find pious and learned men whom she eagerly besought to use their influence and their learning to bring him into nobler and religious sentiments.

One day in particular she learned that there had come to Tagaste a venerable and holy Bishop, whose name has not reached us. He was esteemed above all for his eminent piety, and for his knowledge of the Christian dogmas and the holy Scriptures; moreover, before his admission into the Catholic Church he had professed Manicheism.

Monica hastened to visit him, and besought him to come to the aid of her son, and lead him to the true Faith. But the venerable Bishop, whose knowledge of the guidance of souls was even greater than his secular attainments, answered, while shaking his head, that the time had not yet come : that her son had been too recently associated with this sect to change so soon his religion because of the pride and presumption for which it was noted. " Leave him alone in the meantime," he said ; " only pray for him, and pray much."

But these words did not satisfy the saintly woman. She continued to weep and implore of the man of God to go and speak to him, and urge him to return to God by the profession of the true Faith.

" Go, go, then !" said the Bishop, moved also to tears, " for it is impossible that the son of so many tears can perish."

These words calmed her heart. She considered that it was God Himself Who had spoken by his mouth. They brought consolation to her heart, as they have in all times since brought consolation to the hearts of so many mothers who have wept and prayed for their erring children.

This prediction was in a short time accomplished. Augustine abjured his errors, became a great doctor of the Church and a Saint.

L'Apostolat de la Prière, p. 43.

IX. Parents must Keep a Watch over their Children.

Another duty of Christian parents is to watch over their children, that they may not be led into temptation. The following example is taken from the writings of a holy and learned priest, and will show parents the necessity of watching carefully that they keep away from their children's sight everything that might lead them into evil or teach it to them.

THE SECRET DANGER.

There lived a short time ago a good and wealthy gentleman who had a son who gave early promise of a life of piety. His father, seeing these good dispositions in his child, did everything in his power to foster them, and he had the happiness of seeing the boy grow up a model of every virtue, so that he was the consolation of his parents, and joy of his companions as well as an example for them.

Fifteen years of his life had passed by in this. manner, when suddenly, without any apparent cause, a terrible change came over him. He became sullen and sad ; he shunned the company of his former companions, and even when at home with his parents, he seemed without life, scarcely ever spoke to them, and always kept his eyes on the ground.

This sudden change from joyous gaiety to sadness, from an ever open and pleasant countenance to one of dull despondency, alarmed his father. He thought that perhaps some malady had taken hold of him, and sent for a physician, who, having carefully examined him, declared that he could not discover any disease.

His father then began to fear lest some evil temptation had found its way into his soul, so he went to the priest, and told him what he had observed. This holy man, who had much experience in the conduct of souls, and knowing that those who are the holiest are the ones whom Satan attacks with greatest fury, saw in the conduct of the boy a sign that the devil had succeeded in robbing him of his peace of mind by making him fall into some sin, or at least, as is frequently the case, in making him think that he had done so. So he resolved to visit him.

When the priest entered, Henry's eyes fell on the ground, and he would have rushed out of the room had it been possible for him to escape. The priest spoke to him in that gentle, familiar tone which had been hitherto the joy of Henry every time he met him. But the only response to his kind words was a deep blush on his cheek and a rigid silence. The priest continued to speak to him in the affectionate **tones of a father, and was not long in seeing some-**

thing like a tear glistening in his eye. At length it burst forth, and Henry was next instant in the arms of the good priest, weeping and sobbing as if his heart would break.

" Oh," he said, " I am the most unhappy wretch that ever was born. I have fallen into terrible sins. Come, Father, I will show you what has been the cause of my fall." And he at once led him into his father's room, where there was a great number of books arranged on shelves. One of these he took down, and handing it to the priest, said to him · " That book has been the cause of all the evil that has befallen me."

The priest looked at the book, and saw that it was one of those bad, irreligious books that even then were beginning to be spread about by the agents of Satan, and which are to be met with so frequently at the present day.

When the priest showed the book to the father of the boy, he was filled with amazement. The book had been sent to him by a friend, but as he was too busily occupied with his affairs to look at it, much less to read it, he placed it on one of the shelves of his bookcase till he would have more leisure to do so, and then forgot all about it. In the meantime Henry, seeing this new book there, had the curiosity to read it, and the reading of it was the cause of the terrible misfortune we have just recorded.

But thanks be to God, the evil was detected in time. By the care of the priest the seeds of evil were rooted out of the young man's soul. By a good Confession he blotted out the evil he had done, and with peace of conscience came also his former joy as well as his natural gaiety. But as he grew up to manhood, there was a seriousness in his conduct which those who knew him attributed to what had occurred to him in his boyish years.

X. Parents must Correct their Children.

To correct their children is one of the chief obligations God has placed upon parents. " O parents," writes a pious author, " if you love your children for God, be careful to reprimand them when they do wrong, and correct them. Sometimes it may be necessary, especially in their earlier years, to chastise them, that they may be turned from their evil ways. Oh, how terrible have been, for parents as well as for children, the punishments God has sent for this neglect !"

THE AWFUL PUNISHMENT OF HELI.

" Now the child Samuel ministered to the Lord before Heli, and the word of the Lord was precious in those days ; there was no manifest vision.

" And it came to pass one day when Heli lay in his place, and his eyes were grown dim, that he could not see ; before the lamp of God went out Samuel slept in the temple of the Lord, where the ark of God was.

" And the Lord called Samuel. And he answered : ' Here am I.' And he ran to Heli and said : ' Here am I : for thou didst call me.'

" And he said : ' I did not call : go back and sleep.' And he went back and slept.

" And the Lord called Samuel again. And

17—2

Samuel arose and went to Heli, and said : ' Here am I : for thou calledst me.'

" He answered : ' I did not call thee, my son : return and sleep.'

" Now Samuel did not yet know the Lord, neither had the word of the Lord been revealed to him. And the Lord called Samuel again the third time. And he arose and went to Heli, and said : ' Here am I : for thou didst call me.'

" Then Heli understood that the Lord called the child, and he said to Samuel : ' Go and sleep ; and if He shall call thee any more, thou shalt say : ' Speak, Lord, for Thy servant heareth.' So Samuel went and slept in his place.

" And the Lord came and stood : and He called as He had called the other times : ' Samuel, Samuel.'

" And Samuel said : ' Speak, Lord, for Thy servant heareth.'

" And the Lord said to Samuel : ' Behold I do a thing in Israel ; and whosoever.shall hear it, both his ears shall tingle. And in that day I will raise up against Heli all the things I have spoken concerning his house : I will begin, and I will make an end. For I have foretold unto him that I will judge his house for ever, for iniquity, because he knew that his sons did wickedly, and did not chastise them. Therefore I have sworn to the house of Heli, that the iniquity of his house shall not be expiated with victims nor offerings for ever.'

" So Samuel told him all the words, and did not hide them from him.

" And he answered : ' It is the Lord : let Him do what is good in His sight.' "   1 *Kings* iii.

XI. On Catholic Education.

THE NOBLE CONDUCT OF THE FLEMISH.

The proposal to introduce the godless school among the Flemish peasants was met with a protest as universal as it was vigorous. Certainly the time has not come when irreligious education may be expected to find favour in Flanders, and the Flemings understand that the root of society is in tl e child. Their protest as here given is a literal translation of the document they drew up :

" No, they shall never ga'n possession of the beautiful souls of our children, so long as there is one true Fleming in Flanders ; they shall not have them whilst God's sun shines over our country, and there is a single copper left in our purses.

" The school is a battle-field. They seek to snatch from the Church of God the souls of the little ones. We Flemish Catholics will never tolerate such a sacrilege. The blood of those heroes, who gave their lives in defence of the Faith, yet flows in our veins.

" We do not want Flanders to become a den of thieves ; what we do want is that our children, faithful to God and to His Church, be not changed into victims for the scaffold, and into nails to fasten down the lids of our coffins.

" We are ready to die if necessary, but we never will consent to lose our Faith. Till our last breath— till we have one foot in the grave—we will continue to cry out : ' Never shall our children go to a school in which the crucifix cannot occupy the place of honour.' "

THE DYING WIDOW.

The obedient and pious child is the joy of his parents and the support of their old age ; but for the most part this consolation is a recompense which good parents have merited for themselves by bestowing on their children a truly Christian education.

Not many years ago, in the city of Louvain, there was a widow, the mother of five children.   Old age had come upon her after a life spent in piety and the accomplishment of the will of God in the state of life to which He had called her, and she lay on her death-bed.   Two of her sons were priests, and two others occupied honourable positions in the world, whilst the fifth, a daughter, was remarkable for her Christian modesty even more than for the excellent endowments nature had lavished upon her.

Her sons came frequently to visit her, and her daughter never left her bedside, but attended to her with the most affectionate care.

It happened that a certain religious came to pay her a visit to offer her some consolation in her infirmity.   He was led into her room by her daughter, who immediately respectfully retired.

The religious, seeing her weighed down by the pressure of her malady, asked her if she was suffering much pain or weariness.

" My Father," she replied, " how could I feel weary or complain of the infirmity under which I labour ?   My children take away from me all sense of suffering by their filial attention, and I have always an angel at my side."

This angel who thus ministered unto her and

sweetened all her sorrows was her daughter, whose filial love, in the eyes of the mother, appeared to be something begotten of Heaven.

This happy mother, in the evening of her life, reaped the reward of her labours even while on earth. She had brought up the children God had confided to her with tender solicitude, careful, above all things, to give them a Christian education, and she died happily, because she saw her labour had not been in vain. *Schouppe*, ii. 482.

XII. Parents and Vocation to a Religious Life.

Whatever interest a father may have in seeing his child advancing in the world and pursuing an honourable calling, he cannot, without being wanting in his duty to God, complain when He calls any one of his offspring to a higher and holier life. To resist such a call would be an act of rebellion against God, and be productive of many temporal and spiritual evils to himself and his child.

STORY RELATED BY ST. AMBROSE.

St. Ambrose relates to us an admirable example on this subject. There lived in his time a young Christian lady who had to sustain a severe combat raised up against her, not, indeed, by the persecutors of the Faith, but by those who were of her own flesh **and blood.**

She was, on the one hand, frequently urged by them to engage in a temporal alliance with one **in** every way suited to her virtue and position, while on the other she felt within her a strong call from God to consecrate her virginity to Him.

" What are you doing ?" she said to her many relatives who continually pressed her to accept the hand of him they had chosen for her acceptance ; " and why do you take so much pains to try to force me to enter that course of life ? I am already well provided for. You offer me a certain person to be my spouse ; I have chosen another.

" Choose one for me who is as rich and powerful as the one whom I have chosen, then I will see what answer I will make you. But you could not find anyone to compare with mine ; for the one you have offered me is only a man, whereas the One I have chosen is God. Will you, then, take me from Him, or will you take Him from me ?"

These words, continues St. Ambrose, had a visible effect on all who heard them. They all shed many tears at beholding a virtue so firm and so rare in a person of her age and accomplishments. One only amongst them raised her voice and said : " If your father had lived to see this day, he would never have given his consent to your adopting the course you now intend to pursue."

" Ah !" she replied, " no doubt it was because of this very thing that God in His goodness has taken him to Himself before this day, so that he might not become an obstacle to the orders of Heaven, and the designs of Providence upon me."

St. Ambrose de Virginibus.

ST. ALOYSIUS OVERCOMES HIS FATHER'S RESISTANCE.

From his very childhood St. Aloysius desired to belong to God alone, to live for God alone, and as he grew up he felt within his soul a call from God to enter the Society of Jesus.

His father, on the contrary, though pious, and in every way worthy of being the father of a Saint, had already formed other designs regarding him. He looked upon him as one who in the world would bring honour to his house, and although he saw that the boy's thoughts were fixed on the religious life, he hoped, by causing delays and bringing him in contact with the world, that they would gradually change, and that he would live with him to be the consolation and joy of his old age.

In this he was disappointed. These delays only served to confirm the resolution of the pious youth, and his mingling with the world made him only the more despise all temporal advantages.

One day his father, the Marquis de Châtillon, said to him in a tone of authority he had never before assumed, that he had greatly deceived himself if he even for a moment had thought that he would ever consent to the execution of the project he had entertained, and that he must not imagine that he would even agree to consider the matter until he had attained his twenty-fifth year.

This declaration fell upon Aloysius like a thunderbolt ; yet he resolved to be patient, and to submit to it for a time, resigning himself into the hands of **God.**

But a few days afterwards he was inspired to

make a new attempt to gain his consent. The Marquis was confined to bed, suffering from a painful infirmity to which he was subject.

Aloysius, entering the room, sat down at his bedside, and in a tone of great respect, but accompanied with a firmness which was unusual with him, said : " I have come, my lord and father, to tell you that I will ever be submissive to your commands. Dispose of me as seems best to you ; but I assure you that God has most certainly called me to enter the Order of religion I have chosen, and that in opposing my design you resist His Holy Will."

Having said these words, he rose up and took his departure, leaving his father buried in profound thought and weeping. Grace triumphed in the end, and sending for his son, he said to him ·

" My child, you have inflicted on my heart a wound which time can never heal. My son, I love you, and you deserve my love. I had founded on you all the hopes of my family, but now, since you assure me that God calls you elsewhere, go, my son, go whither He calls you ; I will not stand in your path. May God bestow on you every happiness."

Aloysius, not to add to the desolation of his beloved father, immediately retired to his room, where on his knees before the crucifix, he poured out his soul in acts of thanksgiving.

Les Écoliers Vertueux.

XXXII

THE FIFTH COMMANDMENT

I " Thou shalt not Kill."

The Fifth Commandment is : " Thou shalt not kill." God alone is the master of life and death, my child. By this commandment He forbids us to take away the life of our neighbour, and even the desire of doing so. He also by it forbids us to do anything that might injure our neighbour in soul or body, such as hatred and revenge, anger, striking, quarrelling, and injurious words. Lastly, and in a particular manner, we are forbidden to give scandal and bad example.

In the first place it forbids wilful murder, a crime which always brings down the vengeance of God upon the murderer.

CAIN AND ABEL.

Cain was the first murderer. He steeped his hands in the blood of his brother Abel, and drew down on himself and his offspring the terrible maledictions of God.

" And it came to pass," says the Scripture, " after many days, that Cain offered of the fruits of the earth gifts to the Lord. Abel also offered of the firstlings of his flock, and of their fat : and the Lord had respect to Abel, and to his offerings. But to Cain and his offerings He had no respect : and Cain was exceedingly angry, and his countenance fell.

"And the Lord said to him : 'Why art thou angry ? and why is thy countenance fallen ? If thou do well, shalt thou not receive ? but if ill, shall not sin forthwith be present at the door ? but the lust thereof shall be under thee, and thou shalt have dominion over it.'

"And Cain said to his brother : 'Let us go abroad.'

"And when they were in the field, Cain rose up against his brother Abel, and slew him.

"And the Lord said to Cain : 'Where is thy brother Abel ?'

"And he answered : 'I know not : am I my brother's keeper ?'

"And He said to him : 'What hast thou done ? The voice of thy brother's blood crieth to Me from the earth. Now, therefore, cursed shalt thou be upon the earth which hath opened her mouth and received the blood of thy brother at thy hand. When thou shalt till it, it shall not yield to thee its fruit : a fugitive and a vagabond shalt thou be upon the earth.'

"And Cain said to the Lord : 'My iniquity is greater than that I may deserve pardon. . . .'

"And Cain went out from the face of the Lord, and dwelt as a fugitive on the earth at the east side of Eden."

Genesis iv.

ST. MEINRAD OF SUABIA.

St. Meinrad was the son of a rich man of Suabia, in Germany. When he was very young, he left his father's castle, and went into a solitary place that he might live alone with God. During the night he was often found reading the Holy Scriptures, for he had received from his father an old copy of that holy book, which had come down to him from his ancestors. Often, too, did he meditate on the virtues and the goodness of the Immaculate Mother of God, for whom he always had a childlike affection. He made his religious vows in the Abbey of Reichenau, and after spending some time there, he returned to his beloved solitude. This time he took up his abode in a little hermitage on the summit of Mount Etzel, where he spent seven years.

During that time the odour of his virtues had spread throughout the whole of that country, and his little hermitage soon became a place of pilgrimage. At first shepherds and woodcutters came to him, then lords and noble ladies, and at last great multitudes of all classes of the people.

This homage of the world was a torment to one whose whole delight was to be alone, and to think only of God and of heavenly things. So one day he secretly left his solitude, taking nothing with him but a statue of Our Blessed Lady, which was the only ornament of his little chapel. He went into one of the thick forests of Switzerland, known by the name of the Dark Forest, where he spent many peaceful and happy days unknown to the world, with God and His holy angels.

It happened that, after spending upwards of thirty years there, he was murdered by two robbers, with whom he had the charity to share the wild fruits of the forest and the waters of his little fountain.

But God did not permit this terrible crime to remain unpunished, though committed so far away from the abode of men, and sent two crows to pursue them. Wherever they went, those birds followed them, and gave them no repose, for they accompanied them through the forests and even into the cities. At length they went to Munich and took shelter in an inn, where they thought that the birds could not penetrate. But their pursuers reached them even there, and harassed them so much that the magistrates were informed of the strange event. Being convinced that they had done some evil, they arrested them and put them into prison. The ruffians then, seeing that they could not escape the anger of God in this life, confessed their crime, and were executed.

In memory of this event, which took place in the year 861, the Abbey of Reichenau, of whose community the saintly Meinrad had been a member, placed the figure of two crows on its seal.

Life of St. Meinrad, Jan. 21.

THE PUNISHMENT OF ACHAB.

The Sacred Scriptures record, in the Third Book of Kings, the murder committed by Achab, King of Israel, on the person of Naboth, and the terrible chastisements inflicted by God in consequence of it.

Elated by the victories he had gained over the King of Syria, and led astray by the pernicious counsels of Queen Jezabel, his wife, Achab was filled with the desire of beautifying his palace and displaying his royal magnificence.

One day, as he was walking in the gardens of Jezabel, he conceived the thought of enlarging them by joining to them a vineyard which was situated in close proximity to them. But this vineyard was the property of another, whose name was Naboth, an inheritance he had received from his forefathers.

Sending for him, the King thus spoke to him : " Give me thy vineyard, that I may make me a garden of herbs, because it is nigh and joining to my house, and I will give thee for it a better vineyard; or if thou think it more convenient for thee, I will give thee the worth of it in money."

Now the law of God did not permit the people of Israel to sell a paternal inheritance, but Achab paid little heed to the law of God, and imagined that Naboth would not dare to resist the wishes of the King. But in this he was mistaken, for Naboth said · " The Lord be merciful to me, and not let me give thee the inheritance of my fathers.

" And Achab came into his house angry and fretting, because of the word that Naboth had spoken to him, saying : ' I will not give thee the inheritance of my fathers.' And casting himself upon the bed, he turned away his face to the wall, and would eat no bread.

" And Jezabel his wife went in to him and said to him : ' What is the matter, that thy soul is so grieved, and why eatest thou no bread ? Thou art of great authority indeed, and governest well the kingdom of Israel ! Arise and eat bread, and be of good cheer. I will give thee the vineyard of Naboth.'

" So she wrote letters in Achab's name, and sealed them with his ring, and sent them to the ancients, and the chief men that were in the city, and that dwelt with Naboth. And this was the tenor of the letters : ' Proclaim a fast, and make Naboth sit among the chief of the people, and suborn two men, sons of Belial, against him, and let them bear false witness, that he hath blasphemed God and the King ; and then carry him out and stone him, and so let him die.'

" And the men of the city, the ancients and the nobles, that dwelt with him in the city did as Jezabel had commanded them, and as it was written in the letters which she had sent to them. . . . And they sent to Jezabel, saying : ' Naboth is stoned, and is dead.'

" And it came to pass when Jezabel heard that Naboth was stoned, and dead, that she said to Achab : ' Arise and take possession of the vineyard of Naboth the Jezrahelite, who would not agree with thee, and give it thee for money ; for Naboth is not alive, but dead.'

" And when Achab heard this, to wit, that Naboth was dead, he arose, and went down to the vineyard of Naboth the Jezrahelite, to take possession of it."

But God, Who was a witness of these deeds of cruelty and injustice, did not permit them to pass unpunished. He sent Elias the prophet to meet him as he went down to take possession of the property so unlawfully acquired.

" And," continues the Scripture, " thus shalt thou speak to him: ' Thus said the Lord: "Thou hast slain, and thou hast taken possession." ' And after these words thou shalt add : ' Thus said the Lord : " In this place, wherein the dogs have licked the blood of Naboth, they shall lick thy blood also. . . .'" And of Jezabel also the Lord spoke, saying : ' The dogs shall eat Jezabel in the field of Jezrahel. If Achab die in the city, the dogs shall eat him : but if he die in the field, the birds of the air shall eat him.' "

Such was the terrible sentence pronounced by God himself against these murderers, by which he showed how terrible in His eyes was the crime they committed. 3 *Kings* xxi.

Although murder is so terrible a crime in the sight of God, and punished with such terrible severity even in this world, there are occasions when it becomes lawful. If a person is attacked by another, he is justified in defending his life, even if in doing so he may take away that of his aggressor.

ST. FRANCIS OF SALES DEFENDS HIMSELF WHEN ATTACKED.

St. Francis of Sales, though one of the gentlest of the Saints of God, knew how to defend himself from the swords of his enemies in the day of danger.

During his residence in Padua, whither his father had sent him to pursue his studies, it happened that certain young men, who seemed to live for no other purpose but to gratify their evil passions, were offended at his humility and meekness, which were a condemnation of their own sinful ways, and which they chose to attribute to cowardice and effeminacy. In their wicked hearts they formed the design of waylaying him, and giving him a severe chastisement, more to inspire him with fear than to do him any bodily injury.

To accomplish their design, they one day, towards evening, took up their position in a thicket near which the saintly youth had to pass on his return to the house wherein he lodged. They, knowing his habitual gentleness, imagined that he would offer them no resistance, and that, after having beaten him severely, they would be able, by running speedily away, to make their escape without being recognized.

But in this they deceived themselves, for they had forgotten, or perhaps were not aware, that the virtue of religion which teaches meekness and humility of heart inspires also courage and intrepidity in the hour of need.

When Francis had reached the spot where his assailants were waiting, they rushed out to attack him unawares, and began by trying to raise a quarrel without any cause ; then they heaped upon him untold injurious words, and finding all these of no avail to provoke him to anger, they prepared to inflict on him the bodily cruelties they had previously designed.

But the pious youth, seeing that this was an occasion when duty to himself required him to resist these attacks, instantly drew his sword, and brandishing it vigorously over his cowardly aggressors, instantly made them fly away in great haste, so unexpected was the resistance offered them. Francis pursued them for a time, but they, finding that they themselves were in danger, turned towards him trembling and full of confusion. They fell at his feet imploring his forgiveness, and promising him that for the time to come they would never be guilty of such unpardonable conduct.

Life of St. Francis of Sales.

II. On the Sin of Anger.

Anger is a certain movement in the soul which causes us to reject with violence that which annoys or displeases us.

In order to triumph over the vice of anger, it is not sufficient to go away from the persons and the occasions which have caused us to be angry, but we must also fight against it, and never cease till we have mastered it.

THE MONK AND THE PITCHER.

We read in the " Lives of the Fathers of the Desert " that a certain good religious, finding in the monastery where he dwelt many things which always made him angry, one day said to himself : " I see it is necessary for me to take up my abode in the desert, for there there will be no one to contradict me or annoy me, and I shall no longer be tempted to yield to this terrible sin of anger."

Saying this, he retired to the desert, and built for himself a little cell, where he spent many happy days by himself, without anyone going near him to tempt him to impatience.

But one day, going to the stream to draw water, the pitcher which he placed on the side of the stream, after filling it, was overturned three times successively.   Immediately his old temptation assailed him again, and flying into a passion, he lifted up the vessel and dashed it to pieces in his anger.

When calm had again been restored, he said to himself : " The Devil has deceived me in making me think that I could overcome this vice of anger by flying the society of men.   No ; the real remedy is to fight it till I have overcome it.   Wherever I may go, I must meet with something which will be a temptation to me ; so instead of flying from it like a coward, I must go forward resolutely and face the enemy, and, with the assistance of God, overcome it.   I will therefore return to my monastery, and for the time to come I will do this."

Saying this, he at once returned to the monastery, and by daily fighting against that vice of anger, he finally overcame it altogether, and made rapid progress in the way of virtue.

Lives of the Fathers of the Desert.

III. On Saying Injurious Words.

The Fifth Commandment forbids, also, all kinds of injurious words, or words which might hurt our neighbours' feelings.

ST. FRANCIS OF SALES AND THE LADY.

St. Francis of Sales had an extreme delicacy on the point of fraternal charity.   Whenever he heard anyone speaking lightly of his neighbours, he showed by his face how much the conversation displeased him, and at once spoke of something else.   One day, when an opportunity occurred, he said to one who was speaking in this manner: " Who gave you a right to amuse yourself at the expense of your neighbour ? Would you like that someone would bring forward your faults, and tear your reputation to pieces ? To amuse yourself in this way is a mark of how little you esteem your own reputation."

Another day a young lady took the liberty of turning into ridicule the natural defects and the ungainly appearance of another. The Saint said to her, in his usual meek manner : " My lady, it is God who has made as all, and not we ourselves, and all the works of God are perfect."

At these words the lady began to laugh, and replied that she did not see anything very perfect in that person.

The Saint answered this time in a voice which showed how much he was displeased : " Most certainly, my lady ; the soul of that person is at this moment much more perfect in the eyes of God than your own soul is."

These words had the desired effect ; the lady hung down her head, and never again in the presence of the holy Bishop said anything to the injury of her neighbour. *Life of St. Francis of Sales.*

ST. ALDERIC AND HIS COMPANIONS.

When St. Alderic was quite a little boy, he began to practise mortification. Whenever he sat down to table to take his food, he always left a little portion of it in order that he might mortify himself. Sometimes he would even leave what was most pleasing to the appetite, and eat only that which **was plain and common.**

His companions soon noticed this, and gave him the nickname of " Little St. John," meaning that he was trying to live, like St. John the Baptist, on the plainest food.

Their words, spoken in a spirt of mockery, did not make him angry ; his only answer to them was : " Oh, you are giving me too much praise. I wish I were really as good as the great St. John the Baptist." ·

IV. ON THE FORGIVENESS OF INJURIES.

If your neighbour offend you, my child, it is not allowed for you to take revenge. A good Christian must always pardon, for the sake of Jesus Christ, those who have injured him.

THE TWO LITTLE SCHOOLBOYS.

A little boy who was a companion of the Blessed Sebastian Valfre, and who attended the same school as he did, had a quarrel with another, and his heart was so full of anger against him that he would not forgive him.

When Sebastian heard of this he became very unhappy, because he knew how much it must grieve the good God, and he thought he would try to make peace between them. So he went to his schoolmate and asked him if he had said the " Our Father " that morning.

The boy, not knowing the reason why Sebastian had put this question, replied quite promptly : " Yes, of course I did."

" Did you say it very carefully ?" said Sebastian,

trying to speak with great love and gentleness, that he might not offend him.

The boy again answered, as before, that he had done so. " Surely you did not notice these words, ' Forgive us our trespasses, as we forgive them that trespass against us,' " added Sebastian earnestly.

These words reached the heart of the boy, and struck him with shame and repentance. He at once asked pardon of God for his sin, and, going to his companion, asked his forgiveness, and became reconciled to him.　　　*Life of B. Sebastian Valfre.*

V. On Scandal and Bad Example.

Scandal is spiritual murder, for it attacks the soul, and takes away the life of the soul, which is much more precious than that of the body.

" woe to him who led me astray !"

Thomas of Cantiprensis, a pious man who lived in the thirteenth century, relates that he knew a young man who was led away by a bad companion, and in the end died a miserable death.

This young man had pious parents, and had received from God many great gifts of soul and body. He was sent to school, and that he might grow up piously, his parents chose for him one which was considered to rank among the first in that country for virtue and learning. But, alas ! even in the best schools the Devil succeeds too often in introducing some whom he has already led astray, and uses them as a means of leading others from the path of virtue. There was one of these in this school who, under the appearance of piety, corrupted the hearts of many of those who till then were innocent, and among these was this young man of whom the above-named writer speaks.

At first he contrived to hide the terrible change which had taken place within him from his masters, and was considered one of the most exemplary students in the whole school, but in course of time he threw off the mask and appeared in his true colours, and became a scandal to all his companions.

His parents and his friends, who perceived the change, besought him in the name of God to return to the path of piety, but all their words were in vain. At last God sent him a severe illness, during which He spoke to his heart and urged him to repentance. But the young man's heart was hardened, and he would not accept these graces.

The time of mercy at length came to an end, and the unrepenting sinner reached the gates of death. A strange and painful malady seized him and caused him to scream, so great was the pain he endured. His friends ran to his assistance, and a priest was sent for in haste. When he arrived, he asked him what was it that made him utter such fearful cries.

The dying man turned towards the priest, and in a terrible voice, which seemed to reach the hearts of all who were present, he cried out : " Woe to him who led me astray !"

The priest, in words of burning zeal, tried to speak to him of the mercy of God, and begged the poor wretch to repent before he entered eternity. But it was of no use ; the dying man exclaimed in still more terrible accents : " It is useless for me to ask God to forgive me. It is now too late ; I see Hell open under my feet ready to receive me. Oh, woe to that one who led me astray !"

Saying these awful words, he died in despair.

Works of Thomas of Cantiprensis.

THE TWO SCHOLARS.

Augustus and Henry were two scholars who went to the same school in the North of France. Henry was passionate and cruel, and one day, having quarrelled with his comrade at a game, he became so angry that he challenged him to fight a duel. Augustus refused, saying that it was forbidden by the Church to do that terrible thing. But Henry would accept no refusal. " If you will not fight this duel," he cried, " I will blow your brains out with this pistol." Augustus, seeing no way of escaping, took the weapon in his trembling hand in order to defend himself, for he saw how awfully in earnest his companion was.

They drew lots who was to fire the first shot : it fell to the lot of Augustus. Taking the pistol in his hand, he fired it into the air, for he did not wish to hurt his companion.

When he had done this, Henry, in savage fury, said : " It is now my turn ;" and, looking on his innocent companion with the eye of a tiger, he prepared to take aim.

" What will your mother say when she hears of your death ?" cried out the inhuman boy. " She shall die in despair, and I shall be happy, for I shall have had my revenge."

Saying this, he fired the pistol, and poor Augustus lay dead at his feet.

Oh, what cruelty in one so young ! Yet, my child, what is that in comparison with the cruelty of one who gives scandal to another, or who is the cause of another falling into sin ? Oh, never, never be the cause of scandal to anyone, that you may not have to answer to God for his soul at the Day of Judgment.

ST. AUGUSTINE AND HIS FRIEND.

St. Augustine, before his conversion, led a life of great dissipation, reviling the things of God, and seeking only the vain pleasures of this life. After his conversion, he wept bitterly for the sins of his former life ; and for the instruction of others, he wrote a book, in which he declared before the whole world the evils he had done, that others, by reading it, might be led to the grace of repentance. Among other things he relates the following :

" When I was at Tagastus, there lived there also a young man for whom I conceived a great affection. We were both young and of the same age, and I had known him when I was only a child. It seemed to us that we were born for each other alone. We had been at school together, and we had played together when children. He loved me so much that he did everything I asked him ; and when I proposed to him to renounce the Catholic faith, in which he had been born, and which he had practised all his lifetime, he did it for my sake."

When they had lived for about a year in this way, and constantly in each other's company, the young man became ill, and was soon brought to the point of death. For some days all hope of his recovery was abandoned, and Augustine sat day and night at his bedside waiting till the end would come.

But God wished to prolong his life for our example and instruction. A favourable change came over him, and his consciousness returned. When he had so far recovered as to know those around him, his eyes fell on Augustine "As soon as he saw me," writes that holy Bishop, "he turned his eyes from me in horror, as if I had been his most deadly enemy, and with a firmness which surprised me, who so little expected this treatment from so dear a friend, he declared to me that if I desired to be his friend, I must henceforth for ever abstain from speaking against the Catholic Faith.

"I was annoyed at this, but the grace of God at the same time spoke to my heart, and I saw the evil I had done in drawing away a soul from God by my bad example and my evil words, and I left his bedside to weep in secret over my sin."

Augustine was absent for a few days ; but being anxious to see his friend again to encourage him in his pious resolution to live for the future a holy life, he went to visit him. When he approached his friend's house, he saw everywhere signs of grief. God had called the young man to Himself during his absence. *Confessions of St. Augustine.*

A YOUNG GIRL IN DANGER.

A young girl, who was the idol of her father, went with him one day to a dinner-party, to which he had been invited. Her mother had watched over the tender years of her childhood, and brought her up in great piety and virtue, so that the world and all its vanities were entirely unknown to her.

During the time of dinner the conversation was very gay and cheerful, yet nothing was said that could be dangerous to anyone. But when it was ended, all restraint was laid aside, and the gossip of the world and vain and frivolous topics were spoken of, as, unfortunately is too often the case, even amongst people calling themselves pious.

The young girl did not seem to understand at first the meaning of what they were saying, but being very anxious to learn, she listened with great attention to them.

It happened that her father, who was at the other end of the room, looked towards his daughter, and, seeing her listening with so much eagerness, saw immediately that she was in danger of hearing things she ought not to hear. So he called her to his side, and she remained there for the rest of the day.

But the evil was done. That young girl had learned much during the few moments she had been in that company, and the beautiful piety which till then had been the charm of her childhood became clouded. She began to speak more of the world and less of God, and to wish to be with the gay and the worldly rather than with those who were pious and good. It was a long time before her parents were able to root out of her soul the evil that had entered it during those few moments when she allowed herself to listen to things that were hurtful. But, thanks be to God and to the watchful care of her good parents, she saw the vanity of all human things, and she is now a pious woman. The counsel she most frequently gives to her own little ones is this : " My children, take care never to listen to those who say what is wrong, or who praise the vanities of this world."

A BROTHER'S WORDS OF MOCKERY.

A young woman of sixteen was going to the church to make her Confession. On the way she met her brother, who was a little more than a year older than herself.

" Where are you going ?" he said to her.

" I am going to the church for Confession," she replied. " To-morrow is Easter Sunday, and you know that we must all go to our religious duties at this time."

" Oh, you silly girl !" he exclaimed, in words of mockery ; " surely you know that no respectable person goes to Confession nowadays. Don't be so foolish."

These words made his sister hang down her head, as if she were ashamed of what she had said. She did not go to Confession, and her Easter duties were omitted that year.

THE LITTLE SHEPHERD.

A little boy, to whose care his father had one day confided his sheep in his absence, heard a bird singing beautifully in the woods. Being anxious to see the bird, he left the sheep and went into the wood to look for it. In the meantime a wolf, which had been watching for an opportunity, fell upon the unprotected flock, and slew some of them.

As soon as the bird had flown away, the boy returned to the field, when, to his horror, he saw what the wolf had done.

When his father returned and saw what had happened, he chid his son severely for allowing himself to be led away by the sound of a bird. The boy repented of his foolishness, but it was too late, for his tears could not restore to life the sheep which the wolf had killed.

Many Christians, my child, resemble that boy. The words they hear often make them neglect their duty towards God, and the Devil comes and destroys the good they have already done. They repent only when it is too late, and frequently have to suffer for all eternity in punishment of their folly. Ah, then, take care not to be led away from the path of duty by the bad example of others.

" ONLY ONCE MORE."

Father Bourdaloue relates the following sad story : A young man, who at first led a pious life, happened to meet some bad companions at school, and, although his parents told him not to go with them, and not even to speak to them, he was often found in their company. In a short time he was as bad as themselves, led away by their bad example.

One day, being tormented by the voice of his conscience, he resolved to renounce their evil company for ever, and to return to God by a good Confession.

He went to a Jesuit Father, and, with tears of sincere repentance in his eyes, told him the sins the bad companions led him to commit, and begged of him to hear his Confession. The good Father appointed the day and the hour, and the young man went home to prepare himself to make a good Confession. In order that he might not forget any of his sins, he wrote them on a piece of paper, and spent a long time in weeping over them.

When the time appointed was drawing near, he rose up to go to the church. On the way, he had to pass by a house where he knew some of his former wicked companions dwelt, and where many of his sins had been committed. Satan, seeing his opportunity, again tempted him. " Go in," he whispered to him in his heart—" go in and do once more—only once more—what you have so often done already. It will be easy to add that one sin to the number you have to mention when you are at Confession, and then it will be forgiven with the rest."

The young man went in, and the evil was done. His bad companions made him fall again into sin.

In the meantime the priest, who was waiting for him, seeing that he had not come, and fearing that he had lost courage, went out to look for him. He saw a large crowd of people standing before the door of a certain house, and inquired what had happened.

They answered · " A young man has just fallen down the stairs, and is killed."

At that moment they were carrying the body out of the house. The priest looked on the face of the dead young man, and saw who it was. He also

knew that this was one of the places where much
evil was done, and he soon learned the rest. The
young man had almost certainly lost his soul because
he did not keep away from bad company, for the
Holy Ghost says : " He that loveth the danger shall
perish in it."

It is not only from those who are wicked that
you must keep away, but also from those who are
worldly-minded, and are always speaking of the
vanities and pleasures of the world, because they
also will keep you from serving God as you ought.

VI. On the Reparation of Scandal and Bad Example.

When a person has had the misfortune to give
scandal, he must have the courage to make reparation for it, as far as lies in his power, whatever
trouble it may cost him in doing so.

USTAZADE.

During the persecution of Sapor, King of the
Persians, many Christians suffered martyrdom for
their faith. One of these Christians, whose name
was Ustazade, had the misfortune to yield in the
midst of the tortures to which he was subjected,
and renounced his faith. This man had formerly
been the King's preceptor, and was at that time
Grand Master of the palace.

It happened at this same time that St. Simeon,
Archbishop of Seleucia, was seized, brought before
the tyrant, and accused of being a Christian. Sapor
condemned him to death. As he was being led back

to prison to await the day of his martyrdom, he was met on the way by Ustazade, who respectfully saluted him ; but the holy Bishop, instead of speaking to him or returning his salutation, cast upon him a look full of sadness and reproach.

This look seemed to reach the very soul of Usta zade, who immediately, and on the very place whereon he stood, took off the rich white garments of his office and threw them on the ground. Then he cast about him a black cloak in sign of grief, and broke forth into loud cries of dismay, aecompanied with sighs and tears. He struck his breast, and cast himself upon the ground, crying out in tones of anguish : " Woe to me ! What hope can I now have of ever finding God's grace again—that God Whom I have so cowardly renounced—when even one of my best-beloved friends, Simeon, the holy man Simeon, passes me by without speaking to me, and casts upon me such a look of horror ?"

The King, having been informed of what had occurred, sent for Ustazade, and asked him what was the cause of his great affliction, and if any untoward event had happened which caused him so much grief

" No, my Prince," he answered ; " no family disgrace has fallen upon me to make me suffer as I do now. Ah, would to God that I had nothing more serious to complain of than the loss of some temporal possessions ! Would to God that all possible evils of that kind had come upon me ! Then, indeed, my tears would soon be dried up. I weep because I still live, and I ought to have died through shame. I weep, not because my life has been an unhappy one, but because it has been criminal.   But now I hate and detest the crime I have committed, and I protest openly in the face of Heaven and earth that nothing in this world will ever cause me to be ashamed of my Faith, or ever to renounce it again.''

This change in his favourite, so sudden and un-expected, roused up to a higher degree than ever the fury of the King against the Christian religion ; and Ustazade, faithfully resisting all his induce-ments to apostatize, assured him that he would never adore any creature to the prejudice of his Creator.   The tyrant, foreseeing that any further endeavours would be of no avail, condemned him to be beheaded.

As he was being led to the place of execution, he besought those who were to execute the King's commands to stop for a few moments, as he desired to communicate to Sapor some important informa-tion.   This was granted, and one of his eunuchs, who had always been faithful to him, was chosen to convey his message to the King.

It was in these words : '' O Prince, I do not imagine that it is necessary to seek for any other witness than yourself to testify to the fidelity and the zeal I have always, from my youthful years, manifested towards your Majesty and to the King, your father.   If my care, and the inviolable devo-tion which I have at all times shown towards your self and him, have found favour in your eyes, I beseech you to bestow on me as a recompense one only favour, and this favour is that you will make this publicly known, lest those who see me thus ignominiously put to death may think that you have condemned me to this punishment because I have not been loyal to my King. Be pleased, therefore, to command that a public crier will precede me, and proclaim to everyone who shall see me die that Ustazade has always been faithful to his King and his country, and that he dies because he is a Christian."

The King could not refuse this request, either in justice or in policy. He even persuaded himself that by doing this all the Christians in Persia would at once abandon their faith that they might escape death, to which he would assuredly condemu·them, since he had not spared even his own preceptor and beloved master.

But the design of Ustazade in asking this favour from the King was of a different nature. He had every reason to think that many of the Christians had been scandalized by his apostasy, and might also imitate him in denying their religion if called upon to do so or suffer torments and death; but now that they saw him repentant, and about to die for the sake of Jesus Christ, they might be inflamed with the generous resolution of imitating him, and he resolved to suffer every torment, and even death itself, rather than obey the wicked mandate of the tyrant.

It was in these sentiments that he received the stroke of death, and thus made reparation for the scandal he had given.

The news of his edifying death was brought to St. Simeon in his dungeon, and gave him great consolation. Very soon afterwards he also was led forth to execution, and received the martyr's **crown.** *Acta SS., an.* 345.

TOUSSAINT ON HIS DEATH-BED.

Toussaint was the author of many impious works and books against the Catholic Faith. He was lying on his death-bed, afflicted by a serious malady, which for more than a year had caused him much pain, but which was the means employed by a merciful God for his salvation.

When he saw that his end was approaching, he showed every sign of true repentance, and received the last Sacraments of the Church with every sign of sorrow for the past and hope for the future.

On the last day of his life he called together his friends, and asked pardon from them for all the scandals he had ever given them by his writings and by his worldly life. Then he told his son, a youth of some fifteen years, to come near him to receive his last words.

" My dearest child," he said, " hear and keep in mind the last words you will ever hear from your father's lips. I am about to appear before God, and to give Him an account of my whole past life. I have, indeed, grievously offended Him, and I have great need of His merciful forgiveness. . . . I have given you scandal by my conduct, so void of religion, and by my maxims, which have been so worldly. Will you forgive me ? Will you do all in your power to procure my pardon from God ? Will you promise me to live a different life from that of which I have given you the example ?

" Listen, then, to the counsels I now give you, which I should have given you long ago. I attest to you before that God Whom I am about to receive in my last Communion, and before Whom I must soon—perhaps even to-day—appear, that if I outwardly appeared un-Christian in my actions, my discourses, and my writings, it was not from conviction, but through human respect, and through vanity, and in order that I might please the world and obtain its applause.   My son, kneel down before me, and unite your prayers with those who are listening to me, and who are looking upon you.   Promise God that you will attend to these, my last instructions, and ask of Him to forgive me, your repentant father."   L'ABBÉ MIGNE : *Dict. d'Anecdotes*, col. 17.

THE DYING LADY.

There was once a young lady who was pious and good, and shunned vice of all kinds.   She was careful to go with no companion who did wrong, and everyone said she was an excellent Christian.

But she had her defects, and one of these was that she was a little vain, and was pleased when she heard herself admired.   Those who were her constant companions, although virtuous, were, like herself, fond of the admiration and praise of others, and their conversation was more frequently of worldly things—dress and amusements—than of the things which alone deserve the attention of a child of God.

It happened that the young lady became very ill. Her face, which had been so often admired, was pale and disfigured by a hideous ulcer, and it was evident to all that the days of her life were coming to an end.   Like a good Christian, she received the news of her approaching end with resignation, and prepared for it with fervour and piety.

Her companions came every day to visit her, because they all loved her. One day she said to them : " My friends, we have lived together for a long time, and you have been my constant companions, but your company has not done me any good, and I wish now that you had been very different from what you are. I am now about to leave this world, and to give an account to God of all those vain words and actions in which we spent so much of our time. Take my advice, then : it is that of a loving companion who is dying. Shun the company of those who are vain, proud, and worldly, for Satan can drag souls into Hell by that kind of company, as well as by the company of those who openly sin against God. My last request is that you should pray for me, that God may forgive me the sins I have committed by all those vain, foolish, and worldly words and deeds of which we have so often been guilty."

VII. On Setting a Good Example.

My child, a good example has sent to Heaven thousands of souls on whom the most eloquent sermons had but little effect. You cannot often preach the Word of God by your words, but you can always do so by a good example. A good example is called " the Gospel in practice."

THE SOLDIER AND THE CHILD.

There was once a little girl who had lost both her parents, and who was entrusted by them on their death-bed to the care of an old soldier, a man who possessed a kind heart, but had for a long time given up the practice of his religious duties.

The girl loved the old man, and used to call him her father. She was a very pious child, and her simple ways had won the entire affection of the soldier, and he always called her his little daughter, his little Saint. In her presence he was careful never to swear or say an unbecoming word, and even sometimes said his prayers along with her when she asked him.

One day he went into the church ; he could not tell why he went, for he had not entered a church for many years. The first person he saw there was his own little girl, kneeling like an angel before the altar. " I wonder what she is praying for," he said to himself. " Perhaps she is asking God for my conversion, for she has often told me that that was the only object of all her prayers."

A tear came into his eye and flowed down his furrowed cheek ; it was a tear which brought re-pentance with it. From that moment he became a fervent Christian, and one day, not long after-wards, he was kneeling at the altar by the side of his darling child, receiving his Divine Saviour in Holy Communion.

As he was leaving the church that morning after making his thanksgiving, joyful and happy, with his hand firmly clasped in that of the child, some of his old companions met him. They told him that they were astonished to see one who had led so gay and worldly a life become so virtuous in his old age.

He answered them : " How could I do otherwise ? It is quite impossible to resist the good example of this little Saint ; she would convert Satan himself, if it were only possible for him to be converted.

Such was the effect of a little girl's good example.

MARY'S LITTLE APOSTLE IN THE FIELDS.

In his young days the Curé of Ars had to take care of his father's flocks. There was one particular place where he delighted to lead them, a lovely little valley at some distance from the village where his father dwelt.

His young companions, who all loved him, used to hail his approach as he appeared amongst them, with a staff in one hand, and his little image of the Blessed Virgin in the other, pressed to his bosom.

On a little hillock, by the side of an old willow which is still to be seen there, he placed his dear Madonna upon an altar of turf, and having knelt to pay his homage to her, he invited all the other shepherd boys to do the same.

Never was he so happy as when he saw them kneeling around his beloved image. Then, having said a " Hail Mary " with fervent devotion, he would rise and gravely address his young companions, who listened with devout attention, upon the devotion to the Blessed Virgin.

Sometimes, indeed, they would get tired of listening, and run away after a little to play. Then the little boy would console himself by going into some quiet corner, where he installed his beloved image in the hollow of a tree, and kneeling at its feet, he passed long hours in prayer.

This little boy afterwards by his holy life converted a great multitude of sinners to God.

ST. ALPHONSUS AND THE SLAVE.

When St. Alphonsus was a young man, there was amongst those appointed to attend him a slave who was a Mahometan.

One day this slave went to the priest, and told him that he desired to be made a Christian.

" What has caused you to take that resolution ?" asked the priest.

The slave answered : " The example of my young master has made a great impression on me. It is quite impossible that that religion could be false that makes a young man like him lead a life so pure and holy."

THE CHANGE IN THE OLD GENERAL.

An old General was one day asked by a friend how it was that, after so many years spent in the camp, he had come to be so frequent a communicant, receiving several times a week.

" My friend," answered the old soldier, " the strangest part of it all is that my change of life was brought about before I ever listened to the word of a priest, and before I had set foot in a church. After my campaigns were over, God bestowed on me a pious wife, whose Faith I respected though I did not share it. Before I married her she was a member of all the pious confraternities of her parish, and she never failed to add to her signature the words " Child of Mary " She never took it upon herself to lecture me about God, but I could read her thoughts in her countenance. When she prayed every night and morning, her face beamed with faith and charity ; when she came home from the church, with a calmness, a sweetness, and a patience which had in them something of the serenity of Heaven, she seemed an angel.   When she dressed my wounds, I found her like a Sister of Charity.

" Suddenly, I myself was taken with the desire to love the God my wife loved so well, and who inspired her with those virtues which formed the joy of my life.   One day I, who was hitherto without Faith, and was such a complete stranger to the practices of religion, and so far from the Sacraments, said to her · ' Take me to your confessor.'

" Through the ministry of this man of God, and by the grace of God, I have become what I am, and what I rejoice to be."   *Chimes*, 367.

VIII. A Good Example the Best Means of Propagating the Faith.

But you will say to me, my child, " How can I propagate the Faith ?   Can I be an apostle ?" Yes, you can, for the hymn says :

> " And preach thee, too, as love knows how,
> By kindly words and virtuous life."

You can often do more to edify the Church of God by leading a virtuous life than the greatest preacher by his most eloquent sermons.

EXAMPLE THE BEST SERMON.

Father Fernandez was sent by St. Francis Xavier to preach in one of the great cities of India.

Many people flocked to hear him because he was eloquent, but very few of them, at the beginning, became converts, and he had to endure many insults and suffer much ill-treatment at their hands.

One day he was preaching as usual in one of the public squares of the city. A great crowd was listening to him. Suddenly a man went up as if he wanted to speak to him, and when he came close to him, he spat in his face.

The holy priest, without saying a word or showing the least anger, quietly took out his handkerchief, wiped his face, and continued his sermon just as if nothing had happened.

The people at first laughed when they saw what the man had done to him. But when they beheld the meekness with which the holy man bore the insult, and his patience, their mirth was soon changed into admiration.

Amongst those present was a learned doctor, who was a witness of all that passed. He said to himself: " The doctrine which this stranger teaches must certainly come from Heaven ; for a law that teaches its followers such great virtue, and gives them the courage to practise it, must come from God."

So when the sermon was ended, the doctor went to the saintly preacher, and asked to become a member of his religion.

Father Fernandez gladly granted his request, and he was baptized with great solemnity. His example was followed by many others, and the good Father had the consolation of seeing in a very short time a fervent Christian congregation in that city. *Lives of the Companions of St. Francis.*

CONVERSION OF ST. PACHOMIUS.

St. Pachomius was born in the town of Thebes of parents who were pagans. Although brought up in idolatry, he never yielded to the crimes that others committed, and so God led him, as He has led many others since then, into the fold of His holy Church.

When he was about twenty years old, the Emperor raised an army for the defence of his Empire in the East, and many young men were compelled against their will to join the army ; amongst these was Pachomius.

He was put on board a vessel along with other soldiers, and sent away to a distant country.

It happened that the first port they touched at was a place where the inhabitants were all Christians. When these heard that the soldiers had been forced to leave their homes, to go and fight in a foreign country, they were filled with compassion for them. They tried to give them every consolation in their power, and helped them by many acts of kindness.

Pachomius, who had never seen an example like this amongst the pagans, was at first filled with astonishment. One day he asked who these people were who were so kind to them.

" They are Christians," was the reply.

Pachomius had never before heard of Christians, so he asked · " Who are they ?"

" They are people who believe in Jesus Christ, the only Son of God, and who make it a practice to do all the good they can to others, even to strangers."

" And who is to reward them for their gener-osity ?" asked Pachomius.

" They look for no reward in this world," was the answer ; " they expect to receive it from their God in another world, into which they hope to enter when they die."

The young soldier said to himself : " The religion which can make people do as they have done must indeed be true."

Then, touched by the grace of God, and inspired by Him, he said this prayer : " O my God, Creator of Heaven and earth, look on me with an eye of pity, and free me from my misery ; teach me the way of pleasing Thee, for from this time to the end of my life my only desire shall be to please Thee."

From that day forward, when any temptation came to incite him to sin, he called to mind his promise to God, and overcame it.

When the war was ended, he returned home, but very soon he left it again to begin another kind of warfare, under the service of a greater King. He became a Christian, and the founder of a com-munity of holy men, who, following his example, left the world to serve God in silence and prayer.

Petits Bolland., May 14.

You see, my child, how much can be done by a good example to propagate the true Church of Jesus Christ on earth. Strive always to set a good example, and you will do much for God.

XXXIII

THE SIXTH AND NINTH COMMANDMENTS

I. ON THE ANGELIC VIRTUE OF CHASTITY.

By the Sixth and Ninth Commandments, my child, God forbids us to do or think on anything that is contrary to the angelic virtue of chastity. God loves the angels in Heaven, they are so pure and beautiful ; those on earth who are pure resemble these blessed ones, and God has a special affection for them, and has reserved for them a very high degree of glory in Heaven.

THE BEAUTY OF THE PURE SOUL.

One day St. Catherine had a vision. Jesus Christ showed her a soul that was leading a pure life in the world. The Saint gazed upon it for a long time in rapture ; she had never before seen anything so beautiful. " O my Lord," she said, " if I did not know that there was only one God, I should think that this was one."

Nothing is so beautiful as a pure soul. Pure souls will form the circle round Our Lord in Heaven. The more pure we are on earth, the nearer we shall be to Our Lord in Heaven.

A pure soul is the admiration of the most Blessed

Trinity. The Eternal Father contemplates His work. " This is My creature, and the work of My hand," He says. The Son of God looks on it with love, and the Holy Ghost dwells in it as in His temple ; it is the abode of the most Holy Trinity.

Our Lord has always shown a special love for pure souls. Look at St. John, the well-beloved disciple who reposed upon His breast. St. Catherine was so pure that she was often transported into Paradise, and when she died, angels took up her pure body and carried it to Mount Sinai, where Moses received the Commandments. God wished to show by this wonder that a soul which is pure is so agreeable to Him, that even the body in which it dwells deserves to be honoured.

A pure soul is like a child with its mother ; it caresses her, it embraces her, and its mother returns its caresses and embraces.

Spirit of the B. Curé of Ars.

ST. POTENTIANA, MARTYR OF CHASTITY.

Under the persecution of Maximinian, a young woman of great beauty, named Potentiana, who was a slave in the house of a pagan well known for his profligate life, preferred to suffer the most awful torments rather than consent to violate this holy virtue of chastity.

Her master, seeing that he could not obtain her consent to his wicked desires, was filled with great wrath, and going to the Governor of the province, accused her of being a Christian ; at the same time he promised him a great sum of money if only he could persuade her to consent to his proposals.

Brought before the tribunal of the judge, the pious virgin was first cruelly tortured ; but notwithstanding the torments inflicted on her, she remained faithful and firm. Then he ordered a cauldron filled with pitch to be placed on a great fire, that when it boiled she might be cast into it.

In the meantime, while this was being prepared in her presence, he said to her : " Obey the will of your master, for if you refuse, you shall be cast into this boiling liquid."

" I did not know until now," she answered, " that there ever lived a man so wicked as to say such words of iniquity, or to punish with so much cruelty one who desires to live virtuously."

The judge, filled with rage at these words of the brave heroine, gave orders that she should be thrown into the cauldron without delay.

" Command your servants," said the maiden, " to put me into the cauldron little by little, clad as I am, and you will see the truth of the religion I profess, and the strength given me by my Lord Jesus Christ, Whom you have not the happiness of knowing."

Her request having been granted, she was slowly lowered into the boiling pitch, and lived in the midst of this terrible torture for the space of three hours, sustained by the mighty power of her Heavenly Spouse. He, at the end of that time, took her to Himself crowned with the double crown of virginity and martyrdom.   PALLADIUS : *Hist. Laus.*, iii.

II. On the Great Hatred Satan has for the Pure Soul.

Satan hates a pure soul. Whenever he sees one he rushes against it like a roaring lion, placing before it terrible temptations, that he may rob it of this treasure of Heaven, and awful is the destruction he causes through them among the children of God.

A TRAVELLER IN THE COUNTRY.

One day, in the summer-time, a traveller left his home in the city to travel in the country. When the morning dawned, he had already left the city far behind him, and had reached the beautiful country, with its green fields and its trees covered with fresh green leaves, and all nature round him, as far as his eye could reach, was smiling and gay.

As he was passing under a tree which grew by the wayside, he heard a little bird singing gaily ; and looking up; he saw it sitting on a branch near its nest, in which were its little ones, all happy and content ; and he said within himself : " How happy is that little bird as it sits on the tree and sings so sweetly, with its little ones near it, all so happy !"

A little farther onwards he saw a little child, with his face all smiles, and so happy that no sorrow or trial seemed ever to have reached his innocent soul. He was surrounded by a little flock of lambs white as snow ; the lambs skipped about in the meadow, and the little boy played with them. The man passed on, saying to himself : " I will return this evening by this same way and see them all again."

When evening came, he returned to the place where he had heard the bird sing. It was singing still, but its notes were no longer the joyful strains he had heard in the morning ; sad and plaintive now they were. The traveller stopped to see what had made this change ; he looked up to the nest, but there were no little birds there now; it was empty: some bird of prey had been there, and had stolen all the young ones from the nest.

As he pursued his way he met the little shepherd boy. He, too, was no longer joyful as in the morning. " What ails you, my child ?" said the traveller, as he stopped to speak to him.

" Oh, sir," replied the boy, " I had a little lamb which I loved more than all the rest ; it used to follow me wherever I went, and would eat out of my hand, and sleep on my breast. To-day a wild beast has killed it, and that is why I am so sad."

The man continued his journey homewards, and as he proceeded on the way he thought of something he had often seen in the city, of which these two sad events were only the emblems. " How often have I seen little children gay and happy in the morning of life, with their mothers smiling at their sides, and in a short time, when I looked again, I saw that the smiles of the mothers had given place to tears, and that the once happy children had lost all their comeliness ! What was it that had caused that terrible change ?"

The answer to that question is this : Purity had passed out of those young souls, and Satan dwelt therein.

ST. CATHERINE'S TEMPTATION.

It is not a sin to be tempted ; it is a sin only when we give way to temptation. It is when we are tempted most that God is nearest to us, because He wants to be near us, His children, to help us when we call upon Him.

St. Catherine of Sienna was one day tempted very much with bad thoughts, but by God's holy grace she put them all away.

Not long afterwards, Our Blessed Lord was pleased to appear to her in a visible manner. As soon as she saw Him, she cried out : " O my God, where were you when the Devil was tempting me with those wicked thoughts ?"

" My daughter," He replied, " I was in the midst of your heart all the time."

" O my dearest Lord," said the Saint, " is it possible that you could have been there in the midst of such frightful temptations ?"

" Yes, my child, I was there watching over you when you were fighting against them, and helping you to overcome them ; and when I saw how much you detested them for love of Me, My heart was filled with the greatest joy."

Ever afterwards, when she was suffering temptation, St. Catherine was quite calm, for she knew that Jesus was in her heart, watching her and helping her.

So, in all your dangers, keep in mind that Jesus is near you and watching over you, and do not be afraid ; but be sure to ask Him at once to help you, for He has promised to help His children whenever they are in danger and ask His help.

Life of St. Catherine of Sienna.

20—2

III. The Unhappy Life of those who are Impure.

Those who live in habits of sin against this angelic virtue seem to be content, but their happiness is not real, and when they die, their portion is with the reprobate, for it is only the clean of heart that can see God.

THE VISION OF ST. ANSELM.

St. Anselm was one day favoured with a vision. God showed him a great ocean, the waters of which were black and filthy. In the midst of the ocean there was an immense multitude of men and women— young men and old men, parents and children. The waters seemed to be always, as it were, agitated like the sea in a violent tempest, and they gave the unfortunate people who were immersed in them no rest, sometimes plunging them into the abyss, sometimes tossing them about on the surface.

But what astonished the man of God above all things else was to see that those who were thus in such a pitiable condition seemed to be full of gaiety, and to laugh and to amuse themselves as if they were happy, and it seemed to him that to possess happiness in such misery was impossible.

But their apparent happiness was of short duration, for suddenly a great and terrible wave came over them, and in a moment they were driven to the bottom of this awful sea, from which they never rose again.

St. Anselm was grieved at this terrible end of these wretched creatures, and with many tears besought God to make known to him what was meant by the vision he had seen.

In answer to his prayer, God made known to him that the turbid sea he had seen represented the world, and that the dark and filthy waters represented the sins and crimes in which so many people of the world indulge, and in particular the sins of the flesh ; that in the midst of all these abominations they appear to the eyes of the world to live happily, but that they are in reality very miserable ; and that suddenly the end comes, and they are cut off in their sins, and are plunged into the abyss of hell, where for all eternity they are punished for having chosen to serve the world and their evil inclinations rather than God.

The Saint made this vision known everywhere, that people who should hear of it might be led to think of the terrible evils they would bring upon themselves in eternity if they allowed themselves to be led by their passions during the time of their trial on earth.　　　　　　　*Lives of the Saints.*

IV. Impurity is Hateful in the Eyes of God.

The vice of impurity is the one which is most odious in the eyes of God, and the one which He punishes with the most terrible chastisements, even in this world.

THE RUINED CITIES.

The valley of the Jordan, which lies among the mountains of Arabia, was at one time one of the most fertile and beautiful places on the earth. In it were two cities called Sodom and Gomorrha, which were also rich and magnificent among the great cities of the East. The Scripture thus describes that country : " And Lot, lifting up his eyes, saw all the country about the Jordan, which was watered throughout, before the Lord destroyed Sodom and Gomorrha, as the Paradise of the Lord, and like Egypt as one comes from Segor " (Gen. xiii. 10).

But the more prosperous these cities were, the more wicked did they become. The abundance and plenty in which the people lived plunged them into a state of sloth, and from this vice arose the still more terrible evil of impurity ; so that the anger of God was raised against them, and He resolved to destroy them with all their inhabitants.

In these cities there was only one family that feared God, and had kept away from that terrible sin. It was the family of Lot. God sent an angel from Heaven to take that family out of the doomed cities before He would destroy them.

The following is the description given in the Scripture of what happened to these cities : " The sun was risen upon the earth, and the Lord rained down upon Sodom and Gomorrha, brimstone and fire from the Lord out of Heaven. And He destroyed these cities and all the country about, and all the inhabitants of the cities, and all the things that spring from the earth. And Abraham, rising in the morning, looked towards Sodom and Gomorrha, and the whole land of that country, and he saw the ashes rise up from the earth as the smoke of a furnace " (Gen. xix. 23-28).

Such, my child, was the awful end of these two

great cities because of the crimes they had committed before God by their impurity. At the present day the place where they formerly stood is marked by the Dead Sea, which is an eternal monument of the malediction with which God visits this terrible vice.

It is said that on the banks of the Dead Sea there grows a kind of fruit which is a true image of this great sin. It has the appearance of an apple, and outwardly is of a brilliant and attractive colour, but when it is plucked and opened, the interior is found to be rotten, and, if eaten, leaves in the mouth an exceedingly bitter taste. Such, also, is the vice of impurity ; it outwardly appears to be pleasant, but when indulged in, the soul is filled with bitterness and remorse, and struck dead by its poison.

CHARLES II., KING OF NAVARRE.

Charles II., surnamed the Bad, King of Navarre, died, in the year 1387, a most terrible death, but one which seemed to be a fit ending to his wicked life. This man was known to have led a most scandalous life, and in a particular manner to have broken the Sixth Commandment in thought, word, and deed.

Having, on account of his crimes, fallen into a painful illness, he besought the physicians to tell him what he could do to obtain relief from the pain. They told him that the only remedy they could suggest which might free him from his intense sufferings was that his body should be enveloped in a linen sheet saturated with sulphur and other antidotes, which should be sewed tightly around him.

The person who was appointed to do this work,

having finished it, wanted a pair of scissors to cut the end of the thread that remained in the needle, but, not finding them, he had the imprudence to bring the thread near the candle which gave him light, that he might burn it.

Unfortunately, the thread, which was also saturated with the inflammable material, took fire, which, running to the linen, in an instant kindled it, and the wretched man was enveloped in flames. He screamed in his agony, and the people of the palace, hearing these screams, ran in haste to.help him. But it was in vain : the voluptuous Charles died in despair before anyone could extinguish the flames which covered him from head to foot.

The terrible fire which consumed that Prince in the midst of unheard-of pain was only a shadow of that eternal fire in which the impure burn for all eternity. O my child, keep away from that awful vice, that you may escape the terrible doom of those who are now suffering for it in Hell.

History of the Netherlands.

V. About Dangerous Books and Pictures.

One great source of evil to a good child, and one that leads him on rapidly towards the terrible vice of impurity, is the bad books and periodicals that are being daily published, and the immodest pictures that are constantly being placed before his eyes. It will be known only at the Day of Judgment the terrible evils these things have brought upon the children of God,. and the multitude of souls that have been lost for all eternity by reading these books and gazing upon these pictures.

THE LADY AND THE PRIEST.

During a mission that was held at Marseilles, a certain lady went to one of the Fathers to speak to him. They had not been speaking together long when the priest discovered that she was given to reading novels of a dangerous and exciting kind, and the following conversation took place between them :

" I see that you have read much, and that you prefer light literature, such as novels," the priest said to her.

" Yes, Father, it is quite true ; but I read them only for amusement."

" Are you quite sure of that ?" he said.

" Oh yes, and for no other reason."

" If such is the case," said the priest, " just continue to read them ; only each time you take up the book be sure to go on your knees before you begin to read, and say to God : ' O my God, I am going to read this novel to please You. I know that it contains unsound doctrines, and bad counsels, and the relation of evil deeds, yet I am going to read about these things for Your glory and the salvation of my soul.' "

She answered : " O Father, that is an impossibility ! Such a prayer would only be a mocking of God."

" No, madam," replied the priest ; " if the reading is not bad, you can, and you ought, to make that prayer."

" But—but——" she began, with some hesitation.

"Oh, I see," interrupted the priest; "you do not seem to be quite so sure now that the books you read are so harmless as you at first pretended they were. Tell me the truth, now. Were you not much more pious before you began to read those books than you are now?"

The lady was obliged to acknowledge that she was.

"And were you not also much happier at that time?"

"Yes, Father, I was."

"And did you not go more frequently to the Sacraments then than you have done since you have begun to read these books?"

"Yes, I must acknowledge that I did."

"Then I have only one answer to give you. You ask me what you are to do to serve God as you ought. My answer is this: Cease to read the books you have hitherto been reading, since they have proved themselves so hurtful to you and so dangerous, and you will soon find your former piety restored to you."

The lady did as she was advised. It was at first very difficult to break off the evil habit she had acquired, but in the end, by perseverance and prayer, she succeeded, and soon became very happy again and a good Christian.   *Catéch. en Exemples.*

THE PAINTER'S SIN.

In Valentia, a city in Spain, there lived an artist who had painted several pictures for the Carmelite Fathers of that city without accepting any remuneration. Out of gratitude to him for his kindness to them they buried him in their church, and offered up many Masses for the repose of his soul.

As the Venerable Father Dominicus of that same Order was praying one night in the church, this painter appeared to him, and made known to him that he was suffering most cruel torments because he had once consented to paint a picture which might become for those who looked upon it the cause of offending God.

The souls, he said, who had by gazing on this picture, been led into sin, and were now lost, had cried for vengeance against him at the time of his judgment, and it was only by the intercession of the Saints, whose pictures he had painted, that he had escaped being condemned to Hell fire, and had been sentenced to suffer in Purgatory. He declared, moreover, that he had been condemned to remain in that place of expiation as long as that bad picture existed.

He mentioned, also, the name of the gentleman who possessed the picture, and added that God had made known to him that, of his three sons, two of them were to die within a month ; and he besought him to visit this gentleman and urge him to destroy the picture as soon as possible, otherwise he also would soon follow his two sons to the grave.

Father Dominicus went immediately to fulfil this request. The gentleman was exceedingly terrified on hearing the words the Father said to him, and at once gave him the picture, that he might destroy it. Within a month from that time two of the sons died. He himself, repenting of the evil he had done, began

to lead a penitential life, Moreover, he destroyed
all his other dangerous pictures, and replaced them
by others which would inspire piety.

Life of the Ven. Father Dominicus.

VI. On Keeping Away from Bad Company.

My child, if you should be in the company of those
who say bad or impure words, be courageous.
If you can make them cease uttering them, do so ;
if not, show them how displeased you are, and leave
their company as soon as possible.

ALBINI'S BRAVE REPROOF.

Albini, a good and pious boy, was one day in the
company of two or three of his companions, who
were of the same age as himself.

At first they were amusing themselves very inno-
cently, and there was none among them who seemed
to be so gay and happy as Albini himself, for he
always entered heart and soul into all his games and
amusements.

But during a halt in their games one of the boys
began to say bad words, and to speak about things
which were very offensive with regard to holy
modesty. As soon as Albini saw the turn the conversation was taking, he turned towards the boy
who was speaking, and said boldly to him : " Stop at
once ; these are not words for you to utter, nor for
us to listen to. Come, now, let us speak of something
else."

But the boy, who was encouraged by his companions to continue, only laughed at the rebuke of

Albini, and called him a silly boy and other worse names, and without the least shame continued to speak as before.

" Since you are determined to continue to offend God," said the pious boy, " I must leave you, for I cannot remain here to listen to words which might kill my soul."

Saying this, he at once left him. One of his companions, who had at first been timid enough to keep silence, now took courage to follow his good example. From that moment Albini was never seen in the company of him who had said the unbecoming words.   *Lives of Pious Youths.*

THE KING'S STRATAGEM.

Hadding, one of the ancient Kings of Denmark, was once besieging a strong city which he found impossible to capture. Seeing all his efforts were in vain, he was about to give up the siege, when a thought came into his mind that he might take it by stratagem.

He observed that every day a multitude of pigeons flew out of the city into the fields and woods to look for food. He ordered his soldiers to catch as many of them as they could, and put them into a cage. When he had in this way procured a large number, he tied to each of them a long ribbon which he had steeped in sulphur, and, setting fire to these ribbons, he allowed them all to escape.

They at once flew into the city and returned to their dovecots ; but the burning ribbons kindled the straw of their nests, and in a short time fire broke out in many parts of the town, and spread with so great rapidity that the place was soon destroyed, and the people surrendered themselves to the enemy.

It is in a similar way that Satan ruins many souls. When he sees that he cannot make them fall into sin by his usual temptations, he sends among them bad companions, who destroy in them the holy virtue of purity, which is the brightest ornament of a Christian.

THE STORY OF HUBERT AND LOUIS.

In a small town in France there lived a young man, whose piety and good conduct were an example to all who knew him.

He was regular in his devotions, a model of obedience to his parents, and charitable to everyone. All his thoughts were fixed on Heaven ; and the end for which all his actions were performed was the honour and glory of God and the salvation of his own soul.

It happened that on a certain day a public entertainment was given in a neighbouring village, at which there were to be fireworks and dancing ; and Hubert—for that was the name of the young man —took a walk over to the place to see what was going on.

He had always been accustomed, whenever he went to any amusement, to go in company with a certain companion of his own age, as good and virtuous as himself, and they always returned home at an early hour. On this occasion he went out alone.

On his way he was met by a young man named Louis, with whom he was slightly acquainted. Now, although Louis had been well brought up in his childhood, he had, by mingling with bad companions, lost all the good habits he had then learned, and was noted over all the country for his bad conduct.

If Hubert had been prudent, he would not have gone with him at all, because he knew well what kind of person he was, and would have easily found some excuse to leave his company. But he found Louis's conversation agreeable, and said to himself " Perhaps, after all, Louis may not be so bad as he is said to be." And so he determined to walk along with him.

At first they talked only about the weather and other such matters, but little by little Louis began to speak more freely. He boasted of the pleasant, free kind of life he led, laughed at Hubert because he was still pious, and told him that he had once been pious himself, but had given it up long ago. " It is very good to be pious when one is a child," he said, " but when one has grown up it is time to throw piety away."

Hubert should have gone away from him immediately. These words clearly told him that the one who used them was no fit companion for him or anyone who desired to be good. But he still remained with him.

When they arrived at the village, they met with a number of Louis's companions, wicked like himself. Hubert was introduced to them, and spent the rest of the day with them.

When evening came, they all went together to one of those places of amusement where many souls meet their destruction. Hubert went also, although the voice of conscience was constantly telling him not to go with them. He ended by yielding to temptation and falling into a grievous sin. Scarcely had he thus offended his God, when by an accident he fell down a stair leading to the house, and was killed.

Louis, who had been the cause of his sin, on seeing what had happened, was so struck with horror and remorse that he took a resolution on the spot to leave the world and sin, and to spend the rest of his days in doing penance. He left the village without delay, and going to a neighbouring monastery, begged to be allowed to enter there to atone for his many sins.

When the Superior came into the room where he was, Louis threw himself at his feet and said, while the tears were running down his cheeks : " O Father, I entreat you, take compassion on a miserable wretch who has destroyed the soul of a brother, and admit me into your monastery, that I may bewail my wickedness for the rest of my life '

The Superior, having heard his sad story, exhorted him to be very sorry for his past life, and to confide in the great mercy of God, but added : " I cannot receive you into this house until you have shown me that you intend to persevere in this resolution, and that it is not a mere passing desire."

" Father," replied the young man, who still continued at the feet of the Superior, " I will remain at your gate as many days as you please ; but never will I depart till you permit me to do penance in your monastery for the rest of my life."

The Superior, moved by the appearance of real repentance he saw in Louis, at length told him that he would admit him for a time on trial. Louis entered, and from that day till the day of his happy death remained there ; but the thought that he had been the cause of the ruin of poor Hubert's soul was always before his mind, and whenever he met any of the religious or strangers passing by the monastery, he used to say to them : " Pray to God to have mercy on me, a wretch, who once destroyed the soul of a brother."

From this example we see what a dangerous thing it is to go into bad company. The most innocent souls have been brought into sin by going with companions who are wicked. And if by chance we may have led others into sin, let us be very sorry and do penance for it, and continually ask God to give us pardon ; for it is a terrible thing to have to account to God for being the cause of the loss of a soul, even one soul, since our dear Lord shed His precious blood to save it. Mrs. Herbert.

VII. On the Danger of Idleness.

One of the most dangerous occasions of the sin of impurity is idleness. When a person is idle, the Devil, who is always busy and always on the watch, goes and puts before his mind thoughts that easily lead to evil.

THE YOUNG SOLITARY.

We read in the " Lives of the Fathers of the Desert " of a young solitary who did not employ his time as conscientiously as he ought to have done.

during these idle moments he was often tempted with impure thoughts.

One day, when he was tormented more than usual with them, he went to his superior and told him about it. The superior, who knew the young monk's disposition to idleness, said he would try to cure him. So he at once gave him much more constant labour, and more heavy work than he had been accustomed to, and commanded him to accomplish it without delay.

A few days afterwards the Superior, meeting him alone, asked him if he were still troubled with the temptations he had complained of to him.

"Ah, no," he replied. "How could I find time to be tempted, since you have imposed on me so many and such continual labours? I have scarcely even time to breathe."

Thus was that young monk cured of his temptations ; and in this way also will those Christians who are tempted in the same manner be effectually cured, if they only adopt the same means.

Lives of the Fathers of the Desert.

VIII. Of the Care necessary to Preserve Purity.

The Saints call the virtue of Purity "a treasure of great price." The Devil is continually seeking to rob us of this precious treasure, so we must be continually on our guard, lest by our negligence it may be stolen from us ; and always keep in mind what Jesus Christ says, that to see God we must be clean of heart.

THE CRYSTAL VASE.

St. Henry, Emperor of Germany, on his return from Italy, went, along with his whole Court, to Cluny to visit the holy Abbot Odilo. During his journey through Europe a certain Prince, to show esteem for so great a monarch, presented him with a crystal vase of magnificent workmanship. The pious Emperor thought that this would be a suitable offering to make to the monastery, so he directed two of his chaplains to carry it to the Abbot. When they had presented it to Odilo, they returned to the Emperor.

The beauty of this vase became at once the subject of conversation throughout the monastery. Everyone desired to see it and to hold it in his hands. As it was thus passing from one to another one of the monks let it fall to the ground, and it was broken into fragments. Odilo was not present when the accident occurred, but when he was informed of it, being afraid that the Emperor might be grieved at the destruction of such a work of art, and also thinking that he might blame his two chaplains for the accident, went to the church and prayed earnestly to God to help them in their difficulty. He then commanded the pieces of the vase to be gathered and brought to him. But no sooner had they gathered them together than the vase was found intact, to the amazement of those who carried it. The Emperor, hearing of what had occurred, thanked God for permitting him to see and dwell under the roof of one who was so dear to Him.

Life of St. Odilo.

21—2

This was, my child, a great miracle ; but it is a much greater miracle to restore the beauty of the soul which has once lost its innocence.

ST. BERNARD AND THE ROBBERS.

St. Bernard, with some of his companions, was once on a journey, and when night came on, they went to a certain house to sleep. The landlady of the house was captivated by the appearance of Bernard, who was very beautiful, and whose face reflected the innocence of his soul.

She appointed for him a room not far from her own, that when the household retired to rest, she might be able to go and converse with him.

When all were in bed, the door of his room was gently opened, and the lady of the house went in.

When Bernard saw her in the room, he immediately began to suspect the reason of her coming there, and, raising his heart to God, he prayed for His grace to overcome the temptation.

Suddenly he cried out as loud as he could the words : " Thieves ! thieves ! robbers !"

As soon as she heard these words the audacious woman fled.

But the people of the house all rose in haste, and armed themselves with whatever weapons they could find, and ran about the whole place in search of the thieves.

After a fruitless search of half an hour, they returned each to his own room, and tried to compose themselves to sleep.

When everything was hushed in silence, the unfortunate woman rose again, and went to Bernard's room a second time.

As soon as he saw her, he began again to cry out even louder than before: " Thieves! robbers! help!"

Again the house was in commotion : a more careful search was made ; but as the woman had run off at the first sound that Bernard had uttered, and regained her room, no robber could be found. But Bernard, not willing to expose the woman, did not tell anyone the reason of his cries.

The same thing happened a third time, and with a similar result ; and by the time they had retired for the third time, the grey dawn of morning had begun to appear, and the danger of another attack was averted.

When the little company had resumed their journey, the companions of St. Bernard asked him what he meant by crying out so often during the night and alarming the whole house, and said that surely he must have been dreaming all the time.

" No, dear friends," he answered. " It was all too true ; there was a robber in the house. Our hostess' was the robber, and she wanted to rob me of a treasure which I esteem more than all the treasures of the world—the treasure of holy purity. Thanks be to God, I escaped : I overcame the temptation."

Life of St. Bernard.

WHY HE WAS LOST.

There was a young man who was brought up in piety, and had learned from his parents and his pastor how to serve God, and to avoid sin. He knew that the way to preserve the holy virtue of purity, which God loves so well, is to keep a strict watch over the eyes.

One day, as he was passing along the street, he saw something that put evil thoughts before his mind. He at once remembered the advice that had so often been given him to turn away his eyes. But he neglected to do this, and continued to look at it, and thus he offended God.

Afterwards, when he saw what he had done, he was filled with deep sorrow, and went to the Sacrament of Penance to obtain forgiveness. He died soon after this, and as he had always led an edifying life, people said that he had died a happy death.

But the unfortunate man was lost. God permitted him to appear to a companion after his death to tell him what had occurred. " When I went to Confession after the grievous sin I had committed, I obtained God's pardon, because I made a good Confession. But when I was at the point of death, the Devil put before my mind the thought of what I had seen, and what had been the cause of my sin. It was a temptation ; and by the grace of God I put it away. It came back a second time, and I also banished it. But when it came a third time, I allowed my mind wilfully to rest on it, and I yielded to a grievous sin of thought, and died."

Saying this, the lost soul disappeared.

O my child, it is in this way that Satan brings so many souls to eternal ruin. Do not permit him to deceive you, but as soon as the temptation comes before you, turn away your eyes from it ; call on Jesus and Mary to help you, and the temptation will go away ; and thus you will persevere in God's holy grace.

My child, a great Saint once said to his disciples that if they wished to reach Heaven, they must keep away from all dangerous occasions of sin. The Holy Ghost says in the Scriptures : " He that loveth the danger shall perish in it."

" FLY ! FLY ! FLY !"

A young man who had very often yielded to temptations against holy purity, because he did not run away when he was tempted, asked a holy man to tell him what he should do that he might never again fall into sin, for he desired most sincerely to save his soul.

" There are three things you must do if you desire to overcome these temptations," replied the man of God. " Firstly, you must fly away ; secondly, you must fly away at once ; thirdly, you must fly away quickly. The way by which you can most readily overcome temptations is to fly away from them."

The young man followed his advice, and as soon as he was tempted to do wrong he went away from the person or the place where he was in danger, and he always overcame the temptation.

So, my child, keep away—fly away from the danger, and you shall never sin.

THE ADVICE OF BROTHER GILES.

A religious, who was much troubled with temptations against holy purity, one day asked Brother Giles what he ought to do that he might not yield **to them.**

" My brother," said the holy man, " tell me what you would do to a dog that was going to bite you ?"

" I would take up a stick or a stone," said the other, " and I would try to drive it away, and I would not cease doing so till it had run away from me ; or I would try to run to a place where it could not reach me."

" Very well," replied Brother Giles, " do the same every time a temptation comes near you. Keep it off by prayer, and run away from it as fast as you can, and the temptation will soon go away and leave you in peace."

ST. THOMAS OF AQUIN'S TEMPTATION.

St. Thomas of Aquin, inspired by God, had put on the habit of St. Dominic, in order to serve Jesus Christ in the state of religion with all the fervour of his soul. He became a friar of Mary, as the Dominicans were then often called, and wore the sacred scapular given by her virginal hands to blessed Reginald of Orleans.

The family of St. Thomas, rich, powerful, and worldly-minded, could ill brook the sight of one of their number in the poor habit of a mendicant friar. They employed every argument to shake his resolution, but to no purpose : the holy youth persevered in his design. His brothers awaited their opportunity, and when St. Thomas was on his way to Paris, to study at the famous University of that city, they seized him, and carried him by violence to one of their castles.

Finding that neither threats nor promises could make him falter in his determination to serve God as a son of St. Dominic, they at last confined him in a dungeon of the castle, where the Saint occupied himself in prayer. Then the Devil put into the minds of his persecutors a design truly diabolical. " If," suggested the Evil One, " you can destroy his virginal purity, you will overcome his resolution ; God, who now strengthens him, will then forsake him." This hideous design was carried into effect. A miserable agent of the Devil was sent into the chamber where the Saint was confined, in order to tempt him to sin. The instant the holy youth understood the wicked purpose of this wretch, without an instant's delay, and invoking the assistance of God, he snatched a burning brand from the fire, and drove the tempter indignantly from his presence. He then, with the charred wood, marked a cross upon the wall, and, falling on his knees, he prayed with the utmost fervour, in words like these : " O dearest Jesus ! I know well that every perfect gift, and above all others that of chastity, depends upon the most powerful assistance of Thy providence, and that without Thee a creature can do nothing. Therefore I pray Thee to defend by Thy grace the purity of my soul and of my body. And if I have ever received any impression that may stain this virtue, do Thou, who art the Supreme Lord of all my powers, take it from me, that I may with a pure heart advance in Thy love and service, offering myself on the most pure altar of Thy Divinity, to be chaste all the days of my life."

Whilst the Saint thus prayed alone, other visitors entered his chamber. He had driven forth the emissary of the impure kingdom of the Devil, and behold, angels from that kingdom " wherein nothing that is defiled can enter " fill the prison with glory and with heavenly music. They approach the kneeling form of the Saint bearing a white girdle, with which they encircle him as with a supernatural cincture of purity. As the girdle is drawn around him, St. Thomas experiences an agony of pain, and sinks fainting to the ground. God had answered his prayer. So pleasing in His Divine sight was the generous resistance of the Saint to the diabolical temptation, so fervent had been his prayer, and so ardent his love of purity, that God gave him from that moment an extraordinary gift of chastity, so that never after that moment did he experience the slightest temptation against that virtue.

IX. How to Overcome Temptations to Impurity.

One great means of overcoming temptations against this virtue of purity is to meditate on the four last things—Death, Judgment, Hell, and Heaven. The thought of these truths have saved innumerable souls, either by leading them back if they have gone astray, or by preserving them in their innocence.

ST. EUDOXIA'S CONVERSION.

At the end of the first century there lived in the city of Heliopolis a young woman who was famous for her great beauty and charms, but whose life was one of great sin.

She had left her home in the days of her girlhood to escape the watchful eyes of her parents, that she might have more freedom to gratify the evil inclinations of her heart. So great was the reputation she had gained for evil that it was commonly said that she had been the cause of more iniquity than any other evil-doer in the country. She was also very wealthy, for she received large sums of money from those who admired her.

Eudoxia—for this was her name—was living this kind of life when it pleased God to call her, like another Magdalen, to a life of sanctity.

One night she was lodging in a house which stood quite close to a monastery. It was late, and the traffic of the day being ended, a quiet stillness hung over the city. As the night was calm and beautiful, Eudoxia sat near the open window of her room. Suddenly she heard a sound as of someone reading. She listened ; it came from the neighbouring monastery. It was the custom in that holy house, as elsewhere, for each one of the monks to read a pious book every night before retiring to rest. And it happened that one of these monks whose cell was nearest to the house where the woman lodged, thinking himself quite alone, and that no one was near, read aloud from his book.

Eudoxia listened at first with some curiosity to find out the subject of which he read. It was a meditation on the eternal torments of those who die in mortal sin.

The poor woman began to tremble as she listened to the terrible description read by the unknown voice, and when the monk had finished and retired to rest, happy in the thought that he was not conscious to himself of any grievous sin, Eudoxia also lay down on her bed.

But she could not rest ; the fear of the terrible judgment of God upon sinners drove sleep away from her eyes, and she was tossed to and fro all the night in terrible agony.

As soon as it was morning she went over to the gate of the monastery, and asked permission to see the monk who had read aloud the previous night the description of the torments of Hell.

Germanus—this was the monk's name—was surprised at this unexpected visit, but, in obedience to the order of his Superior, went to speak to the woman at the gate.

" Ah, my Father," cried out the now trembling sinner, " you see before you a woman covered with sins of the blackest dye. Must I, then, be lost for ever ?"

The good monk answered · " Jesus Christ came down from Heaven to seek and to save that which was lost."

" Is it possible, then, that I can escape those eternal torments of which you read last night ?"

" Yes, my child," the monk answered, " by being sorry for what you have done, and by doing penance "

" Tell me, my Father, what I must do."

" You must begin by renouncing sin for ever ; then go and receive instruction and be baptized."

Eudoxia then went in search of a priest who might instruct her in the mysteries of the true Faith, and when she found him, she threw herself at his feet and cried out · " I am the greatest of all sinners, but I have heard that the mercy of God is immense, so I want to be baptized, and to do penance for the abominable offences of my past life."

The priest received her with the greatest kindness. He ordered her to lay aside for ever her gay garments, and to renounce her evil companions ; then he instructed her in the truths of the Christian religion.

Eudoxia received baptism from the hands of the Bishop Theodatus, and from that moment her life was a model of edification to all.

THE OLD MAN'S ANSWER.

A certain hermit who was very much tormented by temptations against the holy virtue of purity went to an old man and asked him how he could best overcome them.

The old man answered : " There is one way, my child, which can never fail. As soon as these thoughts come before your mind, think of the terrible punishments which God inflicts in Hell on those who yield to impurity, and say to yourself : ' O my soul, if you consent to yield to that temptation, you shall have to endure those torments for ever.' "

The hermit followed this advice and became a **Saint**.

ST. BENEDICT'S REMEDY.

prayers Satan brought back to his mind the remembrance of a lady he had formerly known when in Rome, and the remembrance of that woman pursued him so persistently that the union with God after which alone he aspired was constantly disturbed.

To rid himself for ever of these painful distractions and temptations, he lay down amongst the thorns and briars that grew around him, and rolled his body to and fro amongst them till the pain he suffered drove away all sentiments of pleasure which the tempter wished him to experience in order that he might overcome him and gain his soul.

St. Benedict came forth from the terrible conflict victorious, and he received from God as a reward of his fidelity the grace of ever afterwards being exempted from similar temptations.

ST. GREGORY : *Dialogues*, ii.

THE HERMIT AND THE TEMPTER.

In the "Lives of the Fathers of the Desert" we read that there was once a holy hermit who had passed twenty-five years of his life in the wilderness, serving God day and night. The fame of his sanctity had spread far and wide, and everyone spoke of his great virtue.

There was in that country a wicked woman named Zoe, who, when she heard him thus spoken of, said : "You say he is a holy man. I do not believe it. I am sure I could in a short time make him offend God."

Saying this, she went to his cell to tempt him to

sin. But as soon as he heard her deceitful words, he said to her : " Wait a few moments, and come to me when I call upon you."

So he went to a little distance, and kindled a great fire. When this was done, he took off his shoes, and sitting down on the ground, put his feet into the fire. The pain he suffered was so great that he began to cry aloud. Zoe ran to the spot, but when she saw what had happened she started back in horror.

The hermit, in the midst of his suffering, cried out several times : " Oh, what a terrible pain ! If I cannot bear this fire even for a few moments, how shall I be able to bear the fire of Hell for all eternity?"

Zoe, hearing these words, was filled with a terrible fear. She went home, and from that moment began to lead a new life. She lived a life of penance to the end of her days, and died the death of the Saints.

But devotion to the most Holy Mother of God is, amongst all others, the most sure means of overcoming temptations to impurity and of persevering in the grace of God. St. Bernard tells us that it is impossible for one who is really devout to Mary to be lost ; so, my child, endeavour to nourish in your soul a true and constant devotion to her.

ST. ANTONY OF PADUA AND OUR LADY.

Most of God's Saints were often tempted by impure temptations, and many of them won for themselves most beautiful crowns of glory in Heaven often tempted him in this way ; but as soon as he saw the temptation coming he calmly raised up his mind to Heaven, and prayed to his Heavenly Queen for protection : " O my Queen and my Mother, take care of me."

At the end of his life, as he was one day reciting this his favourite prayer, Our Lady appeared to him to console him and to announce to him the great reward that was awaiting him in Heaven, because he had been so faithful to have recourse to her in these temptations. She also obtained for him at the moment of his death the grace of seeing Jesus, and hearing from His Divine lips the happy invitation to go with Him to Heaven. " I see my God," he cried out, " and He is calling on me to come."

Soon afterwards he calmly breathed his last, and went to receive his reward in Heaven.

OUR LADY HELPS US IN TEMPTATION.

The Blessed Virgin once said to St. Bridget · " As a mother who sees her child in danger of being put to death by the sword of an enemy runs forward and does all in her power to save him, so do I also run to the help of my children when I see them— even those amongst them who may have already yielded to sin—in danger of yielding to temptation as soon as they call upon me to help them."

Let this little prayer, " O Mary, my sweet Mother, help me," be on your lips as soon as you see a temptation coming near you, and she, your Heavenly Mother, will enable you to overcome it, and to persevere in God's grace.

XXXIV

THE SEVENTH AND TENTH COMMAND MENTS

I. On the Virtue of Honesty.

THE Seventh Commandment is, " Thou shalt not steal " ; and the Tenth Commandment is, " Thou shalt not covet thy neighbour's goods." The object of these two commandments is to direct us in our duty concerning the property of our neighbour.

In the first place, we must be just towards our neighbour in all our dealings with him.

FRANCIS EGAN, THE HONEST SHOP-BOY.

In a certain great manufacturing city, a youth named Francis Egan, who had recently left college, where he had been instructed in the true principles of a Christian life, had obtained a postion of clerk in the office of a rich manufacturer. He was energetic and willing, and soon won the confidence of his employer.

One day a letter came recalling an order for goods. The merchant handed the letter to Francis, and with a smile said : " Francis, write an answer to this letter, and say that the goods were shipped before the letter countermanding the order came to hand."

Francis looked into the face of his employer with a sad but firm glance, and replied : " I cannot do that, sir."

" Why not ?" asked the merchant angrily.

" Because that is not the truth, for you know that the goods are still here in the shop, and it would be a lie to write what you ask me."

" I hope you will always be as particular," replied the merchant, turning on his heels and going away.

Did Francis lose his place ? No. The merchant, although angry at the time, knew from these words the value of the lad. He not only kept him in his office, but soon raised him to the position of his confidential clerk.

Months and years went on, and Francis by his honesty and his attention to the affairs of his master, made himself very valuable to him, and after ten years' service he was admitted as a partner in the firm, and is now one of the richest men in New York.

Honesty will pay both in this life and in the next.

The Chimes.

II. THE VICE OF STEALING.

We must never take away what belongs to our neighbour, nor keep anything that is his without his consent. It is in this that the sin of stealing consists, and those who begin by taking things that are of little consequence, frequently end by taking that which is of great value.

A STORY, SAD, BUT ALAS ! TOO TRUE.

A young man who lived in a populous part of the country had contracted in his childhood a habit of stealing. At first it was but small things. Sometimes he stole bread and fruit and nuts in his father's house. But when he grew a little older, he sometimes found his way into the gardens of his neighbours, and stole fruit and vegetables. At length he became more daring, and began to steal money in small sums from his parents, and any other thing he took a fancy to which fell under his hands.

He next tried to steal from his companions and his neighbours, and, on account of his cunning, succeeded in escaping without even being suspected.

It is true he often heard of the penalties that were inflicted on robbers when they were discovered—that some of them were imprisoned, and made to endure hard labour, and that many even were, in the end, put to death on the scaffold; but, although he dreaded all these things, he hoped that his cleverness would make him escape them in the future, as it had done till then. Thus he continued his evil life, and with such success that, although he had already plundered much, and had stolen even very valuable things, he had not once been suspected. At length he began to think that all the stories he had heard about robbers and their dismal ends were invented to frighten him.

With this idea in his mind, and taking his past successes as the measure of those yet to come, he boldly undertook still greater enterprises. He chose a certain number of young men, as wicked as he himself was, and formed a gang which infested the whole neighbourhood. Over and over again had things been stolen, but the thieves were never discovered; and as these men kept up the appearance of piety, no one suspected them as being the authors of these depredations.

But the prosperity of the wicked generally comes to an untimely end. One night, as they were engaged in their evil work, it happened that a man who belonged to that part of the country was returning home late, and met the robbers as they were going to the place where they concealed their booty. They had that night stolen a great quantity, and each carried a heavy burden. The man, who knew them, was surprised at seeing them out so late, and knew that they must have been engaged in stealing. They, too, seeing that they were discovered at last, and that if they allowed him to escape, he would inform upon them, and that their career would thus be brought to an end, resolved to murder him. This they therefore did, and left his body on the roadside.

When this murder was discovered, great consternation filled the whole country. The magistrates sent out armed men to apprehend, if possible, the murderers, and they succeeded, in course of time, in arresting them. When they were brought to trial, it soon became known that they were also the robbers who had stolen so much other property, for some of the stolen goods were found in their possession.

At the end of the trial, being found guilty, they were condemned to die on the scaffold. A terrible warning was this to all who heard the history of the unfortunate young man, who had begun his career by taking away what was in itself of but little consequence, and had ended it by the terrible crime of murder.

III. On Coveting our Neighbour's Goods.

Not only must we never take away or keep what belongs to others, but we must be careful not even to covet it—that is to say, we must never desire unjustly or unlawfully what belongs to another.

THE TEMPTATION OF THE TWO BROTHERS.

Two noble knights were one day passing together through a thick forest on their way to a tournament. They were brothers, and each of them possessed great riches.

As they were passing through this solitary place, the demon of covetousness inspired both of them with the same wicked thought—that of killing his brother, in order to obtain his share of wealth.

But, as they were Christians, and feared to offend God, they both resisted the temptation ; but still their consciences were not at rest. So when they reached the nearest village, the one said to the other · " I am going to look for a priest, for I want to go to Confession."

The other one answered : " I also have the same desire in my mind." So they both went to the church and made their Confession.

After both had finished, and were about to continue their journey, one of them said to the other : " My dear brother, I must tell you of a terrible temptation that came into my mind as we were passing through the forest. Satan tempted me to take away your life, that I might obtain possession of your wealth."

The other brother started back in surprise. " My

dearest brother," he said, " the same thought also came into my mind, and I was tempted to kill you, that I might become possessed of your property ; but I, like yourself, banished the temptation."

This revelation filled them both with such a horror for wealth, which so nearly was the cause of crime, that on the spot they both resolved to renounce for ever the riches of this world, so dangerous in time and for eternity, and went to live together in a hut which they built for themselves in the forest.

Thus was begun the famous monastery in the forest of Molesme, in the middle of the eleventh century.   *Lives of the Saints*, Mar. 28.

THE THREE ROBBERS.

Three of the inhabitants of the city of Balke, in Tartary, were one day travelling together, when they by chance found a treasure by the wayside. They divided it among themselves, and continued their journey, talking together of how they would spend their newly-found riches. It happened that, as they were speaking in this manner, they began to feel hungry, and it became necessary for them to procure provisions. So one of them was sent to the neighbouring village to purchase food. He was the youngest of the three.

When he was wending his way to the village alone, he said to himself : " I am now very rich ; but I would have been three times as rich if I had been alone when the treasure was found, for then I should have had all the money to myself. My companions have the other two parts. I wonder if it would be possible for me to get their share as well

as my own ?   Yes, I can easily do so ; I have only
to buy some poison, and put it into the provisions I
am going to purchase.   At my return I will tell them
that I have already dined in the village, and my
two companions will eat what I give them without
any suspicion that there is anything wrong, and they
will both die ; then, instead of having only a part
of the treasure, I shall have it all.''

In the meantime the two robbers, who were seated
under a tree awaiting his return, thus spoke to each
other : '' It is a pity that that young man was with
us when we found the treasure, because we should
then have had a greater share of it.   As it is, could
we not take his share and add it to that which
we already have, by killing him as soon as he
returns ?''

As soon as the young man came back, they
rushed upon him and slew him with their daggers ;
then, sitting down, they partook of the provisions
he had brought. Soon afterwards they became
very ill, and saw that they were dying. They
immediately suspected that their younger companion had poisoned them, that he might possess
himself of their share of the money.   They called
to a passer-by to come and help them, but it was too
late, and they died in the midst of most terrible
sufferings, having first disclosed to the stranger what
they had done.   *L'Ami de la Jeunesse.*

IV. THE EFFECTS OF DISHONESTY.

It very often happens that those who have committed the sin of theft are discovered. What a

disgrace this brings upon them even in this life !
No one ever trusts them afterwards, and everyone
seems to shun them.

SIMON, THE LITTLE THIEF.

There was once a little boy called Simon who
had a great inclination to take away what was not
his own, so that whenever he found anything lying
on the ground, instead of looking for the owner, he
was accustomed to keep it to himself.

One day, as he was passing near the entrance to
a blacksmith's forge, he saw a little iron chain lying
on the ground. No one was near, and the boy, as
usual, went to pick it up and appropriate it. Accordingly, he bent down and took up the chain hurriedly.
But he had no sooner done this than he uttered a
loud scream, which attracted the blacksmith to the
spot. The chain had just been taken out of the
furnace, and being hot, had been placed there by
the blacksmith to cool, an instant before the boy
reached the place. As soon as he had taken the
heated chain in his hand, it burnt his fingers, and
it was this that caused him to scream, and brought
the blacksmith to the place. The theft thus discovered was a lesson for him, and the marks of the
burning, which for a long time remained on his
fingers, reminded him that those who take away
what is not their own may one day be discovered,
and be punished, if not in this world, at least in the
next.   *Moëlher,* ii. 334.

V. On the Rewards of Honesty.

Honesty is one of those virtues which brings down from Heaven the choicest blessings of God, and which always procures for those who practise it the esteem and the confidence of men.

THE HONEST FLOWER-SELLER.

During the summer of the year 1856, in one of the most aristocratic parts of Paris, and in the corner of a large doorway, there sat a poor woman selling flowers, which were neatly formed into bouquets, to the passers-by. Beside her was a little boy, her only child, aged about five years. The poor woman depended on the sale of her flowers for the support of herself and her child.

A gentleman, who was evidently a stranger, and belonged to the more wealthy class of society, happened to pass by, accompanied by a young lady of about fifteen years, who seemed to be his daughter. The gentleman, attracted by the flowers in the basket, went near, and taking up one or two of the bouquets in his hand, looked at them, and then laying them down again, as if they did not suit his taste, turned to go away, without noticing the wistful look and the two tears that were falling from the eyes of the poor woman. His daughter, however, saw them, and took in at a glance the state of matters. Without pretending to observe the tears that were flowing now in streams from the woman's eyes, she silently let a pound-note fall upon the head of the little boy at her side, and hurried away to join her father, who by this time was a little in advance.

" Mother," said the little boy, showing his mother the piece of paper he had picked up from the ground, " what is this ?"

" Where did you find that paper, my child ?" asked the mother.

" That young lady let it fall as she was going away."

Immediately the poor woman rose up, and, running after the two who had just left her, said to the young lady : " Please, madam, you have lost some money," at the same time handing her the note she had in her hand.

Pretending not to understand what she meant, the young lady told her to go away ; but, as she still continued to follow them, the gentleman looked round, and seeing the note the woman was holding in her hand, and hearing that his daughter had dropped it, he took it from her, and was putting it into his purse, when his daughter, taking him aside, spoke to him in a low voice for a few moments. What she said to him was not known, but the good man, again opening his purse, took out a twenty-pound note, which he gave the poor woman, along with the note she had received from his daughter, saying : " My daughter gave you one pound because you are poor ; I now give you twenty times as much because you are honest. May God bless you, my good woman."

Saying these words, he went away, leaving the poor flower-seller stupefied at the good fortune that had fallen on her all on account of her honesty.

SCHOUPPE : *Catéch.* iii. 564.

ST. ELIGIUS, THE GOLDSMITH.

St. Eligius, or Giles, was a goldsmith by trade. At that time Clotaire II. was King of France. Having heard that Eligius was skilful in gold and silver work, the King sent for him, and asked him to make him a throne in gold of great magnificence. At the same time he gave the Saint as much gold as he thought would be required for the work.

Eligius worked with great diligence, and in a very short time, out of the gold he had received, made two thrones of unparalleled beauty, and brought them to the King.

Clotaire was surprised, not only at the magnificence of the work, but more especially at seeing how Eligius had been able with the material given for making one throne to construct two. The two thrones were weighed, and found to contain exactly the weight of gold that had been given him.

The King said : " This, indeed, is an honest man. While others, for one reason or other, take part of the precious metals supplied to them for their work for their own use, this man has scrupulously employed every grain given to him in this work. It is a sufficient proof," added˙ the King, turning towards the Saint, " that you can be entrusted with matters of the greatest importance."

From that day forward the King entertained for the Saint the greatest esteem and respect, and promoted him to a place of trust in his palace.

Petits Bolland., xiv. 4.

FRANCIS, THE HONEST SHEPHERD-BOY.

Francis Fleury lost his parents when quite a little child. A neighbouring farmer, who had no children of his own, brought the child to his house, and took care of him, for he hoped that when he grew up he might be useful to him.

When he was old enough to take care of the sheep, the farmer sent him to the fields with them every day, and he spent the whole day there, returning home with them only when darkness set in.

One evening a gentleman happened to pass along the road on horseback. Not far from the place where Francis was standing something very bright fell from the gentleman's pocket, but, as he did not observe what had happened, he continued to ride onwards.

Francis went to pick it up, and, to his surprise, found that it was a massive gold watch. An old shepherd, who was with him at the time, wanted him to give him the watch.

But Francis said : " No, the watch is not mine ; it belongs to that gentleman who is riding along the road. I must run after him and give it to him."

So, without waiting even for an instant, he ran off in the direction the man had taken. He followed him for several hours, till at length he reached a village, where he saw at the door of an hotel what seemed to be the horse on which the gentleman had ridden. He went into the house, and saw there one whom he thought resembled him.

Francis, going over to him, said : " Sir, did you lose this watch ? I found it on the road, and I have run to this place, hoping to find the owner."

The gentleman, who was a rich merchant from Dunkirk, immediately recognized the watch, but for a moment pretended that he knew nothing about it, to see what the boy would then do.

" It is quite possible you may have mistaken the person who dropped it," he said, as he put on a look of indifference.

" Then," said Francis, " I must run on and try if I can find the owner." Saying these words, he turned to go out.

The boy's honesty touched the heart of the stranger. He called him back.

" Who are you, my child ?" said he, gently stroking the boy's head.

" I am a shepherd-boy," he answered.

" Where does your father live ?"

" Up in Heaven with the angels, and my mother also."

" Have you any other relatives ?"

" Oh no, sir ! I am living with a farmer a very long way from this place. But, sir, I must go at once, for in my hurry to overtake you I forgot about my sheep, and they will be hungry and perhaps go astray, and this never happened before."

" My good boy, perhaps you are even more hungry than they are." Having said these words, he told the boy that the watch was indeed his, and praised him for his honesty. He was about to give him a reward for what he had done, but thinking that he must need something to eat, he went first to procure some food for him. Francis took this opportunity of escaping, and without as much as looking behind him or waiting for a piece of bread,

ran off with such speed that, although the gentleman followed him for some time, he was soon lost
to view.

In the meantime Francis arrived, tired and weary,
at the place where he had left his sheep, but they
were nowhere to be seen. He then went to his
master's house. His master met him at the door
with a heavy stick in his hand, and seemed to be
very angry

"O master," he said, "you must not punish me
because I left the sheep without anyone to take care
of them. It was not my fault. I found a watch,
and I had to go after the gentleman who lost it, that
I might give it back to him. Only he went so fast
that it was a long time before I could overtake him.
So I could not help it."

"You could not help it, you say! I will teach
you that you must mind your work next time that
you find anything."

Saying this, he raised the stick to strike the boy.
But, fortunately, at the same moment the gentleman himself rode up to the door. He had followed
the boy on horseback, because he was determined
not to lose sight of one who was so good and honest.

"Don't strike the boy," he cried out as he saw
the farmer raise the stick; "it was entirely my fault."

Then he told him the whole story, and asked the
farmer to be allowed to take the boy with him.
The farmer after a little time agreed, and Francis
accompanied the gentleman to his house. He grew
up there in virtue and honesty, and in course of
time became a wealthy merchant and a generous
benefactor to the poor of the city in which he dwelt.

VI. On the Obligation of Restitution.

When one has taken away what belongs to another, the sin cannot be forgiven, unless that which has been taken away is given back to its owner when it can be done. This is called " making resti tution." This is many times very difficult to accomplish, especially when one delays till some future time. O my child, read carefully the following examples, that you may ever live an honest life before God and man :

THE RICH MERCHANT ON HIS DEATH-BED.

A certain merchant, who was very rich, fell dangerously ill. His friends, perceiving that his malady was likely to be fatal, exhorted him to enter into himself, and prepare to appear before God. He promised to do so, but deferred the execution of his promise from day to day.

Several learned and prudent confessors were recommended to him, but the sick man, under various pretexts, refused to see them.

In the meantime a certain missionary of great renown for sanctity happened to pass through the town. The merchant being informed of it, and conscious that his end was drawing near, consented to receive his visit.

The missionary having inspired him with confidence, he opened his heart to him, and said : " Father, my conscience has been for a length of time much troubled respecting many things connected with my business."

" Be pleased," answered the missionary, " to

let me know the cause of your uneasiness and doubts."

The penitent immediately began, but after explaining one or two points his ideas suddenly became confused, and the remainder of his discourse was totally unconnected. The confessor was greatly embarrassed. "If I propose to him any questions," thought he, "I shall only increase the confusion of his mind." In this perplexity he determined not to interrupt the penitent, and whilst the latter continued to speak, he fervently besought the Almighty to direct him as to the best means of promoting the salvation of his soul.

The rich man having ceased, the confessor waited a little while that his mind might become somewhat composed, which happily took place soon after. Then, addressing his penitent, he said : " My dear friend, you are a man distinguished for intelligence and prudence in the management of commercial affairs ; moreover, you are gifted with a fair and upright mind. If one of your friends should, on his death-bed, consult you upon the case which you have just proposed to me, what would you answer ?"

" I would tell him," said the sick man, " that he should make unconditional restitution. Things now appear to me in a far different light from that in which I formerly viewed them."

" Well, my good friend," replied the confessor, " adopt in your own case the same measure which you would recommend to another. The eternal reward which awaits you in Heaven is infinitely more precious than all the riches of this world."

The merchant profited by this salutary advice, and, sending for a notary, caused a formal declaration, agreeable to the dictates of his conscience, to be drawn up. He then, with the assistance of the zealous missionary, made a humble Confession; but no sooner had he ended than the light of reason which Heaven had afforded him became suddenly eclipsed, and he heaved his last sigh in the arms of his confessor. *Mrs. Herbert*, p. 231.

THE DYING MAN AND HIS THREE SONS.

Monsignor de Segur relates the following example :
There was a father of a family who had become rich by unjust means. In the midst of his evil ways he became very ill, and began to fear lest he might die. His body was covered with sores, from which he suffered much, and all the remedies he applied were without effect.

The priest who attended him told him that he was in great danger of death, and that he must restore what he had so unjustly acquired if he wished to receive absolution and die a good death.

The only answer the wretched man gave was this one, which he constantly repeated : " What would become of my children if I made restitution ?"

The priest had recourse to the following stratagem to save his poor soul. He said to him that there was a certain remedy which was in ancient times considered very effective in curing the disease from which he was suffering, but that it would cost an immense sum of money to procure it.

" Oh, get it for me, even supposing that it were to cost hundreds—yea, thousands of pounds, for I would part with every penny in my possession to obtain relief. What is this great remedy ?"

" It consists in melting a little of the fat of the arm of a living person, and covering with it these open sores. A very small quantity will suffice. If you could get anyone to allow his arm to be thus melted in the fire for only a quarter of an hour, you would be cured."

The dying man looked at the priest incredulously for a moment, and replied : " That seems a strange remedy. But where could I find a person willing to undergo such a painful operation even for all my fortune ?"

" I will tell you what you will do," said the priest calmly. " Send for your oldest son ; he is to inherit all your wealth. Surely he will not refuse to do this for his father, who is to leave him so much money. But if he refuses, then ask your second son, and tell him that if he consents to do what you ask him, you will make him your heir instead of his elder brother. If he also refuses, ask your third son ; for such a reward he most certainly will consent."

The request was accordingly made to the three sons in succession, but they naturally all refused with horror to allow such a thing to be done to them, even to save the life of their father. The father then said to them : " What ! to save my life, you all refuse to suffer a little pain for a few moments, and I, to procure you a comfortable living, will go to Hell for all eternity ! Indeed, I would certainly be a great fool to do such a thing !"

He at once made full restitution of all he had unjustly acquired, without for a moment considering what would become of his family.

The three sons acted also very wisely. To have consented to do what was asked of them, even for the short space of a quarter of an hour, was a sacrifice greater than human nature could endure ; but to choose to burn eternally in Hell rather than restore what belongs to others is an act of folly which no tongue could express.

MONSIGNOR DE SEGUR : *Œuvres Complètes.*

THE WILL REVOKED.

There was a certain rich man who had amassed his means by fraud and injustice. The end of his life came, and he began to be afraid of the awful judgment that awaited him if he did not make up his peace with God before he died. So he sent for a priest, and prepared to die well, by making a last will and testament, in whch he commanded his heirs to make full restitution of all that he had unjustly acquired, and also to give a great portion of his riches to various charitable works, in order that he might in this way restore to the full all that he had unlawfully obtained.

When the will was finished, it happened that his wife heard of what he had done, and that, instead of the great fortune which she had looked forward to possessing at her husband's death, she would receive only a very moderate income.

She at once, taking her little ones with her, went to the bedside of her dying husband, and in the midst of their tears and her own, she cried out : " Oh, what will become of us now ? We shall be left to pine away in poverty and misery."

The dying man ought to have answered : " And

23—2

what will become of my soul if I die in my sins ?''
But he had not the courage to say these words.
His wife, forgetting altogether the ruin of her husband's soul in eternity, and thinking only of the
pleasures of the present life, gained his consent to
revoke his will, and to make another, in which there
was no question of restitution or pious legacies.

Not long after he had signed this new will the unfortunate man, filled with remorse and despair, died,
and went to give an account of his life to the Just
Judge, who renders to everyone according to his
works.   SCHOUPPE : *Catéch.*, ii. 550.

THE DEATH OF THE USURER.

There was once a famous usurer at the point of
death.   He saw that his days were numbered, and
having hitherto professed the Catholic Faith, he was
anxious to die a good death.

A priest was sent for, who, having discovered that
the riches he had amassed had been obtained bv
unjust means, urged him to make restitution before
he died as the only way of securing his salvation.

" But what will become of my children if I do
this ?" said the dying man.

" The salvation of your soul is of infinitely more
importance to you than the temporal well-being of
your family," answered the priest.

After a few moments of silent reflection he roused
himself, and said to the priest : " I cannot do what
you ask, and I will take the consequences upon
myself."

He turned his face towards the wall, and in a few
minutes he was dead.

O my child, what a terrible death ! Oh, how those should tremble with fear who have made themselves rich by means of fraud and injustice !

MEVAULT : Conjuration de l'Impiété.

A WITNESS FROM THE GRAVE.

Towards the beginning of the year 1070 St. Stanislaus, Bishop of Cracovia, in Poland, had pur chased from one of the citizens named Peter a piece of ground whereon he might build a church for the glory of God.   He paid in full the price of the land, but did not exact a receipt for the payment.   Three years had now passed since the death of the former possessor (Peter), when his heirs, seeing that Boleslaus, an unjust and cruel Prince, was very much irritated against the Saint on account of the continual reproaches he made him for his scandalous conduct, thought this a fair opportunity of enriching themselves at the holy man's expense. They drew up a legal process against him, accusing him of having taken possession, without any right to do so, of lands which belonged to them.   The King was very much pleased at seeing this case brought before him ; and as the Bishop had neglected to receive an acknowledgment of the money being paid, because he had not foreseen this act of deceit, he had nothing to present in his defence, and was therefore condemned either to pay over again the price of the land, or to restore it to the heirs of Peter, who sold it to him. Stanislaus, by an inspiration from Heaven, said to the judges that, as he could not obtain justice from the living, he would ask it from the dead.   " Give me," said the holy man, " but three days, and I will bring before you the man who sold me the land, and he shall justify me." The judges laughed at his request, and as they imagined that such would be impossible, readily granted it.

The man of God immediately returned home, and assembling together his clergy, asked them to join with him in fasting and prayer to God for the space of three days, to obtain from Him justice in the sight of his enemies.

" O my Lord and my God," he prayed, " the cause is not mine, but Thine ; it is against Thee and Thy Church that these wicked men have risen up ; it is Thou Thyself Who art wronged by this unjust demand : be pleased, therefore, to rise up in Thine own defence, that Thy enemies may be confounded."

On the morning of the third day he offered up the most Holy Sacrifice of the Mass with the greatest solemnity. Then, still retaining his pontifical vestments, he went in procession to the cemetery, accompanied by his clergy, and followed by an immense multitude of the people who had been informed of what had taken place.

On reaching the grave, he commanded the stone to be removed, and the grave to be opened. When they reached the place where the body had been laid to rest, nothing was to be seen but a few dry bones mingled with the earth. The Bishop then knelt down, and raising up his eyes to Heaven, again fervently besought God, Who is Almighty and can do all things, to be pleased to work a miracle in the sight of all the people, for the glory of his Name and the cause of justice.

Then, stretching forth his pastoral staff, he touched

the bones, and cried out in the words of the prophet Ezechiel : "O dry bones, hear ye the word of the Lord your God. In the name of the Father, and of the Son, and of the Holy Ghost, I command you to rise up, that you may give testimony to the truth."

In an instant, at the command of the Bishop, the bones began to move into their places, and the dust lying round about became changed into flesh. The man who had been dead stood up on his feet, and, coming out of the tomb, went forward to the Bishop, and reverently saluted him. The procession was again formed, and they all returned to the city. They proceeded in the first place to the church to thank God for this manifestation of His power and goodness, and then to the tribunal of the King.

At this time the King was in his palace, surrounded by his nobles and the magistrates. A messenger entered in great haste, and with trembling lips announced to him that the Bishop and clergy were coming towards the palace, accompanied by an immense multitude of the people, and with them Peter, risen from the dead.

Consternation fell upon the King on hearing this. At first he would not believe it, although trembling in every limb at the announcement. In a few moments the Bishop entered, leading Peter by the hand.

Being come before the throne, he spoke thus · "Sire, behold, I have brought into your presence Peter, from whom I bought the land. He was indeed dead, but he is risen again, and in very truth stands before you. Ask him now if what I said be not the truth ; he himself will bear testimony that I paid him

entirely the price of the land. The man is sufficiently well known to you all, and the grave from
which God hath raised him up is open. His word,
therefore, ought to be a more infallible evidence of
the truth than any document could be, or the testimony of any witnesses that could be adduced.

Then Peter raised his voice, formerly so familiar
to many of them, and said : " Be it known to you,
O King, and to all the people, that I received the
entire price of the land which I sold to the Bishop
whereon to build his church, and therefore my
nephews, Peter, John, and Stanislaus, have no right
whatsoever thereunto."

Then, turning towards the heirs, who were present,
he said : " As for you, unless you do penance immediately for your evil deeds, you will be overtaken
by a sudden death, because God, Who cannot be
deceived, will most certainly punish you with terrible severity for daring to molest His holy Bishop
in the peaceful possession of what belongs to him."

The astonishment of the multitude could not be
expressed, and in their hearts they thanked God
for coming to the assistance of His servant. His
accusers were fixed with dread and terror to the
spot on which they stood, and the King himself,
trembling from head to foot, rose up and gave
sentence in favour of the Bishop.

Peter still remained standing in the presence of
all the people. Turning towards him, the Bishop
asked him if he would desire to live a few years
longer in this world ; that, if so, he would ask God
to grant him this favour. But he answered that
he would prefer to return again to the grave rather

than remain in this life, so miserable and so dangerous. " I am as yet in Purgatory," he said, " and I have some things to suffer in satisfaction for my sins. But I would much rather be sure of my salvation, as I am now, although I may have to suffer yet many pains and torments, than commit myself to the hazards and dangers of the stormy and tempestuous sea of this wicked world. But I beg of you, O holy Bishop, to beseech Our Lord to pardon me, and remit the rest of my punishment, and release me soon out of that prison, and bring me to enjoy His glory in the blessed company of His Saints."

St. Stanislaus promised to intercede for him.

When he had ended, the Bishop and the clergy, along with the people, reconducted him to the grave in silence and fear. The prayers for a departing soul were then read, and while they were being offered up Peter laid himself down in the tomb, and in a few moments returned to the condition in which he had been found.

Not long afterwards it was revealed to the Saint that by his prayers and the prayers of the faithful, Peter had been relieved from Purgatory, and was with God in Paradise.

Life of St. Stanislaus, May 7.

THE UNSEEN WITNESS.

On a certain occasion it happened that a man who had bought some property set out on his way to the offices of his solicitor to pay the price agreed on, which was twelve hundred pounds. This money, which was mostly in coin, he carefully placed in sealed bags, and, having entered his conveyance, in due course reached the town to which he was going.

As he was passing near a church he saw a great multitude of people entering, and on inquiring the cause, he learned that a celebrated missionary had come thither, and that he was about to preach. Anxious not to lose the opportunity of hearing him, he at once left his conveyance, and going to the house of an intimate friend who lived in the neighbourhood, confided to his care the bags of money, for which he said he would return as soon as the sermon was ended.

The man readily consented, and having carefully placed them in a secure place, which he pointed out to him, said : " You will find them there on your return."

About an hour afterwards, when the sermon was concluded, the man returned to his friend's house, and after relating to him some of the chief sentences of the discourse which had particularly interested him, and having paid a tribute of praise to the learning of the eloquent preacher, he began to think of his money.

" Will you be so good now as to give me the money, that I may take my departure ?"

" What money do you speak of ?" said the other, feigning to be surprised.

" The money I left in your care while I went to assist at the sermon—the twelve hundred pounds you placed in that drawer."

" Oh, if they were placed there, without doubt they will be there still. Go and take them."

On opening the drawer, there was nothing to be

found. The owner at first thought that his friend had acted thus through frolic to frighten him for his amusement, but when, in a few moments, he perceived that he still denied having ever seen the money, or even heard of it, he saw at once that he had been robbed.

" Go out of my house immediately," said the other in a tone of anger. " Do you take me for a thief ? You never brought that money into my house. You speak of twelve hundred pounds. Go and look elsewhere for your money, and do not come here to accuse of theft one who is innocent."

The man left the house in dismay. He betook himself, not to a solicitor, but to another friend whom he had observed at the sermon, and who at the same time was on intimate terms with the preacher, who providentially entered at that moment.

" Your sermon, reverend Father, was a most excellent one, but it has cost me dear ; it cost me twelve hundred pounds." Then he related to him what had just taken place.

" Wait here for a few moments," said the priest. " I will soon return."

He went at once to the person who had taken the money, and said : " Sir, I have come to ask you to give into my hands immediately the twelve hundred pounds which a certain gentleman confided to your care while he went to hear a sermon about three hours ago, and which you have declared that you never received. You thought that there was no witness to your cowardly action, but there was, and He saw everything you did.

At the word " witness " the man became pale.

" Restore your ill-begotten treasure," continued the missionary with greater energy, " otherwise your honour and good name is for ever lost, for the witness I will bring forward will not spare you."

Then, taking from under his mantle a Crucifix which he carried, he added : " It is Jesus Christ Himself Who is the witness ; it is He Who saw you. Unless you instantly restore the money, you will not only lose your reputation before men, but you will lose your immortal soul in eternity."

The man could no longer deny the theft. He brought forth the money from a room in which he had secreted it, and placed it untouched in the hands of the Father, who immediately restored it to the rightful owner.

D'HAUTERIVE : *Catéchisme*, vii. 212.

VII. ON RESPECTING THE PROPERTY OF OUR NEIGHBOUR.

My child, it very often happens that people become rich and succeed in their temporal affairs at the expense of others. They are accustomed to call this shrewdness and wisdom in taking advantage of a favourable opportunity, but it is more frequently unjustly possessing themselves of the property of others and enriching themselves at their expense.

THE HERMIT'S BARLEY-FIELD.

In the year 1757, during the Seven Years' War between Frederick the Great, King of Prussia, and other European Powers, it happened that a cavalry officer was commissioned to go forth on a foraging expedition in one of the provinces occupied by the troops.

When he reached a certain valley where he had expected to find abundance of corn, he discovered that the whole country as far as his eyes could reach was barren and uncultivated. He was about to return to the camp, when his eyes happened to fall on a hut almost hidden in the dense foliage of a thicket not far from the rough path on which he rode.

Going up to the door, he knocked, and it was opened by a hermit, whose hair and beard, white as the driven snow, showed that he had reached the evening of life.

"My Father," said the officer, "could you point out to me any place in the neighbourhood where I might be able to procure provisions for our horses?"

The old man informed him that at some distance there was a field of barley, and offered his services to accompany him and his men, and point it out to them.

When they had proceeded about the distance of a mile through the valley, they came to a field on which was growing a magnificent crop of the cereal they wanted.

"Ah," cried out the officer, on seeing it, "this must be the place. What a splendid crop!"

"No, sir," replied the hermit, "the field to which I am leading you is still at a little distance, but we shall soon now reach it."

About half a mile further on they came to another field, covered also with ripe corn, but not so luxuriant as the one they had passed. Here the hermit stopped, and pointing to it, said: "This is the field of which I spoke to you."

The men dismounted and cut down the ripe crop;

then, binding it in large bundles, placed them upon their horses, and returned by the path they had come.

When they were passing near the other field, the officer thus accosted the hermit : " My Father, you have made us take a useless journey in bringing us so far, when here, much nearer to your abode, is a field of barley even more abundant than the one you brought us to."

" Yes, sir," replied the old man, " the barley in this field is certainly better than that which you have taken ; but then, this field belongs to someone else, whereas the field you have harvested belongs to me."

The officer, struck with astonishment at these words, and filled with admiration at the conduct of the pious old man, uncovered his head, and bowed it towards him in token of his profound respect. He had observed with scrupulous exactness during his whole lifetime every point of honour exacted by his position, but he had never before seen an example of such admirable disinterestedness displayed by those among whom his rank caused him to be associated. " This is indeed the sublime fruit which the love of God and of His law produces," he said, " in the hearts of those who love God and serve Him perfectly."   Filassier : *Dic. d'Éducation*

AN ANCIENT FATHER OF THE DESERT AND TWO OF HIS DISCIPLES.

It happened that a certain solitary, already advanced in years, was passing through one of the deserts of the East along with two of his disciples.

The sun was casting down on them its burning rays, and they could nowhere perceive any place which could shelter them from its heat, or even the smallest streamlet of water to quench their burning thirst.

As they continued their journey, they perceived at last in the distance what appeared to them to be a house situated in the midst of widespreading palm-trees. They directed their steps towards it, and as they drew near they saw that around the house was a garden full of trees laden with ripe fruit.

Immediately one of the young men said : " Let us ask the people who dwell in this house to permit us to pull some of the fruit, that we may obtain for ourselves some refreshment in our great need."

So they went to the door and knocked, but no one came to answer their call. They knocked a second time, but with the same result. Then one of the young disciples said : " It seems that no one resides here ; let us therefore pull from the trees three apples—one for each of us—and this will refresh us after our long journey."

Saying this, he put out his hand to pull the fruit ; but the old man cried out : " My son, do not touch it. You know God's commandment : ' Thou shalt not steal.' It is not lawful for us to take even a leaf of these trees which do not belong to us, much less to eat of the fruit they produce ; let us therefore content ourselves with resting under the shade they afford us. This will sufficiently refresh us."

The three then sat down under the shade of the trees to rest. Meanwhile the old man spoke to his disciples of how the first sin came into the world by our first parents in the Garden of Eden eating the fruit which God had forbidden them even to touch, and how we ourselves ought always to try to restrain our natural inclination, so prone to procure for the appetite what is most agreeable to it.

The two disciples, encouraged by these words of the aged anchorite, laid aside all thoughts of the refreshment they so much desired, and continued to rest silently under the shadow of the trees.

When they had thus given themselves a little repose, they arose to pursue their journey; but as they were about to depart, suddenly the door of the cottage opened, and the master of the house, who was a pagan, came out to speak to them.

After kindly saluting them, he said : " My friends, know that I was in the house all the time you have been here. I silently watched you, that I might discover how you would act with regard to my fruit upon these trees. I have seen all, and I have heard all, and your words will ever remain deeply engraven in my heart. Come, now, into my house, and partake of a refreshment I have prepared for you, which you so much need in your exhausted condition and so much deserve."

They gladly accepted his invitation, and with his own hands he gave them bread and milk and fruit as much as they needed.

When they had finished their acceptable repast, the pagan said to them : " To what religion do you belong ?"

The solitary answered : " We are Christians, and we believe in Jesus Christ."

The pagan continued : " Let me learn more about

Jesus Christ and His religion which enjoins its followers to practise such great virtues."

The old man then spoke to him of the truths of our holy Faith, to which the other listened with rapt attention, and when he had ceased speaking the pagan immediately asked to be made a member of that Faith, so magnificent and sublime, which could have no other author but the great God of Heaven and earth.

The solitary baptized him in a stream of water which flowed at a little distance, and the newly baptized Christian joined himself to their company, forsaking his worldly possessions that he might belong entirely to God.

Before continuing their journey, the holy old man spoke to them in these words : " God always rewards every good work we do for His sake. Let your light therefore shine before men, that they may see your good works, and glorify your Father Who is in Heaven."   *Légendes d'Albert Werfer.*

XXXV

THE EIGHTH COMMANDMENT

I. We must Keep a Guard upon our Lips.

The Eighth Commandment is : " Thou shalt not bear false witness against thy neighbour " By this commandment are forbidden all sins of the tongue, such as false testimony, rash judgment, lies, speaking ill of our neighbour, calumny, detraction, talebearing, and any words that may injure our neighbour's character.

ST. JAMES'S WORDS ABOUT THE TONGUE.

" If any man offend not in word ; the same is a perfect man. He is able also with a bridle to lead about the whole body. For if we put bits into the mouths of horses that they may obey us, we turn about their whole body. Behold also ships, whereas they are great, and are driven by strong winds, yet are they turned about with a small helm, whithersoever the force of the governor willeth. So the tongue also is indeed a small member, and boasteth great things.

" The tongue is a fire, a world of iniquity. The tongue is placed among our members, which defileth the whole body, and inflameth the wheel of our nativity, being set on fire by Hell. For every nature of beasts, and of birds, and of serpents, and of the rest is tamed and hath been tamed by the nature of man : but the tongue no man can tame, an unquiet evil, full of deadly poison.

" By it we bless God and the Father : and by it we curse men who are made after the image of God. Out of the same mouth proceedeth blessing and cursing. My brethren, these things ought not to be so." *St. Jas.* iii.

You see, my child, from these words how easy it is to offend God by our words. We must, therefore, if we desire to be perfect, keep a continual watch upon our tongue.

St. James also tells us that he who does not sin by his tongue, the same is a perfect man. It was by a careful watching over their words that many of the Saints became so perfect.

THE LAST WORDS OF A GREAT SAINT.

When Father Angelo of Montelone was on his death-bed, his Superior told him to make known to his brethren in religion for their edification what he considered to be the greatest grace he had ever received from God. Father Angelo, in his humility, was troubled at this command, but not wishing to infringe his vow of obedience, he answered : " My brothers, the greatest favour which I have ever received from God is this : For the past thirty years of my life there has never fallen from my lips one word that was useless."

Fleurs choisies, St. François, 25.

24—2

THE GATE OF THE TONGUE.

One of the brethren of the monastery over which the holy Abbot Sisois presided said to him : " My Father, I desire to keep a guard on my heart."

The Abbot answered : " How can you guard your heart, and preserve it from dangers, if you allow the gate of your tongue to be always open ? The great business of your life should be to keep a guard upon your lips."

The brother went away in silence to put this lesson in practice, and soon became eminent for sanctity.

II. ON LIES.

A lie is to say to another what we believe to be untrue with the intention of deceiving him. Lies are offensive to God, and the Scripture says that the Devil is the father of lies ; therefore, my child, if you love God, you will be very careful on all occasions to tell the truth.

" IT IS ONLY A LITTLE LIE."

A little child of nine years of age was one day weeping bitterly. He had committed a fault by taking something which his father had told him not to touch, and he was afraid that his father would come to know about it, and punish him.

The servants of the house, who saw him weeping, and who knew the reason of his tears, said to him : " If your father asks you if you took it, you have only to deny it, and you shall not be punished."

But the child, looking at them with much indig-

nation, answered · " What is that you tell me to
do ? Tell a lie about it ? No, never ! I would
rather be punished a hundred times than think of
doing such a thing. Let my father do to me whatever he likes. I will never commit such a sin. I
have done enough of wrong already in disobeying
him without adding another sin to the one I have
already committed."

This should be the answer of every Christian child
to anyone who asks him to tell a lie.

˙ THE FLYING OX.

One day a friend of St. Thomas of Aquin cried
out to him by way of amusement : " Thomas, look
at the flying ox."

St. Thomas looked around him in astonishment
to see where that strange animal was, but, of course,
could not see it anywhere.

His friend then began to laugh, and said to
him that he was surprised to see that he was so
credulous.

But the Saint replied : " It is much easier to
believe that an ox could fly than that a Christian
could tell a lie."

ST. FIRMUS OF AFRICA.

St. Firmus, who was Bishop in Africa, concealed
in his house through charity a man whom the
Emperor wanted to put to death.

The messengers of the Emperor, hearing that the
Bishop knew where the man was, went to his house
and asked him to inform them of it.

" I cannot answer you," replied the Bishop, " because I must not tell a lie, nor may I inform you where the man is."

They urged him to tell them, but he always refused. They even put him to the torture to force him to tell them, but he still was silent. They then threatened him with death, but he answered : " I know how to suffer and die, but I do not know how to say one word against the truth or against the charity due to my neighbour."

They then took him before the Emperor, where he spoke with the same firmness. The Sovereign, admiring his great piety, sent him away, and also, for his sake, pardoned the unfortunate man whom the Bishop had concealed.

" NEVER TELL A LIE, MY CHILD."

St. Francis of Sales, as a boy, was so straightforward that he would never even try to excuse himself if found in a fault, and a lie, even of the smallest kind, was never found in his mouth. If it happened that by an accident he would break a glass or some such thing, he preferred to be punished rather than utter the least word contrary to the truth. His mother had often said to him : " Never tell a lie, my child, for a lie dishonours us in the sight of God and before men. A lie comes from the Devil, and the child that tells a lie becomes a child of Satan." These words produced in him so great an impression that he would prefer the greatest chastisement rather than expose himself to become the Devil's child.

ST. JOHN OF KENTY'S LOVE FOR THE TRUTH.

St. John of Kenty made three pilgrimages to Rome during the course of his life. He was accustomed to make them on foot, carrying what provisions he might need for his journey in a sack upon his shoulders.

On one of these pilgrimages he was attacked by robbers while passing through a lonely forest. The robbers took possession of everything they could find upon him, and before departing they asked him if he had anything else which they could take.

He said that he had nothing else, and that they had taken everything from him. They then allowed him to depart in peace.

But he had not gone forward many steps when he suddenly remembered that he had a few pieces of gold, which had been sewed into his clothes, that he might have something to help him in any necessity that might arise. He at once retraced his steps, and, overtaking the robbers, he cried out to them that what he had said to them was not the truth, for he had suddenly remembered that he had a few golden coins sewed into his garments, and he began to look for them, that he might give them to the robbers.

But they, unaccustomed to such delicacy of conscience, were filled with a respect for the old man, and not only refused to accept the coins, but even restored to him everything they had previously taken from him.　　*Life of St. John of Kenty.*

III. Punishment for Telling Lies.

Those who tell lies, as well as those who steal, are very often punished even in this world; for when a person has been discovered telling a lie he will no longer be believed, even although he may tell the truth.

THE EMPEROR AND THE INNKEEPER.

The Emperor Rodolph was one day at Nuremberg, and, as was the custom at that time, those who had any grievance used to go to him for redress.

On this occasion a merchant went to him, and reported that, having come into that city on business, he went to one of the chief hotels, and as he had in his possession about two hundred marks of silver in a leathern sack, he confided it to the care of the innkeeper during the time he was to remain in his house, that he might put it in a place of safety. At the same time, thinking that a man in his position would never yield to the temptation of dishonesty, he did not ask him for a receipt.

When the time came for his departure, he went to the innkeeper and asked him to give him his money, as he was now about to leave the city.

The innkeeper looked at him in surprise, and declared that he had never seen the sack nor the money; and as the merchant had no letter, he found it impossible to prove that he had given him the money. He also informed the Emperor that, being one of the chief citizens, the innkeeper had been chosen to be one of the deputation which was to come that day to offer him the homage of the people.

The Emperor told him to hide himself somewhere where he might be within call, and that he would see what he could do for him.

Not long afterwards the members of the deputation arrived, and the Emperor talked familiarly with each of them, inquiring their names and their professions. When he came to the innkeeper, he said to him in a jocular manner: " I admire your hat very much. Will you give it to me in exchange for mine ?"

The innkeeper was only too delighted to do so, thinking that he was indeed highly favoured. Not long afterwards Rodolph left the room, telling the guests to wait till his return. He met one of the officers of his suite near the door, and said to him · " Run as fast as you can to such and such an hotel, and tell the landlady to give you immediately the leathern sack which her husband has hidden, for it is much needed at the present moment. And as a sign that the case is urgent, show her this hat, and she will immediately recognize it as his."

The officer did as his master had commanded, and went to deliver his message. The woman, seeing her husband's hat, and knowing that no one but themselves knew about the stolen money, thought that her husband had sent for it, and gave it to the messenger without any hesitation, who carried it to the Emperor.

As soon as he received it he returned to the audience-chamber, and calling to his side the guilty innkeeper, and having also sent for the merchant, he related before the company the whole story. The innkeeper at first answered in indignation that

the story was made up to injure his reputation.
Then the Emperor, raising up his hand, in which
was the leathern sack, showed it to him, and to all
those who were present.   The innkeeper was struck
dumb with astonishment, which was only increased
when the Emperor related the manner in which the
sack had come into his possession.

The Emperor then gave him a severe reprimand,
and ordered him to pay a very heavy penalty.   The
action thus exposed brought down on him the
indignation and scorn of the citizens, and he was
obliged to flee from the city as soon as possible.

ST. JAMES AND THE PRETENDING BEGGAR.

Theodoret, in his history of the Church, relates
that St. James, Bishop of Nisibius, in Mesopotamia,
who lived in the fourth century, walking one day
along the streets of a neighbouring city, was accosted by some poor men, who asked him for a
little sum of money to enable them to bury one of
their companions who had just died, and whose
body lay at a little distance by the wayside.

The good Bishop at once acceded to their request,
and gave them what he considered they might need
in their present difficulties.   At the same time he
knelt down beside them, and prayed to God for the
deceased man, fervently beseeching Him to pardon
any sins he may have committed during his life
time, and to receive him soon among the number of
His elect in Heaven.

At the very moment when the Saint was thus
praying for his soul, the unfortunate man, who had
only simulated death in order that he might procure

a generous alms from the Bishop, really died, and when his companions approached him with the money in their hands which the Bishop had given them, they found only his dead body.

Overcome with surprise and terror at what had occurred, and considering this as a punishment sent by God upon them for their deceit, they ran in haste to the man of God, and, throwing themselves on the ground at his feet, humbly confessed their sin, at the same time adding that it was dire want that had compelled them to adopt this means of finding relief. They besought the Saint to forgive them, and by the power of his prayers with God to restore their dead comrade to life.

Following the example of his Divine Master, he immediately forgave them the offence they had committed, and by his prayers restored the life of the man whom God had struck with death as a punishment for their lies to the Saint, His servant.

THEODORET : *Hist. Eccles.*

IV. ON HYPOCRISY.

Hypocrisy is also a kind of lie. It consists in putting on an appearance of virtue in order to gain the esteem of men. A liar deceives his neighbours by words ; a hypocrite deceives him by his actions.

THE ABBOT AND THE YOUNG MONK.

One day a young monk went to the cell of the holy Abbot Serapion to ask him for advice and instruction. Serapion told him to enter, that they might both kneel together in prayer.

The monk said : " O Father, who am I that I should enter the cell of a holy man like you, much less that I should be permitted to pray at your side ? I am a great sinner, and most unworthy of wearing the habit of a monk, or even of looking up to Heaven."

The Abbot saw at a glance that the man before him was not so holy in the eyes of God as he imagined himself to be ; so, to give him a lesson of humility, he said to him : " Do not be kept back by the thought of your unworthiness, my brother. Come in and partake of my frugal meal."

So, leading him by the hand, he made him sit at his side, having first washed his feet after the example of our Lord. When the repast was finished, the Abbot said : " Now, my brother, what is the subject on which you want to receive my advice ?"

The monk answered : " I desire to obtain from you some good counsels, so that I may become more and more perfect."

" Then, my brother," said Serapion, " this is my advice : Go back to your cell, and remain in it. Do not allow your mind to wander on worldly things, as it is now doing ; and do not any longer wander about from place to place, for those who live in this manner are very far from being perfect."

While the Abbot was saying this the face of the monk became very red from subdued anger, which finally burst forth in words, in which he said some harsh words to the holy man. Serapion withstood this storm without showing the least sign of displeasure, and, when it was ended, he calmly said to him : " When there is question of you yourself humbling yourself, you succeed admirably ; but when another one tries to do this, you burst forth into anger. Now I know what you are, and you also now know what you have been. Your pretended piety was, after all, only hypocrisy. By it you might, indeed, succeed in deceiving men, but you can never deceive God. If you now want my advice, this is it : Shun that hypocrisy which has its seat in pride, and seek only to appear in the eyes of men what you are in the eyes of God."

This was a severe but fruitful lesson for the young monk. He returned to his cell, and for the rest of his days sought only to be great in the eyes of God, and to be forgotten by the world.

Lives of the Fathers of the Desert.

V. ON FALSE TESTIMONY.

False testimony is to say on oath that a thing is true which we know or believe to be false, or to declare a thing to be false which we know or think to be true. This is a sin which God punishes with the greatest severity, and sometimes, even in this world, those who are guilty of it bring upon themselves disgrace and other evils.

ST. ATHANASIUS AND HIS ACCUSERS.

In the history of the Church we read the following example : The Arians, wishing to get rid of St. Athanasius, who on all occasions stood up in defence of the Catholic Truth, accused him to the magistrates of having, in his wrath, cut off the hand of a certain man whose name was Arsenius, and, as a proof of what they asserted, they produced the hand of a man which had been cut off, and declared that it was the hand of Arsenius which they had found.

This man had for a long time been concealed by the Arians ; but finding out that they were making use of him as a tool for their wicked purposes, and fearing lest they might really injure him, or even kill him if they found it necessary for their designs, he contrived to make his escape, and hid himself where he knew they would not be able to find him.

But hearing of their designs against the Saint, he secretly went to him and warned him of what they were about to do.   And when the time came when the Saint was brought before the Council and publicly accused by the Arians of the wicked deed which they had invented, Athanasius cried out : " Is there anyone present here who ever saw Arsenius ?"

Many of the people answered that they knew him well.   Then the Saint ordered a door to be opened, and Arsenius came in covered with a long mantle.

" Is this man Arsenius ?" asked the Saint.

" Yes," was the answer that came from every part of the room ; " it is indeed Arsenius."

Then the Saint, lifting up one side of the mantle, raised up the man's right hand, and said : " Behold his right hand ; it certainly is fixed to his body."

Then, taking off the mantle altogether, he raised up the other hand and showed it to them, saying : " Behold also his left hand.   The hand, therefore, that is lying before you cannot belong to Arsenius, for he cannot have more than two hands, so I am falsely accused. What need is there of further proof to show that I am innocent ?"

The Arians were filled with rage when they saw that their plot had failed, and that the multitude began to look on them as liars and impostors. In their anger they resolved to take away the life of St. Athanasius, but he escaped from their hands and· fled to the city of Constantinople.

Lives of the Saints, May 2.

VI. On Rash Judgment.

Rash judgment is to judge evil of our neighbour without a sufficient cause. Rash judgment is contrary to charity, which commands us to do unto others as we wish them to do unto us.

ST. AMADEUS JUDGED RASHLY.

Amadeus was a great lord in the Roman Empire. One day, hearing of the vanity of all earthly grandeur, he on the spot took the resolution of renouncing his riches to serve God in solitude, that he might the more easily reach Heaven.

He took up his abode in the desert of Scete, near a church, that he might have the opportunity of often going there to say his prayers. The priest who served that church, knowing that he had been accustomed to live in great comfort in the world, sent him from time to time little presents of food and clothing ; for he thought that, on account of the. delicacy in which he had been brought up, he would not be able to live in the austere manner of the other solitaries, who had been accustomed to that kind of life from their childhood. Thus he lived for the space of twenty-five years, and became renowned throughout the East for his holy life.

One of the solitaries of Egypt, hearing of his sanctity, and hoping to learn some new austerity from him, went to pay him a visit. When he reached the cell where he dwelt, and saw that he wore clothing of fine texture, and that he slept on a bed which had the appearance of great comfort, and that his food was savoury, he was scandalized, and at once left the place to return home. Amadeus, to whom God revealed the thoughts that were passing in the mind of the Egyptian monk, sent his servant to recall him.

As soon as he entered, Amadeus said to him : " My Father, tell me from what country do you come ?"

" I come from Egypt," replied the monk

" And what kind of life did you lead before you left the world to embrace the religious state ?" asked Amadeus.

" I was a labourer in the fields," he answered.

" And in what manner did you live at that time ?"

" In what manner did I live ?" exclaimed the monk. " How do those live who are poor, and have to labour in the fields ? My bed was the cold ground, and my food was only bread, and water was the only kind of drink that I could obtain. But pray tell me what kind of life did you lead before you came hither ?"

" The wretched being whom you see before you," began Amadeus, " was at one time great in the

Roman Empire. God spoke to my heart, and showed me the vanity of all those things which the world esteems, and I left the city of Rome and came to dwell in this place. When I was in the world, I had every kind of luxury that the world could present to me. I had a bed of down to lie upon, and I wore clothing embroidered with gold. My table was sumptuous, and I drank the finest wines that could be procured. I had many servants to do my bidding, and every kind of comfort that the world could bestow on me. I left all these things that I might serve God here in this solitude. Now, my Father, I pray thee be not scandalized at what you have seen, and at the comforts which I here enjoy, since my infirmities compel me to make use of them."

These words filled the soul of the good monk with the greatest confusion. "I ought to be ashamed of myself, my Father," he said, "since the sacrifice you have made for God is so much greater than what I have made. When I was in the world my condition was so miserable that, instead of the religious life making me suffer more, it enabled me to live in greater comfort; but you, in coming hither, have embraced a life of privations, and exchanged a life of pleasure and enjoyment for one of mortification, poverty, and humility. Oh, how much greater are your austerities than those I practise!"

Having asked his forgiveness for having been guilty of judging his conduct so rashly from outward appearances, he took his departure and re-entered his desert admiring the wonderful ways of God towards His elect.

So, my child, when you see your neighbour leading a life which does not appear to you to be one
of mortification, or when you see anyone enjoying
the pleasures of life, do not condemn him in your
heart, because in the eyes of God he may be doing
more for Heaven than you yourself are doing.

Lives of the Saints.

THE GENERAL'S SNUFF-BOX.

One day a General invited a number of officers
to dine with him. Before they sat down to table,
he showed them a beautiful gold snuff-box that he
had just bought. It was passed from one to the
other, and each one had something to say about it.

During dinner the General wanted to take a pinch
of snuff. He put his hand into his pocket, but the
snuff-box was not there.

" Where is my snuff-box ?" he asked in astonishment. " I thought I replaced it in my pocket."

After looking for it everywhere in vain, he said :
" Gentlemen, would you kindly see if any one of
you has by mistake put the box in his pocket ?"

Immediately they rose up and turned out their
pockets to show that it was not there. One of them
only, who was an ensign, remained sitting, and was
evidently vexed at what was being done. " I will
not turn out my pockets," he said, " but I give you
my word of honour that the snuff-box is not in any
of them."

The company soon afterwards left, and they were
all firmly persuaded that the ensign had stolen the
snuff-box. The General himself looked at him with
a glance which plainly said : " You are the thief."

The young man felt this bitterly, but without saying anything he withdrew along with the others.

Next morning the box was found. When the servant was brushing his master's clothes, he found the box in the lining of the coat. It had slipped through a hole in the pocket which the General had not perceived.

He sent immediately for the young ensign, and told him that he was sorry he had suspected him of having taken it. " But tell me," he said, " why you did not show that it was not in your pockets, as the others did."

" Since you have asked me, my General, I will tell you, but you alone. My parents are very poor. I lay past for them my little pay, and at dinner-time I eat but little, that I may be able to give them some food. I had my usual allowance in my pocket, and was on my way to give it to them when you so kindly invited me to your table. If, therefore, I had turned out my pockets as the others did, this would have fallen out, and you can easily see what would have been the consequence. The others would have been surprised, and would have laughed at me."

The General was moved with this touching story. " You are a dutiful son," he said. ." From this day forward you shall dine with me every day, so that you may be the better able to assist your parents."

He then summoned the officers who had dined with him on the previous day, and told them the reason of the strange conduct of the ensign which had made them look upon him as the thief.

·. The young man was filled with confusion, but the General told him that such heroic conduct was worthy of being everywhere made known, as it showed noble and generous feeling ; and " as a testimony of my esteem," he continued, " I present you with this same snuff-box which has been the cause of making such a noble action known to us."

Histoires choisies.

ALIPIUS FALSELY ACCUSED.

St. Augustine relates in one of the books which he wrote the following story, which shows that we ought not to believe too readily accusations made against others, although they may seem at first to be certainly true.

Alipius, one of his disciples, who was studying under his tuition at Carthage, was one day arrested as a robber by the Guards of the Imperial Palace, in the courts of which he at the time was walking, his mind entirely taken up with the lessons he was learning. This is how it occurred ·

Another pupil, who was the real robber, had ascended unperceived to the terrace which overlooked the street known as the Goldsmiths' Street, and with an axe which he had concealed under the folds of his mantle began to cut the lead and other ornaments which adorned it with the intention of stealing them.

The noise he was making in his work reached the ears of some of the goldsmiths whose workrooms were situated near the terrace, and they hurried out to see what might be the cause of it. When the culprit perceived them coming he threw down his hatchet, and succeeded in making his escape without being observed.

In the meantime Alipius also, hearing the noise, went up to the place from which the sounds were proceeding, but before he reached it the young man had disappeared. Seeing the axe lying on the ground, he took it up to examine it, and while doing so the goldsmiths and those who had now joined them came up, and finding him there alone with the axe in his hand, they concluded that he was the one who was guilty. Alipius was accordingly seized and taken before the judge, who had no doubt of his guilt, seeing he had been caught with the hatchet in his hands. He without hesitation condemned him at once to imprisonment.

But God, Who had been the only witness of the innocence of Alipius, came to his defence.

As he was being led to prison, it happened that a celebrated architect, a friend of St. Augustine, was passing by. He at once recognized Alipius, having often seen him at the Saint's house, and taking him aside, he asked him to inform him how he came to be in this position.

Alipius told him all that passed, and the architect, followed by the crowd and the officers of the law, went towards the house where the real thief dwelt, the axe having been recognized as belonging to him. At the door of the house stood a younger brother of the latter, who had known what his brother was about to do, and who had even gone part of the way to the terrace with him.

When the axe was produced and shown to him, and when he was asked if he recognized it, he at once answered : " Yes, it belongs to us."

He also answered in a straightforward manner

the other questions put to him, which brought home the guilt to the real offender, and at once cleared Alipius from all blame and established his innocence.

He from this incident learned by his own experience how much circumspection must be used in ascertaining the truth of any event of which he was not an eyewitness. It is also a lesson for you, my child, in similar circumstances.

St. Augustine : *Confessions.*

VII. On Calumny.

Calumny is to accuse another of a sin which he has not committed, or to exaggerate a real fault of our neighbour. This is a great sin, and those who are guilty of it cannot be forgiven unless they make satisfaction to the one whom they have thus injured, and restore his good name as far as they are able.

THE FALL OF THE CHRISTIAN RELIGION IN JAPAN.

In the days when the first Christian missionaries went to Japan to preach the Gospel to the natives, certain merchants from Holland went to the Emperor and told him that the only aim that these missionaries had was to bring the Portuguese and the Spaniards into the country, that in time they might take possession of it and add it to their dominions.

This great calumny was the source of the ruin of religion in that Empire, and the cause of a great persecution which was raised against the Christians who dwelt in it.

At that time there were 400,000 Christians in Japan ; forty years afterwards there was not even

one to be found in the whole Empire. This was
the result of a lie which was raised by the cupidity
of these merchants, who wished to be the only ones
who would have a right to come into that country.
What an account they shall have to give at the Day
of Judgment of the words which brought so great a
calamity on the Church, and caused the ruin of so
many souls !

Missions in Japan.

ST. MAURUS CALUMNIATED.

When St. Benedict sent Maurus, one of his disciples, into France to establish a monastery there,
Satan raised up certain wicked men who spoke
against them. They said, when they saw the piety
of St. Maurus, " that he was a hypocrite, and put
on this outward show of piety in order that men
might praise him." They said, too, " that he was
ambitious and covetous, and that he came into
France, not so much to preach the Gospel as to
enrich himself at their expense."

It happened that God worked some miracles by
the intercession of the Saint. But even this did
not serve to convince the people. As in our Blessed
Lord's time some of the people, when they saw His
miracles, said that He worked them by Beelzebub,
the prince of devils, so now they said · " St. Maurus
works them by the help of Satan."

In a short time God came to the help of His
servant. Of the three men who were the principal
calumniators, one died, and the other two seemed to
be possessed by the evil spirit, for they became mad.
St. Maurus was vexed to see the punishment
which God inflicted on these poor men. Being

moved with compassion and pity, he prayed to God for them, and asked Him to deliver the two men from the evil spirits that tormented them, and, if it was pleasing to His Divine Majesty, to raise up from the dead the one whom He had taken out of the world.

God was pleased to hear the prayer of His servant, and granted him all he had asked.

Lives of the Saints.

ST. VINCENT OF PAUL CALUMNIATED.

St. Vincent of Paul, that holy man who is worthy of the admiration of all ages, did not escape the consequences of malignant tongues.

A certain judge, in whose house he lodged, having lost four crowns, accused the Saint of being the thief. The Saint's reply was an assertion of his innocence, leaving it to God to prove this in His own good time.

The judge, however, still considered him the guilty one, and spoke of him as such among all his friends and acquaintances, who believed what he told them.

St. Vincent, little concerned about the matter, allowed the calumny to be carried from mouth to mouth without saying anything else in his defence but the words he had already spoken : " I am innocent. God knows I am innocent, and that is enough for me."

For the long space of six years this unjust suspicion hung over him, until God in His own good time manifested his innocence, which brought to the Saint greater renown than he ever before had obtained. The guilty one acknowledged his sin, and exonerated the Saint from all blame. The people who had hitherto believed the calumny craved his forgiveness, and published on every side the sanctity of St. Vincent.   *From his Life.*

GOD REVEALS HIS SERVANT'S INNOCENCE.

The saintly Abbot Paphnucius, who dwelt in the solitude of Scete in Egypt, was so distinguished by his holiness of life and the high degree of sanctity he had attained, that people came from all parts to visit him and obtain his advice.

"But one of our solitaries," writes Cassian, "who was full of jealousy at his great reputation, formed the design of destroying it. One Sunday morning, when Paphnucius was hearing Mass in the church, he entered the holy man's cell, and bringing with him his manual of prayers, hid it under a mat which was on the floor, after which he went to join the others in the church.

"When Mass was over, this calumniator went to the Abbot Isidore, who was a priest in the same desert, and told him that he had lost his book, and that someone amongst the solitaries must have stolen it.

"The Abbot, who was at prayer with the other members of the community, on hearing this, gave orders that all the religious should remain in the church. He then chose three of the oldest amongst them, and told them to go into all the cells to discover if perchance any one of the solitaries had stolen the book.

"They went accordingly, and in a few minutes returned saying that they had found the book concealed in a mat in the cell of Paphnucius.

" Every eye was turned towards him, all being surprised that one accounted so holy should be guilty of such a sin.

" Paphnucius, who was conscious of his innocence, made no reply to this false accusation. He did not seek to justify himself, because he thought that no one would believe him, since the book was found in his cell, and he left the matter in the hands of God, knowing that in His own good time his innocence would be proved.

" He spent the following two weeks in fasting and fervent prayer, asking God to be pleased to make known his innocence, if such were His holy will.

" At the end of that time God, Who was witness of what had taken place, came to the defence of His servant by punishing the author of the calumny with a terrible judgment ; for an evil spirit took possession of him, and compelled him to declare before the assembly of all the solitaries the crime he had committed and the jealousy which had been the cause of it. When this became known, the Saint received more esteem than ever on account of his humility and meekness.

" It was only by the prayers of St. Paphnucius that he was afterwards freed from the wicked spirit which possessed him, and that God was pleased to bestow upon him true contrition and pardon."

CASSIAN, 18 : *Conference* xv.

VIII. ON DETRACTION.

Detraction is to make known without sufficient cause the real but secret faults of our neighbour.

THE BISHOP AND THE DETRACTOR.

A certain Bishop had invited to his table a number of guests. During the repast one of them began to speak of the faults of a person who was absent. When the Bishop heard what he was saying, he called to his side one of those who were serving at table, and said to him in a loud voice : " Go and ask that gentleman of whom they are now speaking to come here."

The guest who had just been speaking suddenly ceased, and looked towards the Bishop, who, casting a severe glance towards him, said : " I have sent for the gentleman of whose faults you are speaking in order that he may be able to defend himself ; for it is unjust to speak of another in that way without giving him an opportunity of doing so."

No one ever after that time spoke of the faults of his neighbour in the presence of that good Bishop.

THE NOBLEMAN'S DEATH.

History informs us that a certain nobleman, much given to the vice of detraction, was admonished in his dying moments to make his Confession and to think seriously of the salvation of his soul ; but he replied that he could not prevail upon himself to do so, and, notwithstanding the many and urgent entreaties of his friends, he remained obstinate to the last.

Then, putting out his tongue, and touching it with his finger, " This wicked tongue," said he, " is the cause of my damnation," which words were no sooner pronounced than he expired, thus leaving an awful lesson to all who are addicted to this fatal vice.

ST. ODILO'S HATRED OF DETRACTION.

St. Odilo's love for his neighbour knew no bounds, and many instances are recorded of his works of charity and mercy towards them. There was only one circumstance in which the holy man was ever seen to be angry, and that was when anyone began to speak of the faults of others or to cause dissensions to arise. " Such people are the pest of society," he used to say ; and although he readily pardoned other faults, he was most severe with those who were guilty of this one.

THE HOLY MAN'S PENANCE FOR DETRACTION.

Evagrius was a holy priest who spent his whole life in winning souls to God.

On a certain occasion it happened that, in conversation with his neighbour, a word of detraction escaped his lips. When he recalled to mind what he had said, he became so full of sorrow that for the space of forty days he did penance for his fault.

Oh that those who so often, and without remorse, speak of the faults of their neighbours should bear this in mind ! What a number of sins they would avoid, and how much punishment they would escape in the world to come !

IX. WHAT THE EIGHTH COMMANDMENT COMMANDS.

The Eighth Commandment commands us to speak the truth in all things, and to be careful of the honour and reputation of everyone.

" JUDGE NOT, AND YOU SHALL NOT BE JUDGED."

In the desert of Thebais a certain young anchorite became very ill. During his illness he suffered much pain, which in the end brought him to the point of death.

Although he suffered so much, he was always calm and never complained, and the nearer he approached the hour of his death the more happy he seemed to be.

His Superior, perceiving this, said to him : " My son, you seem to be very happy."

" Yes, my Father, I am full of joy."

" Would you be angry with me if I said something to you that might diminish your joy ?"

" No, my Father ; say to me whatever you like."

" Well, my child, Satan often comes to us under the form of an angel of light, to deceive us. Perhaps at this moment he is trying to deceive you by taking away the fear of death, which even the greatest Saints felt as their last end drew near. Tell me, then, what makes you so calm at a moment when so many tremble with fear."

" My Father, the reason is very simple. You know what Jesus our Adorable Master says in his holy Gospel : ' Judge not, and you shall not be judged.' These words were for me a golden rule, and I kept them always before my mind. I have been careful all my lifetime never to judge anyone, and hence, when I am now about to appear before the tribunal of the Great Judge Himself, I hope in His mercy to receive a favourable sentence according to His promise."

In saying these words he breathed his last, and is now most surely in possession of the glory of Heaven.

X. On the Obligation of Restoring our Neighbour's Good Name.

The Catechism concludes the Eighth Commandment by this question : "What must you do if you have injured your neighbour by speaking ill of him ?" And the answer to that question is this · " If I have injured my neighbour by speaking ill of him, I am bound to make him satisfaction by restoring his good name as far as I am able."

ST. PHILIP AND THE LADY.

One day a lady went to Confession to St. Philip Neri, and accused herself of having been guilty of speaking about her neighbour's faults and failings.

The Saint said to her : " Do you often commit this fault ?"

She answered: "Yes, Father, it is a habit with me."

The Saint, from his great experience of guiding souls, saw that this bad habit had been acquired more by want of reflection than by malice, and he thought of how he could most easily correct her. To do this more effectually he imagined that the best thing to do in the first place was to enlighten her on the terrible consequences arising from her unfortunate evil habit.

" My dear child," began the Saint, " your sin is indeed great before God, but the mercy of God is much greater still. With a strong resolution on your own part, and by fervent prayer to God, I feel confident that you will easily soon triumph over this evil inclination."

Then he imposed upon her this penance : " Go to the market-place where fowls are exposed for sale ; purchase one that has recently been killed, and which has still its feathers unplucked ; then, going out of the city, you will walk for a considerable distance along the road, plucking the feathers all the time and throwing them away from you as you go along. When you have plucked off all the feathers, even to the smallest, return to me that I may see whether or not you have obeyed the orders I, the priest of God, have given you. That shall be the first part of your penance ; I will then tell you what next to do."

The lady, as may be well imagined, was utterly astonished at this command of the priest, but knowing his reputation of being a Saint, and that he must have had some good reason for so acting, did not hesitate to obey. " My Father," she replied, " I will do as you have ordered me."

She then went to the neighbouring market-place, and having bought a fowl, she went to the outside of the town and began to pull off the feathers and to cast them from her, according to the instructions she had received. The wind, which was blowing violently at the time, soon scattered them in every direction.

When she had faithfully executed St. Philip's order, she at once returned to him, carrying with her the fowl to show him that she had done so, and also very desirous to know why he had given her so strange a penance.

" Ah," said the Saint on seeing her return, " you have done well. But I said there was still another part of the penance yet to be performed ; when you have accomplished it, you shall be cured of your habit of detraction."

The woman expressed her readiness to comply with this also, though still at a loss to know what it all meant.

" You will now go," said the Saint, " and gather up one by one the feathers you have scattered to the winds. See that you do not neglect to gather every one of them."

" But that is quite impossible, my Father," she answered. " How could I pick them all up, since the strong wind has blown them away far and near ? How could you possibly imagine that I could do this ?"

" I well know, my child, that you cannot do this. Well, then, keep this in mind : that the words of detraction you have uttered are like unto these feathers ; when once you have uttered them you cannot possibly recall them ; they are borne in every direction by the tongues of those to whom you have spoken them. Be careful, then, for the time to come, and keep a guard upon your tongue. Go now in peace, and sin no more."

This example was a lesson for that lady. May it be one for you also, my child. Watch over every word you utter, for remember that it is Jesus Christ Himself Who says that for every idle word we utter we shall have to give an account at the Day of Judgment.

XXXVI

THE COMMANDMENTS OF THE CHURCH

I. ON THE LAWS OF THE CHURCH.

ARE we bound to obey the Church ? Yes, we are bound to obey the Church, because Christ has said to the pastors of the Church : " He that heareth you heareth Me, and he that despiseth you despiseth Me." And again He says : " He that will not hear the Church, let him be to thee as the heathen and publican."

THE ANSWER OF THE VENERABLE CARDINAL OSIUS.

The learned and famous Cardinal Osius, who was chosen by Pope Pius IV. to open the Council of Trent in his name, was one of the most faithful of the children of the Church in obeying even the least of her commandments.

As he was accustomed even in his advancing

mother, that thou mayst be long-lived upon the land which the Lord thy God will give thee.' My Father is God in Heaven, and my Mother is His Church on earth. God my Father has laid down for me the law of fasting, and the Church my Mother has marked out for me the days on which I should accomplish this precept. I willingly obey, therefore, both the one and the other. I hope, by my obedience, to obtain hereafter that eternal life in the land of Heaven which God has promised to me as the reward of my obedience."

THE BRAVE GENERAL DROUOT.

It happened on a certain Friday that a traveller entered the dining-room of an hotel and asked the innkeeper to provide him with something to eat. A considerable number of people were seated at a table in the middle of the room, and he took his place beside them.

The innkeeper in a few moments placed before him a plate of flesh-meat.

" Be kind enough," said the stranger, " to give me what the Church permits to be eaten on an abstinence day. You must surely know that to-day is Friday."

The innkeeper for a few moments looked at him in astonishment, for he was not accustomed to receive such an order, but very soon departed to prepare what he had been asked.

In the meantime the others who were at table, to show their independence, and as a mark of their contempt for his action, loudly demanded to be supplied with flesh-meat, although they also were Catholics.

The stranger, although, aware of the cause of their conduct, said nothing, but partook of his meal with all the relish of one who was hungry.

In the conversation which followed, the subject of the laws of the Church was introduced. The traveller, who took part in it, soon charmed all present by his unaffected yet dignified bearing, the gaiety he mingled with his words, and his gentlemanly behaviour. In reply to a question they addressed to him regarding the necessity in these days of submitting to the commandments of the Church, he replied : " As regards myself, I always abstain from flesh-meat on the days forbidden by the Church, and I am very careful to obey her laws in every point, because the Church has received from God the power to make these commandments, and to require our obedience to them, just as I, General Drouot, have received from the Emperor the authority and the right to issue commands to my soldiers who are under me, which they are bound to obey."

These noble words, and in particular the discovery that the speaker was the renowned General Drouot, filled them with confusion. They hung down their heads, and not another word was uttered until the General, having piously said his grace, rose up and took his departure.

THE FIRST GENERAL COUNCIL OF NICE.

The First General Council of the Church was that of Nice, which was convened by Pope St. Sylvester in the year 325, for the purpose of condemning **Arius.**

26 —2

Three hundred and eighteen Bishops assembled in that town from all parts of the world, many of whom bore on their bodies the marks of the sufferings which they had endured for Christ in the days of persecution.

As soon as the Fathers had assembled, they began by thanking God for the peace He had given to His Church, and they besought the Holy Spirit to enlighten the whole universe by sending everywhere holy men filled with the Spirit of God, who might make known to all the people the truths of the Kingdom of Heaven.

Since the creation of the world there never had been assembled together so venerable a company. One church at that moment had assembled under its roof all that was most virtuous and learned from every part of the world. The Emperor Constantine the Great added lustre to the scene by his presence. He came from Nicomedia as soon as he was informed of the arrival of the prelates.

The day which was appointed for opening the Council was the nineteenth day of June, of the year 325. The Emperor wished them to assemble in the royal palace, with all the splendour and dignity of a Church newly delivered from the bondage and slavery of the heathen, and under the protection of the master of the world. In one of the great rooms of the Palace of Nice there were placed two long rows of seats for the accommodation of those who were to take part in the deliberations of the Council. In the middle of the room was erected a magnificent throne, on which were placed the books of the Gospels, representing the Holy Ghost, Who had inspired them, and Who in the present instance was to guide the Fathers in their deliberations, according to the promise of Jesus Christ.

As for the Emperor himself, being inspired by a lively and humble faith, and knowing that he had no part in these solemn deliberations, nor in the judgments that would ensue, he desired to be placed on a little throne at the end of the great hall, which was simple in style, though of great value, for it was of silver.

Nevertheless, this action, instead of lessening their respect for him, only served to increase it. As soon as he entered, the Fathers all stood up in respectful silence, and testified the joy they experienced at his presence. He was unaccompanied by any of his guards, and had with him only a few of his soldiers who were Christians. The beauty of his countenance, which at the age of fifty years had preserved all the freshness of youth, his tall stature, and the majesty of his appearance, caused all in the Council to look upon him with a kind of reverence. His purple mantle shone with the brightness of the precious stones that covered it, and as he sat in his place listening to the words of the venerable Fathers he fixed his eyes upon the ground in religious silence.

In this Council the heresy of Arius was condemned. The Fathers then drew up a formula of Faith, and adopted certain disciplinary rules for the maintenance of order and discipline in the Church.

But as the Fathers did not consider it enough to publish these decrees, they also took steps to see that they were put in practice, and petitioned the Emperor to use his authority for this purpose.

Constantine, therefore, wrote letters to all the provinces of his Empire, saying that the decisions of the Council were everywhere to be received as a Divine oracle, that no one had any right to examine what the Fathers had decreed, and that their duty was to believe and to obey them, for they were the commands of the Church, and the commands of the Church were equal to the commands of God Himself.

II. THE FIRST COMMANDMENT OF THE CHURCH.

There are six principal commands of the Church. The first command is to hear Mass on Sundays and holidays of obligation, and to rest from servile works.

THE MARTYRS OF THE MASS.

During the reign of the Emperors Diocletian and Maximian, Satan tried to blot out the Christian religion from the face of the earth. The Governors throughout the world, in the name of the Emperors, commanded the Christians to deliver up all their religious books, and forbade them under pain of death to assemble for religious worship.

Among those who refused to obey this order was a holy priest whose name was Saturninus. One day as he was offering up the Holy Mass in a private house, he was arrested and brought before the judge along with all the faithful who were present to the number of forty-nine.

The judge spoke first to Saturninus. He said to him : " Is it you who, against the orders of the

Emperors, assemble together the people for worship ?"

" Yes," replied Saturninus, " it is I."

" And why do you do this, since the Emperors have expressly forbidden it ?"

" We do this because we are Christians, and because we are commanded to keep the Sunday holy."

Many more questions were put to him, but to all of them his only answer was : " It is the law of our God, Who commands us to sanctify the Day of the Lord."

The judge condemned the martyr to death. As he was pouring out his blood at the place of execution the other Christians, who were all present, far from being dismayed, became only the more courageous. With one accord they cried out : " We are Christians also, and we were at that meeting."

When the Governor heard this, he put them all to death, with the exception of one little boy whose name was Hilarion.

Among those martyrs was a young woman who was called Victorina. She was remarkable, even among those holy servants of God, for her virginal purity. Her parents had destined her for the married state, but she had consecrated herself to God from her earliest years. When the night which her parents had appointed for the marriage came, she escaped from the house by the window, and fled to the church, where she renewed her consecration to God. Burning with the desire of suffering for the sake of Jesus Christ, she went to the tribunal of the judge without being sent for, and boldly declared herself to be a Christian. Her brother, who had heard of what she had done, wishing to save her, ran to the tribunal, and said to the judge " O judge, do not believe what she tells you, for she is mad."

" No," replied Victorina, " I am not mad. I was always a Christian, and I will never change my Faith."

" Would you not like to return home with your brother ?" said the judge, wishing to spare her.

" No," she answered, " I am a Christian, and I recognize as my brothers only those who are Christians like myself."

The judge, seeing that he could not prevail on her to offer sacrifice, ordered her to be sent to prison, and afterwards to be executed.

There still remained one more, the little boy Hilarion. When the judge asked him if he, too, had been in the assembly of the Christians, he boldly answered : " Yes, I am a Christian. I was at that assembly, and I went there of my own free accord, and no one forced me to go."

The judge, thinking that he had only an ordinary little child to deal with, and not knowing that God often speaks by the lips of the lowliest of his little ones, threatened him with those punishments that so easily frighten timid children. " I will pull out your hair, and I will cut off your nose and your ears, and you shall be a terrible object all the rest of your life, if you will not for ever renounce that superstition."

But the child answered, with a smile on his coun

tenance · " You can do whatever you like to me ; I will ever remain a Christian."

The judge, in great anger, ordered the boy back to prison.

As they carried him away he cried out over and over again : " O my God, I thank Thee that Thou hast made me suffer something for Thy name's sake !"   SCHMIDT : *Rep. du Cat.*, v. 105.

" I, ALSO, AM GOING THERE."

In Edessa, a city of Mesopotamia, there was, in the fifth century, a church dedicated to St. Thomas the Apostle, which had become a place of pilgrimage, and which multitudes of the faithful Catholics frequented to assist at the Divine mysteries of religion, according to the commands of the Church.

When the Emperor Valens heard of this, and discovered that that vast multitude detested the heretical sect to which he belonged, he sent for the Prefect who ruled in that city to ask him why he permitted men to assemble in so great numbers who held a doctrine which he (the Emperor) hated.

The Prefect endeavoured to pacify the anger of the Emperor, but without effect, for he immediately gave orders that they should all be put to death without mercy. The Prefect returned home with his heart filled with sadness, for his mind revolted from perpetrating so cruel a deed. But in order that he might not incur the anger of his imperial master, and at the same time save the lives of so many innocent people, he privately sent information to the Catholic worshippers not to assemble there for the future, because he had received orders from the Emperor to slay all whom he found there.

Thinking that they would all disperse on receiving this information, he on the following day marched at the head of a detachment of soldiers to the church. But what was his surprise to see even greater multitudes than ever going towards it. On the way by which they were marching he overtook a poor woman running as fast as her weary limbs would permit her, and dragging a little child by the hand.

" My good woman," said the Prefect, " whither are you going in such haste ?"

" I am going to the same place to which all the others are going."

" Have you not heard," said he, " that the Prefect is going to put to death all whom he finds assembled there ?"

" Yes," she replied, " and it is for that very reason I am going thither. My only fear is that I may arrive too late to receive the crown of martyrdom with my brethren."

The Prefect ordered his men to return to their quarters ; then, going to the Emperor, he related to him what he had seen and heard, and besought him not to stain his royal name by putting to death such a multitude of people purely because they differed from him in belief.

The anger of the Emperor melted away on hearing the recital of fidelity of the Christians to the practice of their faith, and he annulled the order he had given.

SUNDAY AMONG THE SAVAGES OF PENOBSCOT.

Monseigneur de Cheverus was a missionary in America before he was elected to be Archbishop of Bordeaux.

On one occasion, after having visited all the Catholic tribes in his own extensive mission, he resolved to penetrate further into the country to gain, if possible, more souls to God.

When he reached the distant country of Penobscot, in the company of a guide, he was astonished, one Sunday morning, to hear the distant sounds of music familiar to his ear. As he proceeded onward the music became more and more distinct, and he was soon able even to recognize the words of their chants. His astonishment became greater still when he drew near the place where they were congregated and saw a great multitude of the savage people assembled together in an attitude of great devotion. The words they sang and the music were those of the Holy Mass, as sung in the great cathedral churches of his native country.

Over fifty years before, that tribe had learned them from the pious missionaries who had visited these countries, and in their wandering lives they had ever remembered them. They had learned, too, the obligation of keeping the Sunday holy, and although deprived of pastors to instruct them, they adhered to the lessons they had learned, and through these many years, and in the midst of their many wanderings, had ever been faithful thus to solemnize the Lord's Day.

" How great will be the dismay of many Christians," remarked the holy missionary in relating this event, " when they shall appear before the judgment-seat of God, who, while possessing every opportunity of hearing Mass, had endeavoured to find vain excuses for neglecting it ! These poor savages will most certainly rise up against them and condemn them."

HAMON : *Vie de M. de Cheverus.*

THE PARALYZED PRINCE.

The Prince de Beauvan, who occupied a high position in France towards the beginning of last century, became in his old age paralyzed, so that he could not make any use of his limbs.

Notwithstanding this, he did not neglect to be present at Mass on Sundays and holidays. As long as his bodily health permitted, he caused himself to be borne to the church by his servants, who remained by his side during the oblation of the Holy Sacrifice.

This conduct of the pious Prince was the admiration of all the people of the city, and his example encouraged those amongst them who were pious never to be absent from Mass ; and those who were indifferent were aroused from their tepidity to a more exact observance of this law of the Church.

L'ABBÉ DUMONT.

HOW A YOUNG MAIDEN ASSISTED AT MASS.

A young maiden once said to her confessor that she never could hear Holy Mass as she ought.

" Tell me, my child," he said to her, " how you occupy yourself when you assist at Mass."

" I do nothing else all the time of Mass but weep for my sins."

" Continue, my child," he said to her—" continne to do this always, and you will hear Mass well."

HOW A PIOUS LAY-BROTHER HEARD MASS.

There was once a simple lay-brother who had but little learning though much piety, who used to say that during Mass he occupied all the time in trying to read three letters. " The one is black," he said, " the other is red, and the third one is white."

The black letter put him in mind of his sins, at the remembrance of which he was filled with fear, and which he begged God in His mercy to forgive. This letter was before his mind from the beginning of Mass till the Offertory. The red letter brought before him the memory of the passion of Jesus Christ, and he imagined he saw the sacred blood of Jesus flowing from His wounds and dropping down upon him. This occupied his attention from the Offertory till the Communion of the priest. The white letter was one which brought great joy to his mind, which continued till the end of Mass, for then, if he did not receive his Divine Master sacramentally, he received Him into his soul by a spiritual communion, which united him to Jesus Christ here on earth, and was to him a pledge of the eternal union he could confidently look forward to when the days of his exile were ended.

This pious religious followed this practice day by day, and although he was very ignorant according to the world, he excelled in that learning which before God is alone worthy of being esteemed—the science of the Saints.

It is not only an obligation imposed upon us by the Church, my child, to hear Holy Mass on Sundays and holidays, but we are also bound to hear it with attention and devotion.

ST. AMBROSE REPROACHES A GREAT LADY.

St. Ambrose, Bishop of Milan, was always filled with great zeal for God's honour, and never failed to promote it by every means in his power.

One day, passing along the streets, he met a rich lady on her way to hear Mass. She was adorned with all the splendour of her condition, wearing gorgeous apparel, and covered with brilliant jewellery.

" Where are you going ?" he said to her, when he had approached her.

" I am going to the temple of the Lord," she answered.

" I would have imagined, from your apparel, that you were on your way to a ball or some great secular entertainment," continued the Saint. " Return home, O sinful woman ! Do not dare to enter the house of God in that attire. Go and weep for your sins in secret, and do not insult the most holy God by appearing before Him in such pomp, and invested with such vanity."

It is not recorded how the lady acted, but it is a lesson for all those who, while assisting at the adorable Sacrifice, are more attentive to consider what others may think or say about them and the raiment they wear than of the great God they have come to worship, and who, instead of speaking to God in humble prayer, spend their time in vain and worldly conversation.

ST. JOHN CHRYSOSTOM'S ADVICE ABOUT HEARING MASS.

The following words are from a sermon by the great Doctor of the Church, St. John Chrysostom :

" Behold the conduct of those who are anxious to obtain some great favour from their Prince, or a position of trust in his palace. How careful they are to please him ! how assiduous to serve him ! How anxiously they endeavour to gain the favour of those who are his special favourites, that they may interest them in obtaining the grant of their petition !

" And you, my brethren, how do you assist at the tremendous mysteries of the Altar ? In the presence of the kings of this world, how great is your recollection ! You do not even dare to utter one word before them, nor even to whisper. Your eyes are fixed upon the ground, and you are careful not to allow them to wander from side to side, and your posture is one of profound respect.

" Surely, then, it is not too much to ask of you to conduct yourselves with at least as much respect in the presence of the King of Heaven on the Altar as you would do before an earthly Prince seated on his throne."

III. The Second Commandment of the Church.

The second command of the Church is · " To fast in Lent and Advent, on Ember-days and Vigils, and to abstain from flesh on Fridays."

Fasting-days are those on which we are allowed to take but one meal, and that not before midday.

St. Antony in the Desert.

When St. Antony was twenty-one years of age, he left his home to spend the rest of his life in the desert to prepare for Heaven.

From that time he began to fast rigorously. The only food he ate was a little bread mingled with salt, and his drink was water. He took this only once a day, and that after sunset. Sometimes he did not touch food for two days at a time, and sometimes not for three or four.

Satan often came to tempt him. He tried at first to frighten him by making a loud and dismal noise ; then he would strike him till he was covered with wounds, and often left him half dead. But nothing ever troubled the Saint. " You cannot do me the least harm," he used to say to the evil spirit, " for nothing that you can do to me shall ever separate me from Jesus Christ my Lord."

This holy man had many disciples, whom he trained up to live as he himself did. " Believe me, my brethren," he often said to them, " Satan is more afraid of the fastings, prayers, and good works of the servants of God than of anything else they do, because these holy exercises inflame their hearts with the love of Jesus Christ, and overturn all the powers of hell."

St. Antony died on January 17, 356, at the age of 105 years, and although his life had been one continual fast, he never suffered from those infirmities which are generally the lot of old age.

From his Life.

Days of abstinence are those on which we are forbidden to eat flesh-meat, but are allowed the usual number of meals.

FERDINAND, KING OF NAPLES.

About thirty years ago King Ferdinand was going from Rome to Naples ; his son was with him. They were travelling in disguise, so that no one knew them, and were in great haste, being on business of great importance.

On the way an accident happened to one of the wheels of the carriage, which caused them to stop at a wayside inn while it was being repaired. The King and his son in the meantime went into the inn to take some refreshments, and sat down at a table where others were dining.

It was a Friday, and although there were some Catholics present, they seemed to have forgotten the law of abstinence, and were partaking of food forbidden by the Church. Only one of them, a young man about eighteen years of age, was dining on food allowed on that day. The rest of the company began to mock the young man, and to say that he was very foolish to make any distinction between Friday and the other days of the week.

Their railleries made no impression on the young man. " You may do as you choose," he said to them, " but I will act up to what my religion requires of me as long as I live."

The King listened to the conversation for some time in silence, but when the young man had said these words he also spoke, and praised him, saying that a man who was faithful in this way to God could be always trusted.

When the carriage was repaired, the King rose from the table without making himself known to them. He told the young man to follow him, and asked him where he was going, and what he was about to do.

" I am going to Naples," he answered ; " I am going to seek admission into the army of King Ferdinand. Although I am by birth a Florentine, I do not wish to enter the army in my native city, because the soldiers are so careless about their religious duties."

The King took a piece of paper from his note-book, and, writing on it a few lines, sealed and addressed it ; then giving it to the young man, he said : " Take this letter to the place indicated on the address ; it may be of some assistance to you when you reach Naples."

The King departed, and the young man continued his journey towards Naples. When he reached that city, he delivered his letter to the person to whom it was addressed, who was no other than the Commander-in-Chief of the King's army. Having thus fulfilled his commission, he turned to go away, but to his surprise he was told to enter the Commander's room, and was received by him with marked honour and respect. The letter contained a command from the King appointing him to the rank of Lieutenant, and he was immediately installed in that office.

This adventure, instead of making him proud, served only to confirm him in his resolution to persevere in the firm and constant practice of his religious duties for the rest of his life.

HISTORY OF THE VENERABLE ELEAZAR.

The following narrative is taken from the Sacred Scriptures (2 Mac. vi. 18-31):

" Eleazar, one of the chief of the scribes, a man advanced in years, and of a comely countenance, was pressed to open his mouth to eat swine's flesh. But he, choosing rather a most glorious death than a hateful life, went forward voluntarily to the torment ; and considering in what manner he was come to it, patiently bearing, he determined not to do any unlawful things for the love of life.

" But they that stood by, being moved with wicked pity, for the old friendship they had with the man, taking him aside, desired that flesh might be brought, which it was lawful for him to eat, that he might make as if he had eaten, as the King had commanded, of the flesh of the sacrifice : that by so doing he might be delivered from death ; and for the sake of their old friendship with the man they did him this courtesy.

" But he began to consider the dignity of his age, and his ancient years, and the inbred honour of his grey head, and his good life and conversation from a child ; and he answered without delay, according to the ordinances of the holy law made by God, saying that he would rather be sent into the other world.

" ' For it doth not become our age,' said he, ' to dissemble, whereby many young persons might think that Eleazar, at the age of fourscore and ten years, was gone over to the life of the heathens ; and so they, through my dissimulation, and for a little time of corruptible life, should be deceived, and hereby I should bring a stain and a curse upon my old age. For though, for the present time, I should be delivered from the punishments of men, yet should I not escape the hand of the Almighty, neither alive nor dead.

" ' Wherefore, by departing manfully out of this life, I shall show myself worthy of my old age, and I shall leave an example of fortitude to young men, if with a ready mind and constancy I suffer an honourable death for the most venerable and most holy laws.' And having spoken thus, he was forthwith carried to execution.

" And they that led him, and had been a little before more mild, were changed to wrath for the words he had spoken, which they thought were uttered out of arrogancy.

" But when he was now ready to die with the stripes, he groaned, and said : ' O Lord, Who hast the holy knowledge, Thou knowest manifestly that, whereas I might be delivered from death, I suffer grievous pains in body, but in soul am well content to suffer these things because I fear Thee.'

" Thus did this man die, leaving not only to young men, but also to the whole nation, the memory of his death for an example of virtue and fortitude."

WHAT A PIOUS CHILD CAN DO.

A certain mother having been invited to dinner, took with her her little girl, who was just ten years old. It was an abstinence day, and the only food on the table was flesh-meat.

Those who were present partook of the forbidden food, except the little girl, who refused to touch it ; and when she was asked why she did not do as the rest did, she said that it was because the Church forbade the use of flesh-meat on that day. Frequently during the course of the meal did they ask her to lay aside her scruples, as they were pleased to call them ; but the child remained firm.

Her mother even, who ought to have given her better example, also asked her to do as she herself was doing ; but to no purpose, for the little girl remained firm. This resistance on the part of the child soon had its effect on the guilty mother, and her conscience began to reproach her for what she was doing.

As soon as they left that house to return home, she said to her daughter, at the same time embracing her with great affection : " My dear child, I am truly grieved for what I did to-night, and especially for asking you to transgress the law of God's Church ; but it shall never happen again. You were right, my dear child, in refusing to obey me, and I committed a great sin in showing you such bad example, and in asking you to do what was wrong. But I promise you, my own dearest child, never to do this again, and for the rest of my life you shall never see your mother be so weak as to break any of the commandments through human respect, or for any other motive."

The penitent mother did as she promised, and she was won over to the path of duty by her little girl, who so faithfully kept the commandments.

THE FAITHFUL CHILD.

In one of the chief towns in France there was a little boy who was preparing for his first Communion. His parents had both ceased to practise their religion, and in consequence of this, neglected to obey the commandments of God and of His Church. They made no distinction between Friday and the other days of the week, but ate flesh-meat on it, and made their child do so likewise

When he went to his Confession before going to Holy Communion for the first time, he had to accuse himself of this sin, and told his confessor that his parents had been the cause of it. The priest then laid down certain rules for his conduct for the future, and the child promised to do what lay in his power to observe them.

Next Friday, according to their usual custom, the dinner that was prepared consisted of flesh-meat. When they offered some of it to the boy, he gently but firmly refused to eat it.

The father said to him · "Why do you not eat the food I have given you ?"

· "My father," said the boy, "there is a commandment of the Church which tells us to abstain from flesh-meat on Fridays, and I must observe it. To-day a piece of dry bread and a drink of water will be enough for me."

These words made the father exceedingly angry. " Begone !" he cried out—" begone from my presence at once !" And, rising up, he put him into a room, telling him that he should have to remain there till next day, and that he should not be allowed even a piece of dry bread.

The child made no resistance. He was suffering persecution for God's sake, and God gave him courage and consolation.

A few hours afterwards his mother began to feel compassion for her poor boy. She went secretly to his room, unknown to her husband, with some food which is permitted on days of abstinence. At the same time she told him it was all a foolish fancy he had taken into his head, and besides that, it was wrong to go against his father's orders as he had done.

" My own dear mother," replied the child calmly, " if my father had ordered me to do something I could lawfully do, I would have done it at once. It was not through obstinacy that I refused to eat the food he placed before me to-day, but because God forbids me to eat it. When he put me into this room, he told me I was to remain here without eating anything till to-morrow morning. I must obey him in this, because God tells us to be obedient to our parents in all that is not sin. So, dearest mother, I cannot eat the food you have brought me."

When his mother heard these beautiful words,

she stood as if rooted to the spot, and did not know how to answer him. She suddenly left the room, that her son might not see the tears that were forcing themselves from her eyes. She went straight to her husband, and told him all their son had said to her.

The father's heart was also moved, and he said to his wife : " Yes, that boy is much better than either you or I."

Saying this, he immediately rose and went to the room in which his son was confined. When he opened the door, he took the boy into his arms and tenderly embraced him. " My child," he said, " I have done wrong in treating you in this way. Tell me the name of the priest who gave you these pious lessons, for I must go and thank him."

Soon afterwards the father was at the priest's house. " I have come, in the first place," he said to him, " to thank you for all the beautiful lessons you have given my son." He then told him what had happened, and in the end said : " Now, my Father, you must hear my Confession, for I desire to imitate my son, and for the future to live accord ing to the principles of our holy religion."

The pastor's heart was full of joy at this conversion. Next day the boy's mother was also at the priest's feet making her Confession, and that family became one of the most fervent in the whole of the city.

Happy indeed was that boy, who, by faithfully obeying the laws of the Church, was able to bring back his beloved parents to their religious duties.

THE ABBÉ MARGUET.

THE KING AND THE OLD OFFICER.

An old officer in the time of Louis XVI., King of France, who though a child of the Church, was not too scrupulous in obeying her commands, took it upon himself to speak to his master with regard to the abstinence he was careful to practise when enjoined by the Church.

" My liege," he said, " why do you act as the meanest of your subjects do in regard to this matter ? Has not Our Lord in the Scriptures told us that ' that which enters the mouth does not defile a man ' ?"

" These are indeed his words," replied the monarch in a serious tone ; " but you must know that it is not eating the flesh-meat that is the sin, for one may at other times partake of it without offending God ; but the evil lies in the fact that by doing so one rises in revolt against legitimate authority by violating a formal command of the Church. You who seem to know the Gospel so well must have read in·it these other words : ' He who heareth not the Church, let him be to thee as a heathen or a publican.' "

This answer was indeed worthy of a Christian monarch.
Life of Louis XVI.

" WE ARE CHRISTIANS," REPLIED THE BOY.

Several young men were returning home from college for the midsummer holidays, happy and full of joyful anticipations of amusements, which make **those days of vacation so welcome.**

On reaching a town on their journey homewards,

they entered an hotel to partake of some food. It was Friday. Sitting at the table were a number of men who partook of flesh-meat in open disobedi ence to the laws of the Church, as if they were pagans and not Christians.

Seeing this, one of the boys, who seemed to be leader among his companions, who were all indignant at this profanation, loudly called upon the mistress of the hotel to bring them food which they could conscientiously partake of on an abstinence day.

The men, in their astonishment at this order, began, in a tone of mockery, to utter among them, selves words which were a testimony of their little regard for God, His Church, or His commandments. Although they were uttered loud enough to be heard by the boys, they replied not, but continued their meal in silence.

At length, one of the men, turning towards them, said : " Well, boys, how can you sit there and listen undisturbed to these words of ours which you cannot but have heard ?"

" We are Christian scholars," replied the leader of the young men ; " and our firm resolution is to obey the laws of the Church."

" Well said !" was the answer. " I also have a son whom I love with the greatest affection, and my greatest desire is that he would grow up piously and be like you. Continue, then, to persevere faithfully in the duties your religion requires of you. Would that every young man might resemble you."

L'Apostolat des enfans chrét., p. 140.

THE PRISONERS OF THE LOMBARDS.

St. Gregory the Great tells us the following story : About forty years ago, forty countrymen, who were fervent Catholics, were taken prisoners by the Lombards, and ordered by them to eat of meat which had been offered to the heathen gods. These good men would not do this, nor even touch it, although their enemies threatened to put them to death if they refused. They preferred the eternal life of Heaven to a short life in this world at enmity with God, and the certainty of eternal death in the world to come. They were put to death, but they are now living with God in His eternal kingdom.

Lives of the Saints, Mar. 2.

IV. THE THIRD COMMANDMENT OF THE CHURCH.

The third commandment of the Church is, " To confess our sins at least once a year."

The obligation of going to Confession at least once a year is a command of the highest wisdom, because, since man is so great a sinner, there is for him the absolute necessity of having recourse to the sacrament which God has appointed as a remedy for sin, and also because of the impossibility that sometimes happens of having recourse to this remedy at the end of one's life, on account of sickness and the temptations of the enemy of our souls.

CONRAD AND HIS FAVOURITE COURTIER.

Venerable Bede tells us of a pious monarch, whose name was Conrad, who had among his courtiers one whom he esteemed and loved more than all the others.

This Prince was a worldly-minded man, and neglected his religious duties, although the good King was always entreating him to amend his life.

At length he was attacked by a dangerous sickness. The King went again and again to visit him, to try to induce him to go to Confession, especially as he was in such great danger of death. But his visits produced little or no fruit. One day he found him so ill that those who were waiting on him thought that he could not live many hours. Then the religious King besought him in the name of God not to put off a moment longer, lest he should die in that awful state.

The dying man remained silent for a few minutes, as if thinking what he should do. Suddenly looking on the King with eyes terrible to behold, he cried out · " There is now no longer time ; I have delayed too long, and my portion must now be with the reprobates in Hell."

When he had said these terrible words, he expired in impenitence and in despair, a warning to all those who, like him, put off their return to God till a future time, and who neglect to obey the command of God's Church to go at least once a year to Confes sion.   *Life of Venerable Bede.*

HE DID NOT REQUIRE TO GO.

When one neglects to go to Confession at least once a year, he not only disobeys one of the commandments of the Church, but exposes himself to the danger of dying in sin.

In the island of Sardinia there was a young man who, though well instructed in his religious duties, began to neglect the Sacraments, and to lead a life of sin. His friends were grieved when they saw this, but hoped when Easter came that he would go to Confession, and begin again a new life. In this they were disappointed. " I do not need to go to Confession," he said, when they spoke to him about it. " Besides, I intend to go later on."

As time went on, he became still more hardened ; from one sin he fell into another, until in the end he had ruined his health by his life of dissipation, and lay at the point of death in the hospital of Cagliari.

A priest who lived in the town was sent for. They told him that there was a man dying who refused to see a priest or to receive the last Sacraments. He hastened at once to the dying man, and saw that he had not many hours to live.

He spoke to him with gentleness of the danger he was in, and besought him to make a good Confession. " I will help you," he said, " and it will be very easy, and God will show you mercy and forgive you, and then you shall be eternally happy with Him in Heaven."

" I do not need to make my Confession," said the dying man coldly.

" My dear friend," said the priest, " everyone requires to go to Confession, especially when one is sick, and on the point of appearing before God. Surely you would not like to die without making your Confession."

" There is no necessity for it." .

" For God's sake," said the priest earnestly, " delay no longer, for the hour of your death is near."

It was of no use ; the only answer the priest received was, " I do not need to make my Confession."

The priest went away full of sorrow and praying for the impenitent sinner. He returned on the following day, hoping that he might still be living and in better sentiments ; but alas ! a white linen covering, which concealed a form lying on the bed, told him that all was over.

He looked on the others who were in the room, and they were ghastly pale. " O, Father," they cried, " if you only knew what happened last night ! That unfortunate man died a terrible death. About midnight he cried out, ' Give me a sword that I may kill him.' "

" ' Whom do you want to kill ?' we asked.

" ' Don't you see that black man who wants to kill me ?'

" ' If you make your Confession,' we said, ' you shall have nothing to fear.'

" ' Confession !' he cried out ; ' what need have I of Confession ?'

" When he had said these words he became silent. Suddenly he screamed out, ' Help ! help ! he is going to seize me !'

" These were the last words he said. A terrible trembling came upon him, and in a few minutes he was dead."

Such was the death of one who neglected to go to Confession.　　　　　SCHOUPPE : *Inst.,* iii. 38.

V. The Fourth Commandment of the Church.

The fourth commandment of the Church is : " To receive the Blessed Sacrament at least once a year, and that at Easter or thereabouts."

THE VISION OF THE LOST SOUL.

The holy Pope Gregory the Great was one day offering up the Holy Sacrifice of the Mass, in St. Peter's Church at Rome, for the repose of the soul of one who had died 180 years previously, and who had by his last will left a sum of money, on condition that every year, on the anniversary of his death, Holy Mass should be offered up for him.

St. Gregory came to the words of the Introit, " Eternal rest grant to him, O Lord, and let perpetual light shine upon him." When he was saying them, he heard a voice which answered, " Never, never shall I have rest, nor see the light of Heaven."

The Saint, thinking that this might be a delusion of the Devil, repeated the words of the Introit. Again he heard the same voice crying out in the most doleful accents : " There shall never be rest nor light for me, for I am lost for ever."

St. Gregory, on hearing these words, was filled with a great fear ; but he continued the Mass he had begun, and when he came to that part where the souls of the faithful departed are commemorated, he asked God to tell him why that unfortunate man had lost his soul.

God, in answer to the prayer of the Saint, and for the instruction of the faithful, revealed to him that

that soul was in hell for having once, by his own fault, neglected to make his Paschal Communion because he had refused to forgive one who had injured him.

Life of St. Gregory.

" CAN SUCH A THING BE POSSIBLE ?"

Father Amadeus left his happy home in France, and his parents whom he loved, to go and spend his life in the lonely islands of the Indian Ocean, among the savages.

These poor people had never heard of God Who made them, nor of our dear Lord Jesus Who died for them ; and willingly did this good priest exile himself from all he held dear on earth, that he might teach them these great truths, and show them the way to Heaven.

For many years this faithful apostle laboured amongst them ; and these poor savages soon learned to love him because he was so kind and so good.

As soon as they heard that he was coming to any of their villages, the news was immediately spread on every side, and some of these simple people were known to have come upwards of twenty miles to see and hear him. He was accustomed to stay in each place he thus visited for several weeks at a time, and it is almost incredible how eagerly they listened to him and how readily they embraced the Faith.

Before leaving any of these villages, Father Amadeus used to baptize those whom he saw to be best instructed and disposed. One day a poor savage came to him and knelt down at his feet.

" Father," he cried out, " could I be made a son of the Great Spirit ?"

" Yes, my child," he replied. " If you promise to obey and serve Him faithfully all the days of your life, I will give you the grace of Baptism, and then you will be His son."

The poor savage could not contain himself for joy at this good news. Father Amadeus catechized him, and was amazed at the knowledge he already possessed of what our holy Faith teaches, so that after his baptism he thought he might admit the young neophyte even to Holy Communion.

After many admonitions on the part of the missionary, and after many promises of fidelity from the savages, Father Amadeus gave them his blessing and left them.

A year afterwards he returned to the same place. He was received with transports of joy by these poor inhabitants of the forests, who crowded round him to welcome him.

Suddenly a young man was seen running in great haste towards the place where the Father stood. He pushed through the crowd and fell down at his feet, and, taking them in his hands, kissed them in the most affectionate manner. It was the poor savage who had made his first Communion the previous year.

" O my Father !" he cried out before all the people, as soon as his emotion permitted him to speak, " give me again the same happiness as you gave me last year."

" What happiness do you speak of, my child ?'

" Ah, dear Father, don't you remember the happi-

ness you gave me last time you came here—the
happiness of receiving the Son of the Great Spirit
in Holy Communion ?"

" Yes, my child, I will give you what you ask,"
he answered ; " but before you receive Him again
you must go to Confession. Have you examined
your conscience ?"

" Yes, my Father," replied the young savage, " I
have done so every night as you told me to do."

" Then, my child, you will come to Confession and
tell the sins you have been guilty of since you were
baptized."

" What sins do you speak of, Father ?"

" The sins you have committed against the commandments of God or of His Church."

" Sins against the commandments of God !" said
the savage in amazement. " Do you think it
possible that one whom the Great Spirit has made
His own child by baptism, and who has received Him
in Communion, could ever offend Him again or break
His commandments ? Surely no Christian ever
did that ! Oh no, that could not be possible ; that
could not be possible ; that would be the height of
ingratitude."

The priest said no more, but, going to the altar,
knelt down to thank God who had instilled into the
breast of a poor illiterate savage such sentiments
of generous love. He then offered up the Holy
Sacrifice, at which the young man communicated
with a fervour which made the good priest shed tears
of joy.

We have over and over again said to God that if
He forgave us our past sins we would never sin again,

but always serve Him and be faithful to Him, and we have as often broken our promise. May the example of this poor savage make us more faithful for the time to come. *Catéchisme de Persévérance.*

VI. THE FIFTH COMMANDMENT OF THE CHURCH.

The fifth commandment of the Church is : " To contribute to the support of our pastors."

It is the duty of every Catholic, my child, to contribute to the support of religion according to his means, so that God may be duly honoured and worshipped, and the kingdom of His Church extended.

" THE LABOURER IS WORTHY OF HIS HIRE."

When Christ Jesus sent out His apostles to preach to the people, He said to them : " Go ; behold, I send you as sheep among wolves. Carry neither purse, nor scrip, nor shoes. Into whatsoever house you enter, in the same house remain, eating and drinking such things as they have, for the labourer is worthy of his hire."

In these words the duty of contributing to the support of our pastors is enforced, and laid down as a duty which everyone is bound in conscience to perform. St. Paul repeats the same obligation in various parts of his epistles. " Let him that is instructed in the Word communicate to him that instructeth him in all good things " (Gal. vi. 6).

" Know ye not, that they who work in the holy place, eat the things that are of the holy place ; and they who serve the altar partake with the altar ? So also hath the Lord ordained that they who preach the Gospel should live by the Gospel " (1 Cor. ix. 13).

VII. THE SIXTH COMMANDMENT OF THE CHURCH.

The sixth commandment of the Church is : " Not to solemnize marriage at certain times, nor within certain degrees of kindred."

SOLEMNIZATION OF MARRIAGE.

The times in which it is forbidden to solemnize marriage are from the first Sunday of Advent till the seventh day of January, and from Ash-Wednesday till after Low Sunday.

END OF VOL. III

PRINTED IN ENGLAND

ion can be obtained
ng.com
6A
280217
/00011B/114/P

CPSIA inform
at www.ICGte
Printed in the
BVOW06s09
477348E